Praise for
Celebrating D

'So many older LGBT+ people will be able to relate to Shaun's personal journey; it's why we need to constantly be reminding people of the "not so long ago" past. Celebrating Difference is written beautifully with honesty and passion to make LGBT+ education understandable for everybody, without any barriers or prejudice needing to be in place. Once children have the knowledge and understanding, they will lead the way to becoming the LGBT+ educators of their siblings, mothers, fathers and other family members.'

Dr Carl Austin-Behan, LGBT+ Advisor to the
Mayor of Greater Manchester

'This is not a book, it is a philosophy, and one which I wish had been in place when I was growing up. We can only truly celebrate difference when we face prejudice head-on, including our own.'

Lord Michael Cashman CBE, Founder of Stonewall

'This is an outstanding book. It is highly engaging, and humorous in places. The discussion of the author's personal experiences of exclusion adds to the richness of the text. There is very clear guidance offered to schools on how to implement a whole-school approach to LGBTQ+ inclusion. Questions are used effectively to promote thinking and reflection. This book is a major contribution to the field and the author does not shy away from contentious issues. I thoroughly enjoyed reading it.'

Jonathan Glazzard, Professor of Teacher Education,
Leeds Beckett University

'Shaun Dellenty's whole-school approach to LGBT+ inclusion is a huge stride towards genuine organisational change. Regardless of the stage you or your school are at, this accessible and stimulating book will be highly relevant and of much value.'

Dr Joseph Hall, University of Leeds

'Recommended. Celebrating Difference is essential and valuable reading for every teacher and school leader – a groundbreaking book to help make our schools safer spaces for all young people.'

Peter Tatchell, Director, Peter Tatchell Foundation

Other titles from Bloomsbury Education

Education: A Manifesto for Change, by Richard Gerver

Leading on Pastoral Care, by Daniel Sobel

Mental Health Matters, by Paula Nagel

The Wellbeing Toolkit: Sustaining, Supporting and Enabling School Staff, by Andrew Cowley

Wellbeing in the Primary Classroom: A Practical Guide to Teaching Happiness, by Adrian Bethune

Celebrating Difference

A whole-school approach to
LGBT+ inclusion

Shaun Dellenty

BLOOMSBURY EDUCATION
LONDON   OXFORD   NEW YORK   NEW DELHI   SYDNEY

BLOOMSBURY EDUCATION
Bloomsbury Publishing Plc
50 Bedford Square, London, WC1B 3DP, UK

BLOOMSBURY, BLOOMSBURY EDUCATION and the Diana logo are trademarks of
Bloomsbury Publishing Plc

First published in Great Britain 2019

A catalogue record for this book is available from the British Library.

ISBN: PB: 978-1-4729-6150-1; ePDF: 978-1-4729-6149-5; ePub: 978-1-4729-6148-8

2 4 6 8 10 9 7 5 3 (paperback)

Typeset by Newgen KnowledgeWorks Pvt. Ltd., Chennai, India
Printed and bound in the UK by CPI Group (UK) Ltd, Croydon, CR0 4YY

To find out more about our authors and books visit www.bloomsbury.com
and sign up for our newsletters.

Contents

Acknowledgements

This book is dedicated to Dominic and Roger Crouch, and all those who have suffered, are suffering or will suffer from bullying, prejudice, discrimination, stigma and hate in our world; you deserve better.

With sincere thanks to all those who kindly contributed to this book:

Dr Joseph Hall, University of Leeds
Professor Jonathan Glazzard, Leeds Beckett University
Emma Nichols, Jill Pearson, and staff and pupils of Barnston School
Dr Elizabeth Malone and students of Liverpool John Moores University
Craig Adams, and staff and students of St Gabriel's College
Scott Palmer, and staff and students of Rosendale Primary School
Fernando Rosell-Aguilar, The Open University/LGBTOU
Colin Wong, and staff and students of Liverpool Hope University
Adrian Shorthouse, and staff and pupils of Kewaigue School, Isle of Man
Max Kelly, and staff and pupils of Dhoon/Laxey Federation, Isle of Man
Ben Eyres, Annette Baker, and staff and pupils of Ramsey Grammar School, Isle of Man
Ian Postlethwaite, and staff and pupils of Victoria Road Primary School, Isle of Man
Dan Williams and Sue Hobbs, University of Derby
Hayle Davies and Chiltern Edge School
Amnesty UK/Amnesty Teacher Programme
Peggy Keane

In addition, heartfelt thanks to:

My wonderful editor Hannah Marston, for believing in my messages and for inviting me to share them via this book
Rachel Lindley and Bloomsbury Education, for their ongoing support and enthusiasm
My parents Daphne and Richard; thank you both for gifting me this life journey
My beautiful husband Michael, for his love, friendship and support, and Tauzerschnauzer too!
Christopher, Gareth, Rose Harris, Sylvia and Dad John, for their love and support
David and the Tindsleys, for everything
Two wonderful teachers, Peter Biebrach and Sheila Hill
Jason C now H!

Greg Hayes

Anna Taylor

All those who took part in the online surveys

Sabrina Sutherland; with one simple request you relit my fire!

Armistead Maupin, for helping me understand that some families are logical and that is okay

Lindsey, Elisabeth, Mason and our global TP family, for their friendship and support

Richard Whent and Vinny Vero, for getting me on social media

Letterbox Library

Guy Dudley and the NAHT

Department for Education

The Huffington Post

Emily Drabble

Gillian Strutton

Paul Sesay and National Diversity Awards

Geoff Moorcroft, Chrissy Callaghan and Karen Riordan at the Isle of Man Department of Education, Sport and Culture

The education and wider communities of the Isle of Man, and the Isle of Man Government

Mayor Sadiq Khan

London South Bank University

Catherine Lee

Angus Swan

Simon Ware and Martin Lunnon, Amnesty LGBTI

Councillor Dora Dixon-Fyle MBE

Points of Light Team at the Cabinet Office

Robert Truelove and ParliOUT

HyperFusion Theatre Company/TIC Box Productions and various *BOY* casts

Brighton Actually Gay Men's Chorus, for the fundraising, support, friendship and songs

Church of England

Faith and Belief Forum

LGBT Consortium

Show Racism the Red Card

Richard Marson

Lord Storey

Mathew Hulbert

Claire Stoneman

Tom Godden at Sugarman Education

Martyn Loukes

Mark Brandon

Dr Sonia Seyfollahi

Jean-Paul Nguegang

Ian Gilbert and the Independent Thinking Team

Leanne Newbold, Nigel Howard and the inspiring Isle of Man LGBT+ Youth Group – stay strong!

Fiona Shelton and Oliver Holz, University of Derby/Homo'poly Project

The organisations named in the body of this book who undertook research about LGBT+ experiences

The work of Jon Kabat-Zinn PhD and Jack Kornfield in helping to enrich my personal response to working with prejudice

University of Bangor

Mindfulness Project London

All the schools, teachers, pupils, governors and trainee teachers who have invited me to speak since 2009; thank you for your belief in my messages and for being on the journey on behalf of your learning communities

My loyal social media followers

And finally, the teaching and non-teaching staff, parents and wonderful young people who inspired and supported my work right from the start (you know who you are); I will carry you in my heart always. Be proud, be safe, be happy, be YOU.

If I have missed anyone out, please accept my apologies and do tweet me before the second edition!

Introduction

This is a book about compassion, upholding basic human rights and empowering young people to be themselves in schools, whoever they may be. This is also a book about changing hearts and minds, in order to facilitate lasting organisational and culture change in support of positive LGBT+ inclusion in education. My ultimate aim is to make schools safer, more inclusive and thereby more productive for all stakeholders.

This book is informed by my personal life journey and by ten years of work (as of 2019) in the field of LGBT+ inclusion. My work was inspired by the suffering of young people in my own school and informed by my own suffering as a child who just always knew he was gay. My work didn't come out of nowhere; it stands on the shoulders of those who strove for equality before me. I hope to support you to make a difference on behalf of your own school communities (and perhaps even beyond), by capturing the strategic journey towards 'celebrating difference' on which it has been my privilege to lead hundreds of schools and other educational settings. I hope to inspire you to build upon your existing good practice to facilitate sustainable organisational change, as a result of which the broad, joyful, natural rainbow of human diversity can be explored and celebrated without exception.

This is not a book about ticking boxes or paying lip service to inclusion; our wonderful young people deserve better than that. My work is also certainly not about diminishing the cultures, beliefs or identities of non-LGBT+ people. Instead, I aim to give you a clearer view of what LGBT+ inclusion work in schools is and, perhaps more vitally, what it isn't. This book is not just about tackling LGBT+ bullying; it is about working proactively to prevent such bullying from happening in the first place. In this way we create a world in which LGBT+ bullying becomes the last thing we talk about as opposed to the first, which is sadly too often the case. This journey requires compassion, patience and resilience. I present to you a focused opportunity to work through some of the 'baggage' surrounding LGBT+ identities to give you a sense of 'permission' and hopefully to enable you to progress with confidence. By the end of the book, I hope you will have formulated your rationale, intentions, actions and outcomes for the potentially lifesaving journey towards positive LGBT+ inclusion, and I hope you will be robust in your defence of the work should challenge arise.

I would like to be clear that this book should not take the place of high-quality LGBT+ inclusion and awareness training for all staff. If you would like me to visit your school to train staff or speak to students you can contact me via Twitter (@ShaunDellenty) or at www.shaundellenty.com. My work takes me not only around the UK but increasingly overseas. Other training providers are available, but this wasn't the case when I started my own work in primary schools.

Throughout the book, I refer to homophobia as an 'umbrella' term for homophobia, biphobia and transphobia. My intention is not to place a hierarchy on human suffering, but to save words. I use the term 'LGBT+ bullying' to encompass homophobic, biphobic and transphobic bullying, and also bullying directed towards human beings who identify as anything other than heterosexual, cisgender or male and female. I will mainly refer to 'identity' not 'sexual orientation'; I believe categorising human beings based upon 'sexual preference' encourages negativity towards highly complex individuals based upon one limited aspect of their existence. I refuse to define people by whom they love, how they look or whom they sleep with.

I aim to be as plain-speaking as possible; hopefully you won't find too many academic quotes or diagrams! What you will find is an accumulation of ten years of multi-award-winning work in the field of positive LGBT+ inclusion in education. I don't claim to know it all or to be an academic or expert; learning is lifelong and rapid change surrounds us. You will encounter very personal thoughts and reflections, and I make no apology for this; on first mooting a book, many people asked me to keep my story and my voice front and centre. I hope I have honoured these requests.

In preparation for this book, I have received a number of case studies from the following schools and other organisations with whom I have worked since 2009, for which I am extremely grateful:

- Barnston School, Wirral
- Liverpool John Moores University
- St Gabriel's College, Lambeth
- Rosendale Primary School, Lambeth
- The Open University
- Liverpool Hope University
- Chiltern Edge School, Oxfordshire
- Kewaigue School, Isle of Man
- Dhoon/Laxey Federation, Isle of Man
- Ramsey Grammar School, Isle of Man
- Victoria Road Primary School, Isle of Man
- University of Derby
- Amnesty Teacher Programme.

I am also very grateful for the contributions of Dr Joseph Hall from the University of Leeds, who was present at the very beginnings of my work and remains a friend and highly respected colleague to this day. In undertaking his PhD, Dr Hall independently scrutinised the impact of my then emergent approach to LGBT+ inclusion.

When researching this book, I undertook an online survey entitled 'LGBT self-awareness', which received 261 responses, and another entitled 'LGBT+ teachers' survey', which elicited 242 responses. In addition, I revisited many thousands of staff feedback forms and conversations gathered from staff and young people from the hundreds of schools I have supported across the UK since 2009. Using the case studies, Dr Hall's contributions, survey data and feedback forms, I hope to illustrate in this book the factors that lead schools to initiate my approach, the strategies they deploy to drive the work forward, the impact that the approach makes and the challenges that they face.

Why have I written this book?

To get us thinking about why LGBT+ inclusion is so important in schools, here are three starter questions for you to think about (feel free to grab a cuppa and a pen and notebook):

1. Why should schools ensure that all stakeholders within learning communities feel safe, supported and included, including those who identify as LGBT+ or those who are perceived to be?
2. How can schools ensure that all stakeholders within learning communities feel safe, supported and included, including those who identify as LGBT+ or those who are perceived to be?
3. What might the impact of this work be upon children and young people, parents and staff?

Reread the questions, noticing what arises for you as you do so, and jot your responses down. As you progress with this book, please keep your notebook close by to notice and reflect upon your thoughts and feelings towards the themes raised. Our responses, both as human beings and as professionals, are as important as the themes themselves. This sets the tone for the whole-school journey ahead.

Now cast your own minds back to the day your parents dropped you off at school for the first time; on that anxious first day, what was it they really needed to know? I would wager that you were safe, felt validated and included, were happy, and were free to make friends. You, as a unique human child, with some similarities but also with some differences to other children.

A child recently asked me, 'Why do old people like *you* keep talking about difference? Young people are now all cool with being different.' Whilst perhaps it is true that some young people have more accepting attitudes to human diversity than my generation (I'm now 51) did at school, the 2017 'School report' from the UK LGBT charity Stonewall (2017a) found that almost half of all LGBT pupils face bullying at school for being LGBT, with more than two in five transgender young people having tried to take their own life. In 2018, a study by Leeds Beckett University also found that 40 per cent of teachers had experienced bullying, harassment, discrimination or prejudice in their teaching career as a result of being LGBT+ (George, 2018). 'Difference' (or 'human diversity') is clearly then still a bone of contention for many people. Now take a moment to reflect on your intentions when you bought this book.

I initiate conversations about human diversity all around the world and now, via this book, I have the privilege (thanks to Hannah Marston and Bloomsbury Education) to write about it too! Countless human beings around the world have reached out to me to share heartbreaking stories of the loss of a parent, a sister, a brother, a friend, a colleague or a child due to LGBT+ bullying and prejudice. If I had a pound for every occasion I had been told one of these terrible stories, I would sadly be a very rich person indeed. I find the level of prejudice and bullying that exists deeply shocking, but as a survivor of homophobic bullying myself, it sadly comes as no surprise. Nor, I believe, is it surprising for many education establishments. When commissioning case studies for this book, I asked colleagues to explore *why* they had made the choice to embrace my approach and undertake a journey towards positive LGBT+ inclusion with me. Several key themes emerged:

From schools

- Improvement of student and staff mental health and wellbeing.
- Deconstruction of negative attachments or associations with LGBT+ identities in order to challenge prejudice, discrimination and bullying.
- A need to revise the curriculum offer and to obtain resources representing LGBT+ diversity and diverse families to educate and increase visibility and representation.
- A need to reduce levels of LGBT+ bullying and associated pejorative language (often dismissed as 'banter') and eliminating the use of the word 'gay' as a negative 'cuss'.
- A need to improve student attendance and outcomes by reducing levels of LGBT+ bullying.
- A move towards whole-school foci, school assemblies and curriculum offer to draw attention to the contributions that the LGBT+ community makes to the world, historically and in the present day.

From teacher training faculties

- A need to ensure that newly qualified teachers are trained specifically in LGBT+ awareness and identities during initial teacher training, with the aim of enabling them to foster inclusive and supportive schools.

I regularly encounter a perceived lack of 'permission' from colleagues in facilitating positive LGBT+ inclusion work and from those who openly express skewed perceptions of what positive LGBT+ inclusion work entails. Equal access to high-quality sex education for young people who identify as LGBT+ is a basic human right, but sex education is not what this book is about. In some cases education professionals harbour their own prejudices. The culture of an LGBT+ inclusive school is established by the governing body, school leadership and teachers. This book represents an organisational journey that can empower and elicit change in every detail of school life, whilst modelling expectations to communities beyond the school gates. My ten years of work in the still-emergent field of LGBT+ inclusion, both in the UK and overseas, have taught me that a majority of school staff and stakeholders lack training (and therefore the confidence) to prevent LGBT+ bullying. However, positive LGBT+ inclusion starts at the *very beginning* of education and as educators we serve as role models. If we can't model a top-down, inclusive, compassionate approach to human diversity, then I would question our career choice. In an ideal world, pre-school education about human diversity should be something children are presented with from early childhood. Listening, considering and debating new concepts are a key part of the education process, as is freedom of speech; freedom of speech brings with it the need for civility and taking responsibility for the impact our words, attitudes and opinions can have upon our children and young people, colleagues and parents or carers.

With this in mind, I have not written this book to teach you what to think; instead I hope *engaging* with this text enables you and your whole school community to become more self-aware about your own attitudes, reactions and responses to human diversity. I hope my words encourage *thinking* about *thinking*. The initial focus in this book upon individual reflection may feel exposing and requires sensitivity; from the outset please strive for a non-judgemental approach or we may run the risk of disengaging with key players from the start. The journey towards positive LGBT+ inclusion may not always be easy, but ultimately it is our young people who benefit.

In undertaking targeted anti-LGBT+ bullying intervention, schools sometimes stand accused of placing a hierarchy upon bullying. It is important to meet this accusation head-on. LGBT+ bullying is singled out as an issue purely because it has been made an issue by those who display prejudice towards LGBT+ people. LGBT+ people are not demanding rights above and beyond others; we merely seek *equality of opportunity* in terms of human rights and compassionate attitudes. Nor do we seek to be 'tolerated'; instead we must aspire for acceptance. Who wants to spend their short time on Planet Earth merely being tolerated? Let's have high aspirations for our young people, please!

LGBT+ inclusion work in schools is *never* about 'promoting' anything except the safety, wellbeing and authentic identities of our wonderfully diverse young people, their families and our staff. I enjoy teaching world religions, yet at no point have I attempted to 'promote' one religion over the other. It is possible to teach facts, without bringing personal views to the table. LGBT+ identities are facts of human diversity; teaching that they exist does not involve 'promotion' and therefore does not compromise personal beliefs. There is, I feel, a spiritual element to this work, stemming from a profound sense of connection to the innate goodness within human beings.

Some individuals believe that when I inform young people in a primary school assembly that I am gay, some children magically 'turn' into homosexuals. Although I was voted one of the 100 most influential LGBT+ people in the UK, not even my superpowers can 'turn' children LGBT+, any more than growing up in an overwhelmingly heteronormative world 'turned' me into a heterosexual! This is not how human sexuality works.

I aim to facilitate schools to be able to explore prejudice from the outset, with the aim of making them safer places for *all* stakeholders, whatever their identity, gender identity or orientation. For me this is the bigger win and this is why historically my work was called Inclusion For All, and ultimately why I have written this book.

The values behind my approach

My approach to LGBT+ inclusion is underpinned by ten fundamental values; these personal keystones are informed by my life experience and meditative self-reflection. To share my process authentically with you in this book, it is only right that I first share these underlying principles.

Curiosity

We should take a genuine interest in the lives, stories, beliefs and opinions of others, even when they are very different or challenge our own experiences and beliefs. It is important to notice our thoughts, reactions and responses, and bring our curiosity to moments in which we experience resistance towards human diversity.

Non-judgement

For being gay I've been threatened, insulted and attacked, and faced deeply held prejudice. After bringing curiosity to the causes of such experiences, I strive to remember that human beings think and feel as they do for a complex myriad of reasons. Adopting a judgemental approach is *not* a positive starting point, however fierce the opposition. Admittedly this is not always easy, thus bringing open-hearted curiosity to challenge helps us in asking the following questions: 'Why do people think/feel/act the way they do?' and 'What is required to lead them to shift their thinking?' Of course, this also requires restraint and patience.

Patience

Some people harbour deeply held views, misconceptions and prejudices towards LGBT+ people, colouring attitudes when they learn of schools undertaking work on LGBT+ inclusion. Although we aspire to change attitudes in and around our school communities, the reality is that for some people, the journey to unpick a lifetime's worth of prejudice can take months, even years, and sadly a minority will never shift from their fixed way of thinking. Our aim is to start people off on their journey, but this requires patience. Meditation such as mindfulness is supportive in nurturing the patience we require, in turn contributing to our overall wellbeing. After all, diminished professionals lead to diminished outcomes.

Dignity and respect

A successful school is built upon strong, respectful relationships. When facilitating dialogue around LGBT+ identities in schools, some individuals might feel awkward and embarrassed or express views that may be considered 'out of date' or prejudicial. As role models (for young people and our staff), we must strive to set a respectful and dignified tone from the outset. Rules of engagement and principles for respectful discussion are important in order to avoid discussions aimed at making all children feel safe descending into a forum for airing grievances against one minority. Freedom of speech is a wonderful thing, but we are all accountable for what comes out of our mouths and the potential negative impact our words can have upon other human beings. We are not here to debate the *existence* of LGBT+ people, but to learn about their experiences and identities through compassionate listening.

Many schools remain inactive because some individuals are afraid to verbalise what is in their head about LGBT+ identities. Alternatively they perpetuate a culture in which negative views are expressed and they are simply not open to an alternative view of LGBT+ people. Dignified, structured discussion in the right place and at the right time enables schools to work with the 'elephant in the room' in order to move forward on behalf of their young people.

An open heart

Information and education around LGBT+ identities require us to engage in new learning, keeping up with equalities legislation and shifting labels and identities. LGBT+ identities and the concepts that surround them do not represent a fixed point in time; they exist as a spectrum. The reactions and responses of non-LGBT+ individuals, organisations, health providers, governments, faith groups and education systems also shift over time with regard to how they view and interact with those who do identify as LGBT+. Educators and school leaders must bring what might currently be termed a 'growth mindset', viewing LGBT+ as a source of ongoing interest and learning.

A belief in equality and the right of all young people to be safe

The United Nations Convention on the Rights of the Child (1990) states that all children have a right (Article 28) to an education without exception, including children identifying as LGBT+. They also have a right (Article 2) not to face discrimination. LGBT+ identities are historically surrounded by 'baggage', and educators often choose to place their awareness on the baggage and on the detractors and critics of the work, instead of on those we are actually striving to help: our amazing young people.

Compassion

The experiences and lives of some individuals and some groups of individuals can vary so significantly from our own that it can be hard to bring awareness to our commonality as human beings. As a result we focus heavily upon our 'differences'. Many human beings experience prejudice for a variety of reasons, but if an individual's experience of prejudice is limited (which is a privilege) it can be challenging to empathise with those whose experiences differ. In facilitating LGBT+ inclusion, schools may engage with those who harbour anxiety or prejudice and those who have suffered prejudice-related bullying and discrimination. If these voices reveal themselves, strive to listen in the first instance, bringing compassion and not judgement. This establishes an initial level of trust from which your ongoing journey can stem.

Kindness

In my experience, the vast majority of education professionals model kindness in their work; it is important to bring an equal approach to all school stakeholders. I have met some individuals who expressed the view that I will go to hell or that I am trying to 'sexualise' young people by merely talking in schools about the fact that I am married to a man or that because I am a gay man working with young people I must be a 'paedophile'. These comments have real potential to deeply hurt and sometimes they do; however, I choose to bring my curiosity, awareness and compassion to what underpins these expressions of disdain.

Resilience

The journey to make schools LGBT+ inclusive is usually an exciting and joyful one. There can be challenges and all staff will require high-quality, dedicated training – this is a non-negotiable. It is vital that the workload is shared and is pitched as a sustainable, whole-school responsibility, one that is not driven solely by one passionate individual. A collegiate approach is vital, not only in developing a consistent approach but also in providing peer support. Regular opportunities must be provided to celebrate success and explore challenges. School leadership should work in partnership with allies. If staff are challenged by young people or parents, it is vital that they know they will be supported by school leadership and governors. What we are working towards is whole-school improvement, which benefits everyone.

Honesty

Many LGBT+ people spend much of their lives being forced into inauthenticity by bullying and prejudice. Educators must aspire to create an environment in which all stakeholders can be honest about their whole selves if they wish to be; this will foster positive health and wellbeing. Schools should not be modelling how to lie.

The structure of this book

The 12 chapters ahead will lead you on a journey towards a school context that unashamedly celebrates difference and human diversity. The chapters are structured around a six-tier approach (think of it as a cake!), which I deploy when working with schools. Taking into account feedback from schools, I believe that my six-tier approach works because it does not assume that providing schools with glossy teacher resources aimed at facilitating positive LGBT+ inclusion will alone change whole-school culture and ethos. The six-tier approach makes no assumptions about educators' confidence or willingness to make schools LGBT+ inclusive; instead my approach works with professionals' individual attitudes prior to starting work with formal LGBT+ training resources.

The journey towards positive LGBT+ inclusion is most effective when certain factors are already present or developing, and these form the 'foundation layer' (cake base!) for the six-tier process we are about to undertake. If you do not have these factors already established, please do not wait to have them fully established before getting started; they can be embedded within your strategic action plan later on. Even as you read this book, it's likely that someone in your school is already suffering due to bullying or prejudice or has noticed a rainbow in their heart and is afraid for their future. They need immediate support, validation and representation.

The foundation layer

It is helpful to have the following factors in place in your setting before embarking on the six-tier process, but if any (or even all) are missing, they can be embedded into your action plan as you go along:

- inclusive school ethos, vision and aims
- inclusive behaviour policies
- ethos of early intervention and robust pastoral support and listening services
- human rights education from the start of schooling
- strong, compassionate relationships
- specific ongoing teaching opportunities to develop empathy
- philosophy for children training for all staff
- mindfulness training for staff and a mindfulness programme for students
- links with international schools
- global citizenship
- circle time
- a strong personal, social, health and economic (PSHE) programme relevant to the needs of the students
- use of pupil voice.

Reflect upon these foundations in terms of your own context. What is already in place? What needs to be developed further? What needs to start from scratch and form part of your strategic action plan?

Tier 1: Focusing as an individual

Tier 1 facilitates *individual* self-reflection whilst establishing a more authentic sense of our own attitudes to LGBT+ identities (whether we identify as LGBT+ or not) and the prejudices, myths and misconceptions that often surround them. We take greater responsibility for our thoughts and feelings about human diversity, bringing non-judgemental curiosity in order to work with them positively. Some organisations merge Tiers 1 and 2 to work with all staff at once; the six-tier process is a guide, not a cage, but it is vital that all members of leadership and management undertake Tiers 1 and 2 first, as these tiers set the strategic tone.

Tier 2: Focusing as a team

Tier 2 mirrors the themes of Tier 1 but requires leadership to replicate the ethos and content of Tier 1 at whole-school level via staff training and conversations, consolidating their own rationale, learning and Tier 1 experiences as they do so. Tiers 1 and 2 involve teaching and learning input for all staff around LGBT+ identities and what LGBT+ inclusion work in education involves. Tier 2 also has a focus on enabling authenticity at work.

Tier 3: Strategic development for organisational change

Tier 3 involves application of the individual and team reflection and new learning from Tiers 1 and 2, as well as whole-school auditing using a variety of sources to drive the development of a robust strategic vision for school improvement and a realignment of school ethos and vision.

Tier 4: Implementation

Tier 4 sees the implementation of the strategic action plan (with opportunities for ongoing evaluation and reflection) and the introduction of new learning opportunities across the school in the form of whole-school foci, assemblies and classroom curriculum-based teaching and learning.

Tier 5: Evaluation and realignment

In Tier 5 impact is evaluated and adjustments and realignments are made. Additional top-up training and support are brokered where needed. Short-term aims are revisited and middle- to long-term aims are realigned based upon auditing of sources of impact data.

Tier 6: Celebration and dissemination

Tier 6 encourages shame-free, outward-facing celebration of the strategic vision. New learning, best practice and impact taking place in the school are used to inspire growth and change in local and global education communities.

I hope this six-tier approach will take you and your school on a joyful professional journey towards celebrating difference – a journey that has the potential to save lives.

Let us begin.

Tier 1
Focusing as an individual

Chapter 1
Surviving homophobia

'*There are multiple legitimacies of existence and multiple ways of living lives.*'
Professor Ian Rivers, 2011

In undertaking work on LGBT+ identities we will encounter challenge, prejudice and bias. Prejudice may arise from those around us, but it can also arise from *within*. Prior to starting our strategic journey, let us first bring awareness to our own hearts and minds, to ascertain our own rationale, intent and attitudes. If we fail to invest the time to do so, our journey can be compromised from the start.

The focus of Tier 1 is honest, individual self-reflection of who we are, what we think and feel, and *why* we think and feel in certain ways. Through Chapters 1 to 3 of this book, I will guide you through a process of self-reflection, just as I do when I work with colleagues in education contexts. As part of this process, I wish to share my own life journey with you. I should signpost that my journey has not always been an easy one, and once you have read and digested it, if you notice any charged and lingering negative emotions please prioritise your own self-care and talk to a partner, friend, colleague or an organisation such as the Samaritans.

LGBT+ people are not all the same. LGBT+ identities exist on a spectrum and every LGBT+ individual is a unique human being. We should never be viewed as a homogenous group or defined solely by the labels we use to explain our existence to those who seek to define us by limited aspects of our being. We all have our stories; this is mine.

My journey

In the final days of the autumn term in 2009 my life changed forever. A few days prior to the Christmas break, a teaching assistant handed me a folder of pupil voice questionnaires. It's perhaps rare to recall with such clarity a moment in which one's life changes so irrevocably, but this simple act represents a pivotal moment of divergence, triggering a chain of events in my personal and professional life that, ten years later, leads directly to you kindly reading this book.

Pupil voice feedback of our twice-Ofsted-rated 'outstanding' inner-city London primary school told a shocking story. Seventy-five per cent of our pupils were experiencing homophobic bullying and language daily, in and around school. Nearly all children experienced the word 'gay' used as a pejorative 'cuss'. Children were being called (and calling others) 'faggots', 'lezzers', 'batty boys', 'trannies' and 'AIDS victims' in a derogatory manner to imply that being lesbian, gay, bisexual or transgender represented the lowest common denominator of human existence. My core duty as deputy headteacher was to ensure the safety and wellbeing of all of our wonderful young people, without exception. It was unacceptable that young people in my care should experience suffering akin to that experienced during my own childhood journey through the UK education system in the 1980s.

Training as an educator hadn't originally featured in my career plan. Having barely survived serious and sustained homophobic bullying as a teenager, returning to state education hadn't been a key life goal. Yet by 2009 the roles of 'class teacher', 'deputy head' and 'seconded local authority school improvement consultant' were present and correct on my curriculum vitae and by 2016 I was extremely surprised to find myself in Number 10 Downing Street receiving an honour (and my third major award within the same week) from the British prime minister for my services to the education and LGBT+ communities.

Despite my difficult journey and now aged 51, I am very grateful to be gay; it affords me the privilege of experiencing the universe from another perspective. It was whilst attending my first London LGBT+ Pride event in 1996 that I finally accepted myself; many young people and adults attending Pride events have similar experiences because for the first time they feel validated and like they belong. My LGBT+ identity remains a source of light in my life, whilst only being one part of my life. I am blessed to have the love and support of my beautiful husband Michael, whom I married in the Houses of Parliament in 2016, something that until well into my forties seemed an impossible dream. So please now let me share what they call in cinema 'my origin story'.

Early childhood

I was born in 1968 in Weymouth. Dad was a retired naval officer whose childhood polio and military service had left him physically frail and often unable to work. Mum was a full-time mother to my brother Christopher and me. In July of the previous year, the Sexual Offences Act had resulted in limited decriminalisation of homosexual acts in England.

We lived on Portland Bill in Dorset, in the south of England, then moved further north to a tumbledown house within the grounds of Stowe School, near Buckingham. My early childhood was spent within the grandeur of Stowe School itself and the surrounding ornate landscaped gardens of Capability Brown. Dad was the school caretaker; we had very little in the way of money and possessions, yet our 'quirky', leaky home was bordered by the most magical kingdom within which I could explore my growing sense of self.

Ah yes, myself.

You know, for as long as I can remember being Shaun, I've known I fancy men.

Please take a pause for a moment and notice whether you have any response or reaction to that last statement. Can you notice whether any thoughts or feelings arose? Gently explore them, without any sense of judgement.

I always knew I was attracted to men; that is a fact of my life. When did *you* know who *you* are? If you *are* LGBT+ ask yourself *when* and *how* you first became aware of this. If you are *not* LGBT+ ask yourself *when* and *how* you knew you were *not* LGBT+. As you reflect upon when and how you knew your own identity, notice what arises for you and explore the resulting thoughts and feelings, without judgement. There is no right or wrong to this question; every reader will be different. There is no magic switch that automatically reveals our identity and preferences to us. We emerge in different ways and at different rates, as do our children. We must make no assumptions as to which children might know they are LGBT+ or when this might occur.

Throughout my life, I have been asked, 'When did you know you are gay?' I respond by asking, 'When did you know who *you* are?' When seeking answers from others, we must also be prepared to seek them from ourselves. In asking questions of LGBT+ people (as often tends to happen), bring awareness that you seek to access information that individuals may experience as sensitive or personal. If a young person or colleague chooses to share their authentic identity, listen compassionately and value their identity, rather than question its validity. In the last few years there has been some vociferous debate about transgender and non-binary individuals in the media, much of which centres around debating the core identity of another human being; such debates can be deeply damaging for young people.

Some, like me, *always* knew, whilst for others awareness came later. Some always knew but suppressed their authentic identity in the face of societal, familial, cultural, political or religious disapproval. Others knew early on, but later felt included and safe enough to embrace the authenticity of their own being, but perhaps only within certain contexts. Imagine a heterosexual person who is 'openly heterosexual' at home, but functions as a 'closeted heterosexual' at work or in their church or sports team? Put like this, it frankly sounds a bit silly, but this is the reality for many LGBT+ people around the world. It is also my own experience at various stages of my life.

So *how* did I know I was gay at an early age?

I knew I fancied men on first seeing Benny from the Swedish pop group Abba on *Top of the Pops*, or American film star Burt Reynolds hairy chested and shirtless in a film, or Sean Connery as James Bond – all long before starting formal education. These men 'excited' me in a very specific manner; my pre-pubescent physical attraction manifested as facial flushing, a tightened throat, butterflies in the lower stomach and a comforting warmth in my groin. When I saw Benny, Burt or Sean kissing women, I first experienced jealousy. On attending primary school, it was the dads and male teachers who caught my eye. Educators and parents don't always seem comfortable acknowledging that children can experience attraction whilst still very young; I certainly did.

From aged seven onwards, the quality of the thoughts and sensations associated with my attraction absolutely became more sexualised. I'd secrete photos of men from Mum's clothing catalogues and hide them away. Already I had learned that my natural preferences were unpalatable to society, via unhappy gay stereotypes on television, who were often mocked, beaten, suicidal or killed. Positive LGBT+ role models were completely absent from my childhood.

For a time, I had Christian faith, 'inherited' from Dad and constructed from extrinsic sources: Dad read me Bible stories and taught me prayers by rote. I attended a Sunday school where the Bible was presented as absolute truth. For a while I bought into it, but my same-sex attraction was different, arising instead intrinsically from within my core sense of self. I didn't learn the label 'gay' until my teens. The vocabulary I related to myself I inherited from adult conversations, the media or the playground, the pejorative terms of the 1970s – poof, sissy, queer, bender, faggot, shirt lifter – some of which are still in use today.

My identity as a physical male came into question during primary school. Pre-pubescent little me preferred the company of girls; I felt a greater affinity with them, and the football and war-based games most of the boys played didn't appeal to me at all. I did hang out with a couple of other boys who liked to read *Doctor Who* (a British science fiction series) like me. We were soon labelled 'softies' and 'sissies'. I also enjoyed many of the school activities, clubs and books that teachers in the early 1970s stereotyped as being 'for girls'. My parents' friends would some-times make me feel uncomfortable by staring at me before joking, '*He's* pretty, isn't *she*?' or 'Are you sure *she's* a boy?' This made me begin to question my own gender identity, as it was already clear that I wasn't meeting societal expectations of what a 'real boy' was supposed to be.

I naturally tended to sit with my legs together to one side and crossed them high up. Having been teased for this with 'You are such a girl', I mimicked the wider-spread leg stance that most boys exhibited. I consciously lowered my voice and laugh in an attempt to sound more 'stereotypically manly'. In physically modifying myself I longed to fit in; the less visible I was, the less likely I was to be labelled as 'different' and I hoped I would be safer in school. Society and school were presenting me with only one way to be a boy or man and already I was caving in under the pressure to comply.

I had little interest in sport and games, but I was drawn to reading, writing, poetry, films, dance and crafts. My teachers openly expressed concern and redirected me to activities, friendship groups and clubs that they considered more 'boyish'. Thus, I became resentful of trusted adults, especially when our headteacher examined for herself what genitalia lay in my underpants, in order to ascertain my *physical* sex.

This procedure was done without the knowledge or consent of my parents. It was upsetting, humiliating and confusing; I kept it secret well into adulthood.

As a direct result of this experience, I decided that I only fancied men because I was a girl trapped in a boy's body. I believed that my physical body and my 'soul' were mismatched. As an adult, when listening to transgender speakers, I often reflect on this experience. Although these feelings passed in time, for a chunk of my childhood I genuinely thought my soul and body were mismatched, because I fancied men and other people questioned my 'manliness'. Whatever that means!

I was already rejecting my own self; transgender people may experience similar feelings but often over a more protracted period. The heartbreaking statistics around transgender self-harm and suicides show how difficult it must be to live day to day with such feelings, whilst being condemned and mocked in society.

Aged nine I was well into early puberty, leaving me in no doubt of what I really craved from Benny, Burt and Sean. Visible physical development, including beard growth, meant confusion around my gender identity mostly abated, but by the time my family fragmented, shattering my world at the age of 11, my sense of unease at being 'other' was already deeply ingrained and negatively affecting my mental health. It was when I hit puberty, as I struggled to conceal my increasingly profound sense of self, that my previously very good academic record began to suffer as my interest in learning waned.

In 1979 Mum and I moved to the small Leicestershire town of Lutterworth to be with my stepdad and brothers. Although very hard for me, I hoped for a positive new beginning at school.

Secondary education

On arriving on my first day at Lutterworth High School, an older, much taller boy (let's call him Clip) spat into my face. 'You are one of *them* – a fucking queer,' he yelled. I stood silent, shocked and sweating; how could he know my 'darkest' secret? Having gained power over a vulnerable new arrival, Clip went about gathering the troops. Thus began an almost daily ritual, usually accompanied by spitting, kicking, pushing or punching. My subsequent secondary school experience was punctuated by Clip and his followers (boys and girls) targeting me at school, around town and near home.

I didn't seek help because I thought I deserved to be hit for fancying men. I thought teachers wouldn't be sympathetic; some of them even used the same homophobic words Clip and Co. deployed to humiliate me. I couldn't tell my newly reconfigured family, as some very strong views were being expressed at home about 'poofs'.

I believed I was simply getting what I deserved for being born 'one of them'.

Back then Lutterworth High School physical education department operated on an unwritten policy of 'if you're bad at football you're a nobody and most likely a queer'. After breaking a bone on the school field, my twisted limb was kicked by a male PE teacher who called me 'a fat fairy' and left me alone on the school field to walk the considerable distance back to school. Another pupil finally helped me back to first aid and I ended up in a hospital. These experiences (and others) would put me off physical exercise until well into my thirties. It's a non-negotiable of my approach that physical education departments take a visible lead with LGBT+ inclusion work; LGBT+ people need to keep fit and are very capable of winning medals too! There are now a wide range of 'out' LGBT+ sports people and PE departments absolutely need to make use of them as role models.

In order to become socially acceptable, I 'dated' a number of lovely young women; in reality, we would spend time gossiping about pop stars, singing New Romantic pop songs and working our way through various shades of eyeliner. To some, my new found 'heterosexual credibility' was mildly convincing, but not to Clip or his followers, who had now progressed to scrawling 'Shaun Franks is a queer' on bus shelters and street signs around town (Franks was my surname at the time).

Sometimes I went to friends' houses to clean my blood off my face before going home. I didn't want my parents asking me why I was being bullied. Mum had made her views on 'two men kissing' very clear and my stepfather worked for the criminal investigation department at the local police office. At the time, he held and expressed many prejudices, especially towards LGBT+ people.

As I moved on to Lutterworth Grammar School, I began to externalise the bullying behaviours I was experiencing and my own internalised homophobia onto an older boy who openly admitted he was 'probably gay'. Finally, I had my label, yet in the moment I learnt it, I was deploying it to hurt one of my own kind. I struggled to manage my growing anger and began regularly punching myself in the face in the bathroom mirror, whilst hurling Clip's insults back at myself. My pyre of shame was in rapid ascendance.

I was naturally an acutely shy child, but it was my inspirational middle school class teacher Peter Biebrach who first convinced me to take a role in a school assembly. 'You play a *character*; it won't be *you* up there,' he advised. Onstage, real-isation dawned that performance could function as an escape from suffering and as a mask to hide my true 'unnatural' self. As I became unhappier, my personality and behaviour shifted. Riffing on television characters became second nature; if my peers were laughing at my impressions, they were distracted from my 'otherness'. In the latter stages of secondary school, hiding behind increasingly raucous characters became my survival tactic. My engagement with learning had significantly waned and I became difficult in class. My school reports map my disengagement from education, as day-to-day survival took precedence. I did find unconditional friendship from another student in my year, called Jonny. We shared a love of music that stirred our feet and souls and I can't thank him enough for his calm support. A drama teacher too saw my suffering and encouraged me as an actor. Every child needs a teacher who stands their ground. Mrs Hill did and I remain very grateful.

Well before sixth form I was experimenting sexually with other boys (and occasionally girls) but due to a total lack of relevant sex education or conversations around consent, I was sometimes pressured into sexual activities that I didn't have the coping strategies to say no to. In the process I placed myself in serious danger of contracting sexually transmitted diseases including HIV/AIDS, which at the time was killing many people. It was not uncommon for some of the local lads who were targeting me to approach me on my way home from school (or even by knocking on my front door) to demand that I 'relieved them' either by hand or orally (notice your responses to this), after which they would punch me, spit at me or beat me.

Sixth form

Early in sixth form I met an openly gay student, with whom I shared a love of pop music, and we ended up 'going out'. I didn't really fancy him, but he was a lovely person. In all honesty, I was fearful I might never meet another gay person. In 1986 the age of consent for gay men was 21, raising legal concerns for us; the threat of police or parental discovery (as my stepdad was a policeman, they were the same thing in my case) brought additional pressure. Some of our peers did show compassion towards us, but away from school the ritual of bullying and violence covertly continued, now with additional vicious comments about AIDS, which was hitting the UK hard. With every sneeze or aching limb, I wondered whether I would even be alive by the time sixth form ended. In nearby Leicester I saw gay men visibly wasting away; I feared this was the future for all gay people. It felt like our lives were over, just when they should have been beginning.

In school AIDS or LGBT+ people were not talked about, at least not positively, some of which was the result of legislation called 'Clause 28' or 'Section 28'. Section 28 was an amendment to the UK's Local Government Act 1988, enacted in 1988 during Conservative Prime Minister Margaret Thatcher's administration. Section 28 stated that local authorities 'shall not intentionally promote homosexuality or publish material with the intention of promoting homosexuality' or 'promote the teaching in any maintained school of the acceptability of homosexuality as a pretended family relationship'. As a result, many educators felt restricted from openly acknowledging LGBT+ identities in schools. This in turn led to teachers feeling disempowered when it came to tackling prejudice-related bullying and language and led to many young LGBT+ children (and indeed teachers) feeling targeted, shamed, excluded and discriminated against. Section 28 also had the effect of boosting confidence in those who harboured hate towards LGBT+ people.

Section 28 was enacted at a time when attitudes towards gay people were turning a dark corner. Despite increased visibility in the mid 1980s, the onset of HIV/AIDS in the UK and the associated shaming, blaming and witch-hunting by politicians, the media and other key public figures meant that for a generation of young people, school became a place where their core identity became toxic. As prejudice against gay people took hold (especially in the media), our schools, the one protective factor that could have helped young LGBT+ people feel represented, safe and included, instead had been neutered by prejudicial legislation.

There was widespread, highly passionate campaigning against Section 28 and the UK charity Stonewall was established in direct response. After public demonstrations and campaigning, Section 28 was finally repealed in 2000 in Scotland and in 2003 in the rest of the UK.

Section 28 lives on as a deeply painful memory for those of us who were fortunate to survive the 1980s. Many are not here to tell their stories. Such prejudicial legislation must *never* be allowed to happen again, although sadly I fear it will. One only has to look to some overseas territories such as the USA, Australia, Hungary, Poland and Indonesia to see how recent progress on LGBT+ inclusion can rapidly and dangerously be set back. This possibility places more urgency upon our journey towards inclusive LGBT+ culture change.

Section 28 effectively enshrined into law the untruth that when schools acknowledge and celebrate the existence of LGBT+ people and their contributions to society, this is a form of 'promotion'. Teaching about non-LGBT+ lives involves the dissemination of information. Teaching and learning about LGBT+ people is no different. The intention is purely to promote inclusion, safety, kindness and success. Even in 2019, in some Midlands schools, the emotive word 'promotion' is currently being deployed by some parents of faith to protest against LGBT+ inclusive curricula. I personally believe there is a correlation between the manner in which some faiths historically aspire to recruit and indoctrinate and the misconception that teaching and learning about LGBT+ people involves the promotion of a 'lifestyle choice'.

Against the background of an education system neutered by Section 28, and now aged 17, my parents finally discovered I was gay. As a result, I was not allowed out of the house for a year, apart from lifts to and from school; my relationship was forcibly ended, and overtures were made that I would be taken for clinical 'correction' such as electro-convulsion therapy. I had reached a tipping point where even my own family rejected me.

I became highly anxious, sank into a deep depression and began self-harming. Until my late forties, when I underwent a period of sustained and significant therapy, I would often struggle with depression and anxiety. At times of acute stress or suffering, the unhealthy coping strategy of self-harm that first emerged when I was a vulnerable gay youth would return. To this day I use a variety of techniques to minimise the impact of anxiety.

Bullying and rejection can spoil a playtime, a whole day, a week, a full term, an academic year or an entire stage of formal education and can impair our emotional and physical functioning well into old age if we don't seek support. This is not what I want for the young people we teach; they deserve better, don't you think?

My parents were doing what they thought was right to protect me, but it became too much to bear and one rejection too many. I felt there was little to look forward to; education and exams seemed irrelevant and I looked instead for jobs that would pay enough to help me leave home to find a safe space. There seemed no point in studying to live and work in a world that viewed me as defective and unnatural. A world in which governments made laws to stop even conversations about people like me, as if we were a disease or infection.

My state education came to a sudden end in May 1987, when part-way through my A-levels I was summoned to the Head of Sixth Form, who questioned my increasing non-attendance. Put on the spot, at first, I lied and said my parents were getting divorced, which was upsetting me. Initially he seemed supportive, but then something shifted in my thinking and I decided to take a chance on being authentic for the first time in my life (I respected him as a leader) and tell him the truth. On nervously informing him that I was gay, his voice, body language and physical proximity changed negatively towards me and in that moment I saw no further reason to remain at school. Whilst many teachers were prevented from teaching about the existence of LGBT+ people due to Section 28, in that one moment back in May 1987 I finally lost hope and trust in adults. It was very nearly the end of me.

Walking out of school and running home, I sobbed my heart out for hours, before coming very close to taking my own life with a rusty razor blade. Ultimately it was a glimmer of hope that resulted in me living – hope that a day might come when a young person could study within an education system and live in a world that celebrated the natural diversity of human existence. If I could just hold on and keep swimming, maybe that day would come.

The next time I would enter a classroom at Lutterworth Grammar School would be in July 2013 as an adult. After seeing my LGBT+ inclusion work on national television the school invited me back to speak about my experiences to staff and pupils. It was an emotional day and I was impressed by the work the school was now undertaking on diversity.

But back in 1987 significant life changes had to be made in order to ensure my survival. I took a job in a record shop and moved out of home shortly afterwards. I had no sense of career direction and my A-level exam results were poor. Then, totally out of the blue after a chance meeting in a local village pub, I unexpectedly found real, lasting love and stability with a loving and compassionate man named David. My own ongoing struggles to manage and process the wounds of my youth meant that my focus was still on surviving day to day, as opposed to thriving or growth. My relationship with my own parents would remain strained until my forties and David was not once allowed inside my family home, even at Christmas. We stayed together for 12 mostly lovely years (although he was clearly struggling with his own internalised homophobia, which often had the potential to make me feel even more shameful) and without him I simply wouldn't have survived or ultimately trained as a teacher.

I will always be hugely grateful to David and his family.

Post education

After short-term posts in the civil service and local government I worked as a professional actor. Several directors remarked on my suitability for teaching. I was 26 and facilitating theatre in education in order to stimulate the learning of young people. My faith in the potential of education to positively change lives was in ascendance. I enjoyed the open hearts and creativity of young people; what a privilege it was to make a positive difference to their lives. I loved the way in which children expressed themselves so openly and creatively. Concrete thoughts of entering teaching crossed my mind. However, I was concerned that if I was to enter my chosen age range of primary schools, I might be perceived as a paedophile if parents or colleagues discovered that I was gay. I had heard (and continue to hear) so many people wrongly equate being gay to being a paedophile that I was very fearful. I was once asked by a relative (at the dinner table) whether working with primary-age pupils would result in me looking at the 'little boys changing for physical education'. This question made me feel sick; I knew there was a fundamental difference between LGBT+ people and paedophiles, but the general population apparently did not.

My terminally ill father urged me to train as a teacher and I undertook a Bachelor of Education degree, gaining very good reports for my teaching practices. Dad sadly didn't live to see any of my resulting school class photos, nor indeed the awards that would later come my way for my LGBT+ work. He died of lung cancer aged 69, related to his time in the Royal Navy. I hope he would now be proud of my work, although he too struggled with my identity.

My first year of teaching was at a very challenging (and now demolished) middle school in Northampton. There I witnessed homophobic language being used by some teachers when discussing pupils; I questioned whether schools had really changed much since 1987. Old internal shame and fear arose, and I wobbled, leaving to undertake supply instead, which felt more anonymous. For safety on supply, I would lie about my long-term relationship when talking about my holidays or weekends with colleagues. I would use female pronouns to refer to David. I would also pretend to be single. Lying made me feel ashamed; I felt I was betraying the man I loved. On some days I would sit in the toilet at work and cry about my deceit.

A friend then warned me *not* to lie about David as 'if parents or governors find out you are lying, they will think you are only working in a primary school because you are a paedophile'. It seemed I couldn't win.

I taught in contexts ranging from small village schools, to faith schools, to large inner-city schools, something that brought me a joyfully broad sense of education contexts and management styles. In many schools I would hear staff make comments likening boys who liked drama to 'poofs' or girls who liked football to 'lezzies'. In the late 1990s, it was all still there, just as it had been growing up.

South of the river

I moved to London in 2000, when my 12-year relationship with David morphed into a lifelong friendship. I was asked to undertake a day's supply teaching in a large, relatively new primary school in Docklands. I was first placed in Year 3 and was immediately struck by the number of children with complex additional physical needs. The school was unusually (in my experience) committed to inclusion, including many young people with highly complex additional physical and learning needs in mainstream provision. I was moved by the compassion of very young children towards those less fortunate than themselves. Having experienced life as an outsider, the school ethos of 'strong relationships' resonated deeply and for the first time in my professional life I felt a sense of belonging. Thinking that London would be more accepting in its attitudes, I accepted a permanent role at the school.

I worked as a class teacher initially, then undertook various coordinator roles, before progressing to Key Stage 2 leader, then deputy head and often acting head. Section 28 was finally repealed in 2003, but I still saw no significant LGBT+ education. I was informed by a colleague that the National Front (a far-right extremist organisation) was active in the area local to the school. Indeed, two National Front marches took place in neighbouring streets. Despite this, the school intake was increasingly diverse, with over 35 different languages and multiple faiths; we worked hard to increase the visibility of a range of diverse role models.

Initially I again felt compelled to conceal my authentic identity, as at a social evening colleagues made homophobic jokes at my expense. Over the next eight years I was open with my colleagues on a 'need-to-know' basis. Even as late as 2009 I was investing a huge amount of emotional energy in the workplace into concealing a part of my core identity, energy that really should have been directed into my work with young people.

And then, just prior to Christmas 2009, my life unexpectedly changed, as a result of the pupil voice questionnaires I highlighted at the start of this chapter, which showed that 75 per cent of our primary pupils experienced daily direct homophobic bullying and language in and around school. Nearly all were hearing the word 'gay' used as a pejorative 'cuss', often covertly. For the sake of our young people I knew something had to be done. At that moment my life changed; it was time to really get to work.

Inclusion For All

I distributed staff development questionnaires and the resulting data showed that no staff had received any training on LGBT+ identities, including me! Clearly there was a significant training deficit, so I researched what support or training was available. I contacted several local primary school leaders and asked them whether they had ever had any training on LGBT+ identities and bullying – none had. Several admitted that homophobic bullying and language was a problem but said they did not feel equipped to deal with it. Several headteachers had previously been sent published LGBT education resources but admitted to dumping them. The general feeling was that formal resources were unhelpful without awareness training upfront, to facilitate conversations with staff who potentially might never have used the words 'lesbian', 'gay', 'bisexual' or 'transgender' aloud in an education context. There was a toxic, lingering sense that Section 28 still precluded such teaching and learning, despite being repealed in 2003.

There was a clear training deficit at primary level especially, yet we had a growing problem in the primary sector with LGBT+ bullying. I decided to devise training myself to run in my own school. My experience as a teacher, school leader and school improvement consultant led me to conclude that my training offer must include opportunities at the outset for *all* school staff and governors to explore their thoughts and feelings towards LGBT+ identities and the prejudice, including the myths and misconceptions, that often complicates them unnecessarily.

In my head a question formed: 'If a training scenario is facilitated in which the rationale of positive LGBT+ inclusion is established first, providing opportunities to explore personal beliefs and attitudes towards LGBT+ identities, might this result in a more accepting education sector within which positive LGBT+ inclusion training can be nationally deployed?'

I offered to facilitate an LGBT+ inclusion staff training day in my own school after considering the potential personal safety and career implications of tackling the issue. As a gay man I already ran the risk of accusations of having some kind of 'gay agenda' – whatever that means! Had our pupil voice data related to problems with racist or disablist bullying, we would not have hesitated for a moment, but because we were dealing with LGBT+ we were fearful and briefly hesitant. It is never appropriate to let our own fear hold us back from taking direct action to make schools safer for our children.

Interestingly, I had noticed that staff members who were aware I was gay usually reported incidents of homophobic language to me, as opposed to managing it themselves. Would a school with a black member of staff deem it appropriate for all incidents of racial bullying to be reported just to that one individual? I would hope not. It was also clear that with a majority of non–LGBT+ staff working at the school, they naturally leaned towards heteronormativity in all aspects of school life. I insisted that *all* staff were required to attend my training in order to develop standard procedures and to facilitate a shared and consistent level of understanding. To be most effective for the greatest number of stakeholders, I had to stimulate lasting organisational change. It wouldn't be enough to seek 'tolerance' for LGBT+ identities; who wants to spend their lives being merely tolerated? My aim was to help our school community move beyond tolerance and even acceptance to a mindset where LGBT+ identities could be celebrated each and every day in all aspects of school life, just like everyone else.

Over Christmas 2009 I combined my childhood experiences of homophobic bullying with my learning in the roles of class teacher, school leader and education consultant. This resulted in my first 'Inclusion For All' training day, positioned as part of a wider ongoing strategic initiative around diversity and inclusion. My initiative was informed by my meditation practice, helping me to bring compassion and patience; it had taken me many years to come to terms with being gay – could I really expect those who had not lived life as LGBT+ to go on a journey in a single training session? In the end, many did.

In January 2010 I delivered my training, my confidence bolstered by the introduction of the (then) new UK Equality Act, which for the first time placed sexual orientation and gender reassignment as 'protected characteristics', thus placing a legal duty upon schools to prevent discrimination. Whilst this strengthened my case, my rationale was the prevention of suffering of children. Legislation is, after all, subject to change and whilst we wait for legislators, young people are still getting hurt.

I nervously 'outed' myself to around 110 staff members. Some staff immediately admitted that they didn't understand the terms 'lesbian', 'gay', 'bisexual' and 'transgender'. Others were visibly embarrassed or laughed when using the terminology in front of other professionals. For many, this was their first opportunity to openly discuss these concepts with education professionals. Once the words were spoken, people were visibly more relaxed and empowered.

Over that day (and several other staff meetings) we went on a profound journey. Colleagues shed many of the misunderstandings, fears, anxieties and, in some cases, prejudices they had harboured about LGBT+ people. I remain deeply proud and moved by their honesty. Stonewall came to watch my initial training sessions, taking notes about my approach in a primary context. Feedback was highly positive, and colleagues expressed great relief that we were 'finally talking about these things'. Others stated they had wanted to tackle 'these issues' but had not known how.

Cover supervisor and teaching assistant Peggy Keane was a staff member present on that first day of training. She recalls it well:

> 'I remember at the start of the session some staff refused to believe that there was any bullying at our school and that some of the remarks that had been made by children and adults were just "harmless banter". As the session progressed people's attitudes began to change. By the end it was clearer to most people that homophobic bullying was real and not harmless banter. Before the training, responses to incidents were along the lines of "Don't worry, it's only words, ignore it" or children were sent to Shaun because staff felt uneasy dealing with the situation.'

By presenting our bullying data, by telling my own story and by highlighting the relationship between prejudice-related bullying, mental health, pupil outcomes and attendance, I had not only opened up conversations but also unexpectedly shifted thinking in many of our staff, some of whom previously held negative views on LGBT+ people.

Encouraged, I wrote and implemented a strategic whole-school improvement plan, which emerged out of feedback and discussions at my initial training day and from my self-devised, whole-school LGBT+ visibility audit. I didn't want a tokenistic approach; our strategic plan represented a key element of long-term school improvement, requiring a full commitment from all stakeholders, including pupils, governors and parents.

Peggy Keane observed shifts in attitudes and confidence within staff at the school:

> 'Since the training staff feel confident and better equipped to deal with situations. Staff and children talk openly about their feelings and how to deal with bullying. The attitude of staff has totally changed and any form of homophobic language or bullying is dealt with promptly and sympathetically with both parties involved in the discussion about what can be done to resolve things.'

It was a meaningful, inspiring and exciting journey to be undertaking.

To engage pupils, I shared our school homophobic bullying data in assembly. To make the stakes real, I 'came out' as gay and recounted some of my own childhood experiences. Pupils were saddened and in some cases shamed. Pupils admitted using 'gay' as a cuss, with others admitting that they pretended not to know what the word 'gay' meant when challenged by adults to avoid punishment. We discussed a range of 'out' LGBT+ celebrities they knew from the media to make the conversation relevant to them. We pledged to undertake a school-wide campaign to promote respectful usage of the word 'gay' amongst pupils, staff and parents. I asked pupils to openly discuss my assembly with their parents and carers; the more open we were about our journey towards positive LGBT+ inclusion, the more part and parcel of everyday life in school it would be. We saw no shame in celebrating human diversity or in making children safe. When my assembly ended pupils responded with unprompted applause, bringing tears to my eyes. Afterwards they congratulated me on my 'bravery', some disclosing that they had LGBT+ friends and relatives and because of my assembly they now felt happier talking about them.

As a school community we were noticeably more cohesive, authentic and compassionate. Parents sought advice as to how best to support learning about LGBT+ identities at home. Authenticity in the workplace resulted in my own productivity doubling as finally I was freed from the shackles of inauthenticity. I often wonder what I could have achieved much earlier in my working life had I never had to invest energy into lying and keeping myself safe.

Over the following years we embedded teaching and learning about diversity, human rights, prejudice, LGBT+ role models, stories and history throughout our school ethos and curriculum offer. Visibility and statutory compliance were achieved via realignment of policy and ethos and newly purchased resources reflected a more diverse range of human experiences.

In 2010 my work came to the attention of the Department for Education, Ofsted, the National College and Stonewall, all of whom spent time with me in order to study my approach and see where it aligned with their own provision. My work made the mainstream press and was globally reported via the media and social media. I subsequently worked on positive LGBT+ inclusion in education with teacher trade unions, initial teacher training faculties, and national anti-bullying and youth organisations, and I advised at government-policy level.

In 2011 Ofsted judged my own school's LGBT+ inclusive practice as 'outstanding'. I was by then delivering Inclusion For All as outreach in other primary and secondary schools and was hosting termly in-school training events. Feedback showed that delegates experienced the sessions as 'outstanding'. I couldn't quite believe it. I had never been trained on positive LGBT+ inclusion myself (anything but); however, my journey and my message seemed to resonate and somehow have the power to open hearts and minds.

What a tremendous privilege!

'I was fortunate to attend a professional development session early on at Shaun's previous school, to see first-hand how such a provision could be embedded into a working primary school. This enabled me to confidently inform my students that it can be done, and great results can be achieved!'

Training delegate from Liverpool Hope University

Since then I have trained and coached many thousands of colleagues in hundreds of primary, secondary and faith schools across the UK and overseas. I continue to tell my story to many thousands of young people in school assemblies, webcasts and workshops around the world.

In 2014, whilst travelling by bus to undertake a radio interview for the BBC, I was approached by a man I didn't recognise initially. He was around my age and stared at me for a long while before finally moving to sit next to me. I was anxious about his behaviour and asked him if he was okay. He responded by asking whether my name was Shaun. When I said it was, he asked me whether I used to be called Shaun Franks. When I confirmed that I did he began to cry. I again asked him whether he was okay and he asked me whether I recognised him; initially I did not, but then I saw something around his eyes that triggered some difficult memories from many years before. 'I was one of the kids that bullied you,' he said before admitting, 'I thought you had killed yourself as you disappeared from view. I have never stopped thinking about you and the hurt we must have done to you. I want you to know that I am so very sorry for what I, for what we, did.' I said, 'Thank you' and I told him it was okay, giving him a hug. I told him to let the past go. With that he burst into proper flowing tears as years of shame and guilt began to lift. What we say in jest or in anger in one moment of one day in a playground, classroom or staff room can not only diminish the wellbeing of another, it can diminish ourselves too.

I have now had the pleasure of supporting many of the leading anti-bullying, hate-crime, human rights and safeguarding organisations in the UK in developing their provision around LGBT+ inclusion. My work has been recognised and recommended by Amnesty UK, the Church of England and the Faith and Belief Forum. In May 2016 I was honoured and humbled to become the recipient of three major awards in one rather surreal week. In addition to being named 'LGBT+ Education Champion' at the Excellence in Diversity Awards and also being presented with the Mayor of Southwark's Highest Civic Honour at Southwark Cathedral, I was summoned to Number 10 Downing Street, where I was honoured in person by the then prime minister David Cameron. In a recommendation for my work, the prime minister wrote that my work is:

> '... having a fantastic impact on increasing awareness in schools. By equipping teachers to speak to children about these issues you are helping to make sure future generations will not face the despicable prejudice that you and many others in the LGBT community so wrongly had to endure. I believe it is my duty as Prime Minister to hold up examples of great service as an inspiration to others. Through your hard work and dedication you are making our communities stronger and our world a better place.'

It is humbling to be recognised and have one's work honoured in this way, but I don't undertake my work to seek approval or win awards, lovely as they are; I do it to change and save lives. Therefore, when young people write to me out of the blue, as they sometimes do, these moments mean more to me than anything.

> 'I left school in 2011 and I have so much to thank the school and you in particular for; I found the school such a happy and friendly place to be and after discovering that I myself fall on the LGBTQ+ spectrum, I believe without doubt that the self-acceptance I felt was as a result of the inclusive and loving environment that was fostered. I was never taught or in an environment where sexualities were discriminated against and I therefore never felt any of this towards myself – thank you for this. Only after leaving your school did I realise how uniquely brilliant it was; none of my peers now have been exposed to such diversity in terms of religion, race, special needs and sexuality, and I can tell you how much all of these things have shaped me into the person that I am proud to be now, so thank you. I still remember the assembly in which you came out. It made such an impact on me; when I discovered your website I had to reach out and thank you. You are what teachers are supposed to be.'

> Former pupil

Looking ahead

My work goes on, for whilst we have made significant progress there is still so much more to do. I am currently engaged in a long-term project to support the entire Isle of

Man education system to become LGBT+ inclusive, which is a tremendous privilege. You will read about some of the inspiring practice happening on the island later in this book. I have also recently been working with Sikh and Catholic schools in London and increasingly overseas.

The role of any educator is to be courageous on behalf of all our amazing young people without exception, promoting dignity and respect and challenging injustice on their behalf, whenever we encounter it. We must remain unwavering in our view that LGBT+ young people, staff and parents deserve their time and place on Planet Earth and in our school communities, for complacency and inaction lead only to poor outcomes, depression, self-harm and even suicide.

Educators at all levels share a moral responsibility to enable inclusive and safe spaces within which individuals with non-heterosexual and non-cisgender identities (including emergent identities over time) can be celebrated as equally as their heterosexual and cisgender peers and colleagues. I hope educators reading this book will bring an open heart to undertake a journey towards more positive LGBT+ inclusion (perhaps for the first time) whilst internalising a set of strategies that can be deployed to prevent prejudice-related bullying of any kind, resulting in respectful and safe inclusion for all members of our school communities.

If you have been moved by my story, know that however difficult life gets, each breath brings the possibility of a new moment. Never lose hope; look forward and not back. Reach out for help. Tell your story.

Now it is time for us together to write a happier story on behalf of all the brilliantly unique young people we teach or will ever teach. Please shine brightly for our young people and empower them to shine too.

Time to reflect

Before turning the page, please take a moment to reflect.

Things to think about:

- What is present for you after reading my story in terms of charged thoughts and feelings? Be sure to take care of yourself.
- Did anything surprise or challenge you about my story?
- Reflect upon your own life journey. Have bullying, prejudice and discrimination affected you at school, at work or in wider society? How has this impacted upon your life journey and sense of self?
- What might you do differently as a result of reading my story, both within and outside of the professional environment?

Things to do:

- Explore the experiences of young LGBT+ people via www.rucomingout. com.
- Watch my TED Talk at https://youtu.be/jaBhtT65i6U.
- Find out more about the experiences and identities of young LGBT+ people around the word by visiting https://itgetsbetter.org/.
- Ensure that you are familiar with the United Nations Convention on the Rights of the Child.
- Join a local mindfulness class and get to know your brain.

Chapter 2
The reality of homophobia

'School can be the difference between hope and despair, between life and death for kids.'

Dr John King (as quoted in Bedford, 2018)

Following on from my personal story in Chapter 1, this chapter will consider the impact of homophobia upon individuals, the extent to which it exists in our schools and the moral obligations supporting LGBT+ inclusion; I will also address some common misnomers. Developing this understanding of how damaging homophobia can be is a vital part of the Tier 1 process to explore our thoughts and feelings towards human diversity. Please aim to bring full awareness to your reactions and responses to the topics I raise, bringing non-judgemental curiosity to *what* you think and feel and, importantly, *why* you think and feel it.

In 50 years, I have often accumulated 'stuff' about other humans I actually know very little about, from multiple sources. If we are mindful and self-aware, we can avoid making assumptions and believing in stereotypes, potentially disempowering our own prejudices.

Let's be honest with ourselves: I've had prejudices; haven't you?

Prejudging others leads us to treat people unfairly based upon aspects of their identities that may be exaggerated or untrue. LGBT+ identities and the surrounding debates are complex; notice what challenges or inspires you as you read on and reflect in your notepad. As educators we must strive to develop a more refined sense of our own relationship to human 'difference' and diversity, for when we nourish ourselves, we can aspire to nourish our young people. Let us now take a more detailed look at homophobia, before exploring its extent and impact.

Homophobia

'But we don't have any homophobia in our school.' I have been repeatedly assured of this by school leaders, often in complete denial, for the past ten years. Homophobia exists – in our schools, workplaces and communities – and we must acknowledge it.

The term 'homophobia' was first used by US writer George Weinberg in 1972, who defined it as a 'dread of being at close quarters with homosexuals'. Homophobia is prejudice, stigma and discrimination against lesbian, gay, bisexual and transgender people; the more specific terms 'biphobia' and 'transphobia' have evolved over time, but still don't take into account the wider spectrum of human non-heterosexual, non-binary or intersex identities.

Prejudice is targeted at LGBT+ individuals from *within* and *without* the LGBT+ community, with experiences and impact varying significantly. Many schools are at an emergent stage of tackling and preventing LGBT+ bullying from students who are not LGBT+ and can fail to prevent conflict *between* those young people who identify as LGBT+ entirely. Conflict between members of minority groups can feel impenetrable if we don't identify with the group ourselves. We may worry about causing offence by intervening where we might perceive we are not welcome; however, LGBT+ youth deserve and need our full support in fostering healthy personal and interpersonal relationships.

In our 21st-century world, families come in a variety of shapes and sizes. In discussing family groups with school stakeholders, we must no longer assume that a marriage is between a woman and a man, or that LGBT+ people cannot have children, or that a parent in a male–female partnership cannot be trans-gender, or indeed that a transgender man cannot have periods or a baby. This is our joyful diverse world, but it can seem complex. We can bring resistance when we don't have all the facts we need and our resistance can lead to anxiety, fear and prejudice.

When I first began offering training in LGBT+ inclusion, I hadn't anticipated the number of heads who would shut down the conversation, saying either that homophobia didn't exist in their school or 'We don't have any LGBT+ pupils in our school.' My response was: 'With respect, how do you know?' It turned out that some heads were aware of the problem after all but highlighted a lack of training and perceived permission (a Section 28 throwback) to openly talk about LGBT+ bullying. The first step towards preventing homophobia is acknowledging the problem and understanding the damage it is causing to young people.

There does exist an issue around how we *know* whether we have LGBT+ pupils in our schools. Gaining accurate statistics of the number of LGBT+ students (and indeed staff) in our schools remains an issue because stigma exists, and therefore some young people and adults do not feel comfortable in defining their LGBT+ identities in schools or the workplace. The figure 'one in ten' is quoted frequently when I attend education seminars on LGBT+ inclusion and whilst accurate statistics are useful, I work from the assumption that in any school, in any work-place, whether we are aware of it or not, LGBT+ people will be present. In add-ition, there will be those who have LGBT+ friends and family. It is therefore vital that all schools work to tackle homophobia.

Take a pause

Sit comfortably upright. Either close your eyes or lower your gaze to the floor. When settled, bring your attention to your breathing, noticing where your breath is coming in and out of your body. Try not to control your breathing but notice the coolness or warmth as breath travels in and out of your body and any associated movements of your belly or chest. If you struggle to bring awareness to your breath then use your feet on the ground, or your bottom on the chair, to ground you.

If you notice thoughts popping into your head (and they will), gently guide your attention back to the physical sensations of your body. Label any thoughts that arise as 'thinking' without judgement and let them dissolve.

When your attention is more focused in the present moment, visualise a pond. Visualise how it feels to be standing next to that pond.

Now visualise a smooth stone in your hand. When you have a strong sense of the stone, visualise throwing it into the water. As it breaks the surface ask yourself several times, 'What are my prejudices?' and notice what arises for you, without judgement. Now visualise the stone falling deeper still, well below the surface. Ask again, 'What are my prejudices?' and 'Where do my prejudices come from?' Notice what arises.

Finally, visualise the stone falling to the bottom of the pond, letting it ground itself firmly. Repeat the previous questions and also ask, 'How do my prejudices influence my behaviours?', bringing compassion, curiosity and non-judgement to whatever arises.

When you are ready, bring your attention back to your breath and then your sense of seated self.

This has been your personal exploration. You do not have to share what you have learned with anyone else. Prejudice and bias are ongoing companions for us all, whether we are aware of them or not, and whether we choose to acknowledge them or not.

You may repeat this activity and ask these questions:

1. How do I know when I experience prejudice?
2. How do I experience my own prejudices? (For example, thoughts or specific physical sensations or a combination of both.)
3. When I experience prejudice, how does this impact upon the choices I make?

Whenever you have finished, bring gratitude to yourself for your commitment to self-growth and honesty. Don't forget to use your notepad to reflect upon your personal exploration.

If you would prefer to listen to this meditation, there is a reading available at https://youtu.be/SVvf_jxtLCA.

Being mindful of prejudice

As educators, we have for years instructed young people, staff and parents 'not to be prejudiced' and told them not to say certain homophobic, racist and pejorative terms. However, as we will discover in Chapter 3, page 58, prejudice is not just about saying the 'wrong' thing; prejudices are deep-seated attitudes, assumptions and beliefs that may be conscious or even unconscious. Often our prejudices develop over time, based on environmental factors, such as our upbringing or the way we are influenced by the media. This approach of simply telling people, 'Don't be prejudiced' therefore does not work. People quickly learn to say prejudicial words only when staff are not listening. Instead we must work proactively with our prejudices and encourage all school stakeholders to do the same.

To bring curiosity initially to my own prejudices, I use the 'PPOP' technique. I have now deployed it successfully in many schools. 'PPOP' stands for 'put your prejudices on your palm' and it involves us noticing, allowing and bringing curiosity to moments in which we experience prejudicial thoughts and feelings. I developed PPOP many years ago when I came home by train late one night. Apart from one person in a burqa sat opposite me, there was no one else on the train. As we sat in silence, I became aware that I was experiencing an unexpected level of anxiety. Rather than bury these feelings I visualised them on the palm of my hand and brought non-judgemental curiosity to them. I imagined the colour, shape and texture of my anxiety. I gently explored its origin within myself.

After some gentle self-reflection two pieces of relevant information emerged from my subconscious: firstly, as a child, covered faces and masks had often frightened me and secondly, I could 'hear' voices of some of those I had grown up with who had reinforced negative stereotypes of Muslims. As a result of placing my prejudice in my palm and exploring it, I was then able to undertake some new learning about Muslims, which dissolved my anxieties and allowed me to gain control over the voices of the past. PPOP empowers me to own and work with any prejudice or bias that may arise, rather than allowing my prejudice or bias to dehumanise or disadvantage others.

Think back to the pond and stone activity; did anything arise to which you can try to apply the PPOP technique?

Take a moment to think about LGBT+ identities. Visualise two men or two women kissing one another fully on the lips or a male-to-female transgender person. Should any negative reactions arise, PPOP them in your palm, bring curiosity, own them and then work with them, for if we neglect to do so, there is a genuine risk that that palm could become a fist. Aim to bring the same curious awareness to your judging mind.

Internalised homophobia

In Chapter 1, page 20, I described how societal homophobia eventually led me to verbally abuse another LGBT+ student. A sense of self-worth and a positive view of our core identities are critical for our mental health. The effects of growing up LGBT+ in an often hostile world are so profoundly damaging that many LGBT+ people experience mental distress as a result. Some turn the negativity inwards upon themselves. In time it may reach 'critical mass' and be externalised onto others.

I have encountered internalised homophobia in a number of ways:

- denial of authentic identity
- separation of sex and love
- denial of one's authentic identity to others
- attempts to modify authentic identity or orientation to appear more socially acceptable
- low self-worth
- shame
- low self-esteem
- unhealthy approach to self-care
- underachievement as an attempt to strive for social acceptance
- bullying more visible members of the LGBT+ community
- fear of intimacy
- trying to pass as heterosexual or cisgender
- using alcohol or chemicals to 'blot out' thoughts or feelings
- seeking conversion therapy
- self-regulation and modification of behaviours and mannerisms
- attacking those speaking out for LGBT+ rights
- acting up at school as an attempt to strive for social acceptance
- aggressive sexual acts.

There is an increasing body of evidence to suggest that some of the most homophobic individuals are internally gay and conflict with themselves (see for example Weinstein et al., 2012). Their internal conflict is then directed towards more openly LGBT+ individuals. Even within the LGBT+ community, shaming for being 'too masculine' or 'too feminine' occurs.

By challenging the negative social factors causing this internal conflict, via positive LGBT+ education, we can lessen the damage. Unlike many other forms of prejudice, LGBT+ related prejudice can also manifest within the family home, placing a significant need upon schools as a protective factor.

LGBT+ 'lifestyles'

I received the following as feedback after leading an LGBT+ training session in a Church of England school:

'I understand that children bullying other children is wrong; however I am not convinced that schools are the appropriate institutions to be teaching that gay lifestyles are a normal part of human life.'

I often hear educators refer to LGBT+ 'lifestyles', an offensive, inaccurate term that diminishes LGBT+ identities and fails to account for testimonies of LGBT+ people. It implies that LGBT+ people consciously *chose* a path that might lead to sacking, family rejection, conversion therapy, prejudice, bullying, beatings, self-harm or even suicide. Why would children and young people want to run the risk of such negativity?

I grew up Christian and gay. My Christianity was constructed from extrinsic sources, whereas my LGBT+ identity emerged intrinsically from *within*. My faith was (mostly) my choice; my fancying men was not.

I have made many choices:

- grow a beard
- become a teacher
- study meditation
- become an actor
- buy a schnauzer
- obsess over *Doctor Who*.

These were choices, but there was *no* choice in me growing up fancying Burt Reynolds. I tried to deny it and modify myself in failed attempts to fit with societal expectations, but there was no *choice* involved. I even had a 'type' by the time I was at primary school. 'Being heterosexual is a lifestyle choice' is something no one would say!

Recently there has often been toxic debate in the press about young people supposedly 'choosing' to be non-binary and transgender, as if it is a fashion craze. I have spent many hours talking with young non-binary and transgender people, listening to many stories of extreme suffering. None of them simply woke up one day, clicked their heels and decided to make a 'lifestyle choice' to become trans or non-binary; yes, there are gradual awakenings, but these take place over a period of time, sometimes over a whole lifetime. Sometimes we don't understand who we are ourselves, until we see our own experiences mirrored back at us. Just like the animal kingdom, which so readily meets with our interest and approval, humanity is a joyful, diverse spectrum; sadly, our reactions and responses do not always suggest that we are emotionally equipped for the privilege to live and work with diverse human beings.

Who are we to discount the testimony and lived experience of another individual, however different their life might be from our own? If we bring compassion instead of judgement, our conversations become less damaging to those already suffering. We should never question the validity of a young person's core identity.

Concerns about LGBT+ 'lifestyles' often stem from intergenerational or faith-based prejudice and stereotypes. Individuals can claim that they are 'not homophobic' or 'not prejudiced' whilst being *just* that. These moments are opportunities, if we allow them to be, not for judgement but for *new learning*. I work with faith schools and ask young people whether faith is a barrier to learning about LGBT+ identities; a typical response is that their faith teaches them to respect other people, to love and to be kind.

Until scientists solve the 'nature versus nurture' debate I suspect the term 'lifestyle choice' will prevail, but this should never detract from the fact that UK schools have a statutory duty to meet the needs of all pupils, including those who identify as LGBT+. Even if our young people were 'choosing' to identify as LGBT+, our duty of care would still stand. Finally, it is worth mentioning here how derogatory it is to tell someone their life is a 'waste' simply as a result of their LGBT+ identity; this is a comment that has been made to me so many times throughout my life by some heterosexual women who apparently define me in terms of only one sexual function. It's highly reductive and it can hurt.

The impact of LGBT+ bullying

Students at St Gabriel's College in South London had this to say when I visited in 2018:

> 'It is important for schools to tackle LGBT+ issues because homophobic bullying can really affect people in the LGBT+ community and also in school. They might, for example, miss out on crucial exams and this could have a lifetime effect on their lives and how they fit into society.'

The second comment is especially astute, describing the potential for lasting damage beyond the present moment and well into adulthood. Kovacs and Devlin (1998) agree, concluding that 'a negative event in childhood can remain in evidence for up to five decades and perhaps beyond'.

I have never heard anyone say that children 'deserve to be bullied for being heterosexual' and yet from some educators I hear the view that young LGBT+ people 'bring bullying on themselves', simply by being themselves. Our tolerance for bullying must be set at zero, whilst adopting a curious, compassionate and restorative approach to its root causes.

Take a pause

Reflect on these questions, noticing what arises for you:

1) Were you bullied at school?
2) How did it make you feel?
3) Did you ever report it to anyone? If not, why not?

Whilst working with young LGBT+ people on the Isle of Man in January 2018, I asked them how it felt to be attending schools that historically had failed to represent them or in some cases even acknowledge their existence. Their replies brought me to tears:

- 'We feel invisible.'
- 'We can't be ourselves.'

- 'We don't feel safe.'
- 'No one talks about us in schools.'

The impact of any kind of bullying can result in lifelong damage. Our role as educators is not only to tackle but also to prevent all kinds of bullying. Tackling LGBT+ bullying might seem challenging at first and so it is important when building our own confidence that we are able to identify and communicate what is at stake if we fail to attain our goals on behalf of our young people.

Take a pause

Take a moment to reflect upon the damage caused by bullying behaviours and language related to LGBT+ identities. Using words and short phrases, write down the kinds of damage that you think prejudice-related bullying causes an LGBT+ young person. Record them around the figure of the child below or in your own notebook.

I have already added one to start you off; see how many you can list.

Low self-esteem

Finished? Well done. This simple activity is one of my core activities; I have undertaken it for ten years with many thousands of education professionals and young people. In preparation for this book I revisited 50 versions of this activity I've retained from schools, teacher training faculties and faith organisations.

The most commonly suggested words and phrases are (in no particular order):

- Low self-esteem
- Low self-worth
- Modifying or compromising aspects of true identity
- Feelings of isolation
- Exclusion from peer group
- Poor mental health

- Self-loathing
- Not wanting to attend school
- Surviving becomes more important than learning
- Personality changes
- Self-harm
- Depression

- Feeling 'othered'
- Feeling shameful
- Separation or compartmentalisation of parts of self
- Anger
- Rejection of self or aspects of self
- Feeling helpless
- Feeling confused
- Wanting to withdraw
- Sadness
- Becoming a bully
- Hopelessness
- Trying to hide being LGBT+

- Suicide
- Dealing with physical violence
- Inability to escape online bullying
- Impact of so-called 'banter'
- Less likely to stay on for higher education
- Career path compromised
- More likely to veer towards drug or alcohol abuse with associated sexual health risks
- Post-traumatic stress disorder
- Difficulties in making or sustaining relationships

How did this list resonate with your own?

Mental health

The inclusion of 'poor mental health' in the list in 'Take a pause' is not intended to suggest that LGBT+ individuals experience poor mental health as a result of their LGBT+ identities. It is shocking that only in 1992 did the World Health Organization declassify homosexuality as a mental illness. The declassification of transgender identity did not come until 2018. Poor mental health arises as a result of growing up feeling 'othered' and separated from societal 'norms' and the accompanying prejudice, discrimination and bullying.

'Transforming children and young people's mental health provision', a green paper by the UK Department of Health and Department for Education (2017), concluded:

> 'Lesbian, gay, bisexual and transgender (LGBT) people of all ages are more likely to experience poor mental health than heterosexuals, which indicates that LGBT children and young people have particular support needs. For example, LGBT people were found to be at higher risk of mental disorder, suicidal thoughts, substance misuse and self-harm than heterosexuals.'

LGBT+ inclusion is a matter of keeping young people safe and well. It is not uncommon for an LGBT+ child coming out to an untrained educator to be referred to mental health services, based solely on their LGBT+ status. Consider the message this sends to young people about a part of their core identity. The medical world is taking a slow journey to stop pathologising diverse identities. Schools must do the same. The suggestion (still made by some education professionals) that LGBT+ education represents a subject that is somehow 'sensitive' must be viewed in the context of the above information and the knowledge that LGBT+ bullying can and does affect many young children who are simply perceived as 'different' or who don't comply with gender 'norms'. Schools don't refer to teaching and learning about non-LGBT+ identities as 'sensitive'; it just happens naturally. How often do we hear LGBT+ lives and history described as 'LGBT+ issues'? The word 'issues' implies negativity. Similarly, LGBT+ rights are simply 'human rights'. In 2019, the headteacher of a primary school in Birmingham, when sadly forced to defend LGBT+ inclusion work against parental protest, went on national television and used the term 'LGBT agenda'. Her heart was undoubtedly in the right place but this language only inflames detractors and plays into misconceptions. There is no 'LGBT agenda' here; our agenda is simply the inclusion, safety and wellbeing of our diverse young people. This is a prime example of how we must shift thinking.

The reality of LGBT+ bullying

'It is important to tackle LGBT+ bullying in schools, because then people will learn about what it feels like to be LGBT+ and how some people can use it against you.'
Laura, aged 14, London

The UK has made significant progress in furthering equality for LGBT+ people. In my lifetime, we have shifted from partial decriminalisation of homosexuality to same-sex marriage to greater protections for transgender people, although in the case of the latter group especially, there is still much more to be done. Attitudes and legislation towards gay men have historically differed from those towards gay women, as have attitudes towards gender non-conforming people.

Our current UK Equality Act 2010 (see Chapter 4, page 72) reflects an ongoing need for a governmental and societal response to individuals and groups of individuals whose rights and freedoms have been marginalised. If these groups and individuals were afforded equality of opportunity and were able to live free from prejudice and discrimination, then specific equality legislation would not be needed to protect them. It is called cause and effect and it's something we must teach young people.

According to the Stonewall 'School report' (2017a), the number of lesbian, gay and bi pupils bullied because of their sexual orientation has decreased by almost a third since 2007. Additionally, schools are now more likely to say that homophobic bullying is wrong, and children are more likely to experience education about LGBT+ people in the classroom. This is testament not just to Stonewall but also to the many other individuals and organisations who have been working in the field. However, there is so much still to do. The same report also shows:

- Nearly half of young people are bullied for being LGBT at school, and only one in five have learnt about safe sex at school in the context of same-sex relationships.

- Fifty-two per cent of LGBT students hear homophobic language 'frequently' or 'often' at school.
- Eighty-six per cent of students regularly hear phrases such as 'That's so gay' or 'You're so gay' in school.
- Fewer than a third of bullied pupils said that teachers intervened when they were present during the bullying.
- Sixty-one per cent of lesbian, gay and bi pupils have deliberately harmed themselves.
- Most LGBT pupils are never taught about what LGBT identities mean in school or college.
- Only one in five pupils reported that their headteacher talked openly about LGBT equality.
- Over half of LGBT pupils said there isn't an adult at school to whom they can talk.
- Forty per cent of LGBT pupils have skipped school because of bullying.
- Despite transgender pupils being at increased risk of bullying, self-harm and suicide, 44 per cent of transgender pupils reported that staff in school are not familiar with the term 'trans' and what it means.

These findings not only represent a significant deficiency in raising awareness, but also indicate an inherent failure on the part of some schools in acknowledging their statutory role as protector. Young bullied LGBT+ people will often not tell anyone they are being bullied; they may fear being 'outed' before they really feel safe to be out, or perhaps they are not LGBT+ but fear they might be labelled as such due to the nature of the bullying. Whether LGBT+ or not, these kinds of bullying place young people in a highly vulnerable position in which they feel unable to reach out to adults who would, in any other circumstance, be there to offer support and protection.

The intersection of disability and LGBT identity also results in additional vulnerability for these young people. The Stonewall report indicates that LGBT disabled pupils are more likely to experience homophobic, biphobic and transphobic bullying than non-disabled pupils (60 per cent compared to 43 per cent). As a result, nearly half of disabled LGBT pupils (48 per cent) have tried to take their own lives and 80 per cent have thought about it. Free school meals children also show up as a very vulnerable group in the report. The statistics highlight the need for awareness of the intersections between equality strands and the multiplicity of ways in which young people can experience bullying associated with identity. It is important to be aware therefore that bullying related to LGBT+ identity may often be accompanied by bullying related to other aspects of young people's lives such as social economic background, race, faith, disability or levels of academic achievement.

The Stonewall report also found that whilst 40 per cent of young LGBT people have someone at home to talk to about being LGBT, this figure falls to 28 per cent for black, Asian and minority ethnic young people. Historically some school leaders may have backed away from talking about LGBT+ identities due to fear of causing offence on cultural or religious grounds, but the data findings of the Stonewall survey highlight the importance of placing the safety and wellbeing of the young person absolutely front and centre in this process, even where this may result in challenge.

The findings from the Stonewall report are supported by a survey of 9,000 young people aged 12–20, which was undertaken by the UK charity Ditch the Label in 2018 in partnership with schools and colleges from across the country. The survey found that 43 per cent of people within the LGBT community had been bullied in the past 12 months. The survey also raised some alarming findings about the impact of this bullying on young people's mental health:

- Sixty-two per cent of LGBT youth had experienced suicidal thoughts as a result of bullying.
- Of those within the LGBT community, nearly a third had attempted suicide due to their experiences and half of the respondents reported self-harming.
- Thirty-one per cent said they had developed an eating disorder.
- Seventy per cent said they had developed social anxiety.
- Seventy-one per cent said the bullying had led to depression.

Concerned? We should be.

The Stonewall 'School report' found that in schools where pupils are taught about LGBT identities, LGBT pupils are less likely to experience homophobic, biphobic and transphobic bullying. LGBT pupils in these schools are also more likely to report feeling safe, welcome and happy at school.

It is therefore essential that we facilitate an environment in which young people can develop in a manner that is conducive to good physical and mental health. A child who feels othered, rejected and bullied in and out of school by their peers, teachers, family members, community or faith community will be significantly damaged by the experience, having a direct impact upon their learning potential and thereby standards.

Are schools doing enough?

In 2018, the UK government published a 'LGBT Action Plan', formulated in response to the National LGBT Survey 2017 (Government Equalities Office, 2018). The response to the 12-week survey was unprecedented, with over 108,000 respondents over the age of 16 who identified as having a minority sexual orientation or gender identity or as intersex. This makes it the largest survey of its kind. The resulting data tells a sobering story and whilst respondents were generally positive about the UK's record on LGBT rights, some of the findings made for difficult reading. LGBT respondents were less satisfied with their life than the general UK population and transgender respondents had particularly low scores. At least two in five respondents had experienced an incident because they were LGBT, such as verbal harassment or physical violence, in the 12 months preceding the survey. Twenty-four per cent of respondents had accessed mental health services in the 12 months preceding the survey.

This survey shows that life after school for many LGBT+ people continues to be challenging, with many forced to compromise their authenticity in relationships in everyday life. However, the survey also shed some light on LGBT+ inclusion in schools. Respondents were asked whether sexual orientation or gender identity had been discussed whilst at school in lessons and whether these had prepared them for their lives as LGBT people. The survey asked those who had been in education during the 2016–2017 academic year whether they had faced negativity related to LGBT identities.

The key findings were:

- Only three per cent had discussed sexual orientation and gender identity at school, be that during lessons, in assemblies or elsewhere. 77 per cent said that neither was discussed.
- Where there had been discussion, only nine per cent of respondents said this had prepared them well for later life as an LGBT person.
- Many respondents highlighted the importance of including LGBT-specific content as part of sex education, whilst noting that it had been lacking from their own school experience.
- A third of respondents said they had experienced a negative reaction due to them being, or people perceiving them to be, LGBT. Common reactions were disclosure of their LGBT status without permission and verbal harassment.
- Six per cent reported exclusion from events or activities.
- Two per cent had experienced sexual and physical harassment.
- Thirteen per cent of transgender men and women in education said they had experienced being excluded from activities due to their transgender identity.
- Eighty-three per cent of the most serious incidents within educational institutions went unreported. Common reasons included that it 'happens all the time', 'nothing would happen or change' and that 'it wouldn't be taken seriously enough'.
- The most frequent perpetrators of serious incidents were other students, in 88 per cent of cases; however, nine per cent of negative incidents were committed by teaching staff.

There is clearly still a long way to go in terms of teacher training. The final statistic is especially shocking. I have witnessed staff deploying their own prejudicial views to dehumanise young people. It must stop, and where it doesn't, school leaders must take robust disciplinary action. Personal cultural, religious or political views should never enable prejudice in our professional practice.

The global view

In 2018, the International Lesbian, Gay, Bisexual, Transgender, Queer and Intersex Youth and Student Organisation (IGLYO), who are the largest LGBTQI youth and student network in the world (with over 95 member organisations in over 40 countries), published their 'LGBTQI inclusive education index' and accompanying report (Ávila, 2018). The report concluded that LGBTQI inclusion within education is still lacking in most European countries, with particular focus needed on mandatory teacher training on LGBT+ awareness and compulsory curricula inclusive of LGBT+ people. An increasing body of research in the United States, Canada, Australia and New Zealand reveals that LGBT+ young people (and individuals perceived to be) experience higher rates of bullying, social exclusion and physical assault in schools in comparison to their heterosexual peers. This is then compounded by school staff who either ignore the bullying or, worse still, engage in prejudicial behaviours themselves. There are 53 countries in the Commonwealth and most of them are former British colonies. Out of those, 36 still have laws that criminalise homosexuality. In Chechnya LGBT+ people are experiencing hate and prejudice on a scale not seen since the Second World War. We must remain on our guard and never take our current freedoms for granted.

Transgender and non-binary

The politicised public and media debates that currently exist (and show no sign of abating) around transgender children could lead to challenge for you as you strive to make your own school LGBT+ inclusive. As leaders it is our role to negotiate some of these debates but always refocus back on the dignity, safety and wellbeing of young people.

The reports we have already discussed identify particular concerns around the safety of young trans people. The National LGBT Survey 2017 found 44 per cent of transgender women who responded started transitioning by the age of 24, compared with 84 per cent of trans men and 78 per cent of non-binary respondents, showing what an important role schools must play in supporting them (Government Equalities Office, 2018). However, of the transgender respondents who were transitioning whilst at school, 36 per cent said their school was very or somewhat supportive of their specific needs, and only 13 per cent said their teachers were very or somewhat understanding of the issues facing trans pupils.

The Stonewall 'School report' (2017a) also raises concern around trans, as it found 51 per cent of transgender pupils are bullied at school and 45 per cent have at some point attempted to take their own lives. In the general population, the NHS estimates that 13 per cent of girls and five per cent of boys aged 16 to 24 have made such attempts. A 2017 report commissioned by the Children's Commissioner in England (Renold et al., 2017) highlights young people's changing perception of gender and gender identity, with a majority of survey respondents agreeing or strongly agreeing that 'people my age are more accepting of different types of gender than older generations'. The report suggests a shift in how children and young people think and learn about their own or others' gender identities, including a widening vocabulary related to gender identity and a commitment to gender equality, gender diversity and the rights of sexual minorities. Comments written by young people cited in the report include:

- 'Gender is a social construct.'
- 'If we need to be put into categories why can't we choose the category WE feel fits?'
- 'Gender does NOT matter.'
- 'No matter what you think about religions and sexuality, respect others and who they want to be.'
- 'We might just be teenagers but we're growing up, let us be who we are.'
- 'Gender stereotypes don't define me.'
- 'There are more than 2 genders.'
- 'Gender can change.'
- 'Gender is no longer physical, it's how people feel, not what they look like.'
- 'If there was no judgement for genders then life would be easier.'

The report makes for powerful reading, giving a significant insight into the ownership many young people wish to now take over their own identities. Where this goes well, it can very empowering, but many schools still find the concepts surrounding gender challenging.

These are the most common challenges around transgender and non-binary identities in schools I encounter:

- Lack of appropriate staff training and/or staff prejudice.
- Lack of awareness of appropriate language and terminology.
- School policies and procedures are not trans-specific in terms of meeting needs and upholding basic dignity and rights or compliance with equality legislation.
- Resources, curriculum and teaching do not include, reflect or celebrate trans.
- Support for trans pupils is not available.
- School does not know how to support transition process.
- Uniform/PE kit is not gender neutral.
- Schools are not clear on the importance of respecting pronouns and name changes of trans children.
- Changing rooms and toilets do not allow the trans individual to maintain safety or dignity and to use a space that aligns to their gender identity.
- Accommodation on residential trips does not allow the trans individual to maintain safety or dignity and to use a space that aligns to their gender identity.
- The school views the trans individual as a problem, rather than their own policies and procedures.
- School leaders are unable to meet challenges with resilience, as they have had no training.

When I started my own LGBT+ work I knew little about transgender lives, so it was important that I took responsibility for my own learning to be able to support young people. The earliest signs of transgender identities can emerge very early on in a child's life and therefore dedicated whole-school training is vital.

An increasing number of organisations offer trans-specific training in the UK. My advice would be to approach those run by transgender people or those who have *direct experience* of trans within their own families. The best training arises from a place of authenticity. In the UK, advice and training are available from a number of organisations, including:

- **http://genderedintelligence.co.uk** who for 21 years have delivered trans youth programmes, support for parents and carers, professional development and trans awareness training for all sectors, and educational workshops for schools, colleges, universities and other educational settings.
- **www.gires.org.uk** who are a UK-wide organisation whose purpose is to improve the lives of trans and gender non-conforming people of all ages, including those who are non-binary and non-gender.
- **www.stonewall.org.uk** who are a UK-wide LGBT support charity.

What form does LGBT+ bullying take?

LGBT+ bullying can manifest in many different forms. Firstly, the range of different targets is extensive and can include:

- young people, teachers or parents who are LGBT+
- young people, teachers or parents *perceived* by others to be LGBT+
- young people, teachers or parents who are *perceived* as being 'different' (and, of course, as all people are different, this means we are all potential targets)
- young people or teachers who have LGBT+ parents
- young people or teachers who have LGBT+ siblings or family members
- young people or teachers who have LGBT+ friends
- those who act as 'allies' for LGBT+ members of the school community
- a staff member, leadership team, governing body, multi-academy trust, diocese or local authority fulfilling their statutory duty (in the case of the UK) in terms of positive LGBT+ inclusion
- individuals not conforming to 'accepted' gender norms or stereotypes.

Secondly, the bullying itself can take a large variety of different forms. The following list is gathered from my pupil workshops and assembly feedback in UK schools since 2009, so represents a broad and realistic picture of the type of bullying taking place in our education settings:

- verbal bullying often dismissed as 'banter', including the use of the word 'gay' as a pejorative term
- teasing about LGBT+ identities
- gossip
- jokes about LGBT+ identities
- wrongly labelling someone as LGBT+
- adding negative value to LGBT+ identities
- exclusion from peer group
- being ignored
- defacing property
- graffiti
- looks intended to intimidate
- outing an individual as LGBT+ without consent
- threats of violence
- actual violence
- attempts at 'corrective' sexual contact
- attempts to view or expose genitalia or other body parts of transgender or non-binary pupils
- non-verbal abuse or threats, including threatening hand gestures or mimicry
- death threats
- deliberately misgendering or deadnaming a transgender person.

The Stonewall 'School report' (2017a) found that the majority of bullying takes place in school grounds, including in the corridor and in lessons. Bullying was also likely to happen outside of school or when travelling to and from school, in school changing rooms and via mobile phones.

Cyberbullying

When I was a child experiencing bullying, I could close my bedroom door and shut it out. In the 21st century young people are seemingly permanently connected to mobile phones. According to the 2017 report by Ofcom entitled 'Children and parents: media use and attitudes', 83 per cent of young people aged 12 to 15 own their own smartphone, whilst 55 per cent own a tablet. Young people spend around 21 hours a week online, with 74 per cent of them having social media profiles, whether parents are aware of it or not.

Chat rooms, mobile applications, online messaging systems, online forums and messaging boards all provide new spaces within which prejudice-related bullying can occur. Social media can instil greater confidence in online abusers and trolls due to its perceived anonymity; since 2009 I have been subjected to online abuse and threats as a result of standing up for the safety and wellbeing of young people. As an adult these messages can be upsetting, but as a young person they can be the final straw. Educators and parents spend an increasing amount of their week investing precious time into attempting to unravel and mediate unwelcome behaviours that manifest themselves online out of school hours, in the form of online bullying, sexting and trolling. Two in five LGBT young people have been the target of homophobic, biphobic and transphobic abuse online and nearly all LGBT young people have seen homophobic, biphobic and transphobic content online. Despite this, two in three LGBT young people think that online platforms are unlikely to do anything about tackling homophobic, biphobic and transphobic content or incidents when they are reported to them (Stonewall, 2017a).

We should also be aware that in the absence of teaching and learning about LGBT+ people, our children may turn to the internet, in a variety of ways, to seek this information. Stonewall (2017a) found that nearly all LGBT young people say the internet has helped them understand more about their sexual orientation and/ or gender identity, getting information not always forthcoming in schools. Seeking information online for young people can be a double-edged sword, leading to less savoury corners of the internet.

I advocate the teaching of *responsible use* of electronic devices in schools, but too often as teachers we simply advise young people to *refrain* from unwelcome behaviours, without offering positive alternatives or potentially more influential ways of deploying social media, for matters such as personal learning or social causes. Helping out with social media content for the school can also model respectful usage. It is vital that we encourage pupils to report and block cyberbullies, first capturing and printing any bullying communications, and that we take the time to ensure they know what is and isn't appropriate. We must explore online safeguarding and privacy settings and ensure young people know how and when to report online behaviours that make them feel uncomfortable. Furthermore, sanctions applied to LGBT+ bullying in schools must also be relevant to online bullying.

Hate crime

The Stonewall (2017b) report 'LGBT in Britain: hate crime and discrimination', which was based on a YouGov polling of more than 5,000 LGBT people in Britain, found that:

- One in five LGBT people have experienced a hate crime or incident because of their sexual orientation and/or gender identity in the last 12 months.
- Two in five trans people have experienced a hate crime or incident because of their gender identity in the last 12 months.
- Four in five anti-LGBT hate crimes and incidents go unreported, with younger LGBT people particularly reluctant to go to the police.

Schools must engage in discussions around what constitutes hate crime and provide visible posters and online strategies for young people to report incidents or seek help should hate crime occur in and out of school. In the UK, LGBT hate crimes can be reported online at www.galop.org.uk.

Understanding the reality and implications of homophobia can be eye-opening and spreading this message is an extremely powerful way to encourage and empower teachers to strive for change. This has been successful with trainee teachers at Liverpool Hope University.

Liverpool Hope University

Prior to Shaun's input, this area of equality was not deemed of such high priority or importance by Ofsted, so his sessions were timely for our own Ofsted inspection, enabling us to inform them that the equality agenda was being covered in the curriculum by field experts.

It ensured essential sharing of knowledge for our undergraduate and postgraduate trainee teachers training to become primary and secondary teachers. His sessions proved to be a real eye-opener for many of our trainees who would be dealing with these issues in their schools. Subsequently, they felt adequately armed with resources and the ability to challenge homophobia in schools. Issues surrounding challenging homophobia are now fully embedded and integrated into the undergraduate and postgraduate teacher training programmes. They are also a part of the wider curriculum; for example even in mathematics teaching we can refer to statistics provided about LGBT+ related issues. As an ecumenical university, there may have been a danger that students' personal beliefs might conflict with the core messages of LGBT+ equality. However, all students have responded positively to the messages that we have since gone on to discuss.

Trainee teachers have all heard the positive messages of, for example, 'different families' and take this through to their placement schools and teaching jobs. A generation of teachers have therefore been empowered with information that started with Shaun's initial training.

Time to reflect

Before turning the page, please take a moment to reflect.

Things to think about:

- How might you begin to gather data within your own school context about the experiences of LGBT+ stakeholders and those merely perceived to be?
- How can you communicate the findings of the various survey reports detailed in this chapter in order to build staff confidence in your journey?

Things to do:

- Continue to work with the pond and stone (page 35) and PPOP (page 36) activities and consider how you might share these with staff.
- Undertake the 'impact of LGBT+ bullying' activity (page 40) with staff and gain a sense of existing knowledge and attitudes to LGBT+ identities. Explore with staff what skills and strengths already exist to support work on LGBT+ inclusion.
- Explore options for whole-school training about equality legislation and LGBT+ inclusion in education.
- Explore options for trans-specific training.
- Schedule these training sessions as part of an ongoing commitment to diversity and inclusion in all its forms.

Chapter 3
Pride and prejudice

'Education is the most powerful weapon which you can use to change the world.'
Nelson Mandela

In this chapter I explore the concepts of bullying, gender, identity and prejudice, and our relationship as educators to them. Now we understand the true extent of homophobia in our schools and the impact it can have on our young people from my own story in Chapter 1 and the wider picture in Chapter 2, I would like to explore further how homophobia comes about, the underlying prejudices from which it often stems and how we can better understand LGBT+ identities to help eradicate it.

As part of the individual self-reflection required in Tier 1 of our journey towards LGBT+ inclusion, we must adopt an honest and non-judgemental approach to exploring our own relationship to the key concepts and themes. What do we *really* think and feel about difference in all its forms? We may be accepting but might not be. New learning can help us to accept difference and diversity, although our relationship to diverse identities (and our own) may shift over time. We may know what not to say to avoid causing offence, or not be held accountable for a hate crime, but privately we may harbour unease towards certain people or certain groups of people.

I was once asked by a secondary colleague what more secondary schools could do to tackle homophobia. I answered that Early Years and primary schools should celebrate human diversity as early as possible, for children are not born prejudiced. Children *are* born with biological factors intended to keep them safe. As they live and learn, they internalise and copy prejudicial behaviours from others around them. Article 28 of the United Nations Convention on the Rights of the Child states that *all* children and young people have a right to education. When we *choose* to become educators we do not (I would hope) expect to support only those students who comply with our own personal, theological or political world view, for this is damaging, unprofessional, exclusive and prejudicial.

Prejudice is inherent in the human condition, yet education systems often fail to provide learning that encourages young people to take ownership of and work proactively with their prejudices, rather than pretend they don't exist. As educators we can make a choice to *direct* our school communities 'not to be prejudiced' or we can take the realistic view that prejudice exists *within us all* and facilitate schools that serve as a learning crucible, within which to explore prejudice in an honest, dignified manner.

Meditation or a 'mindful' approach helps foster greater awareness of our own reactions and responses to difference and diversity; I recommend mindfulness training for all staff at the outset of your journey towards becoming an LGBT+ inclusive organisation, alongside mindfulness for children, human rights and philosophy for children programmes.

It is also vital to adopt a fluid approach to ongoing learning about LGBT+ identities. Yes, this can be challenging and time-consuming, but a commitment to ongoing life learning is part of the role of an educator. If we don't take the time to keep up with LGBT+ identities and experiences, we may unknowingly facilitate a school environment in which we condone LGBT+ bullying.

Defining prejudice-related bullying

The term 'bullying' is used frequently in our schools, but how can it be defined?

The UK government (2012) defines bullying as behaviour that is:

- repeated
- intended to hurt someone either physically or emotionally
- often aimed at certain groups, based on, for example, race, religion, gender or sexual orientation.

Bullying can take varying forms, including:

- physical assault
- teasing
- making threats
- name-calling
- cyberbullying – bullying via mobile phone or online (for example, email, social networks and instant messenger).

Take a pause

Do you agree with this definition of bullying in full? Are there any aspects of the definition you would change? What are they and how and why would you change them? Note any thoughts down.

Now draft your own definition of bullying.

Based upon your existing knowledge and what you have learnt from Chapters 1 and 2, can you now draft your own definition of homophobic, biphobic or transphobic bullying?

If you work in a school, do your personal definitions resonate with those of your own school community? Does your school community have a shared understanding of what constitutes homophobic, biphobic and transphobic bullying?

If it doesn't, there is work to be done!

Homophobic bullying can be defined as bullying behaviours motivated by prejudice against a person's actual or perceived sexual orientation or gender. As you know I was homophobically bullied at school, but I also experienced other forms of bullying:

- for having a separated family
- for having a dad who 'looked old enough to be my grandad'
- for going to Sunday School
- for liking *Doctor Who*
- for wearing the 'wrong kind' of trousers
- for liking the wrong pop bands.

These forms of bullying all affected me to various degrees, but not to the extent of homophobic bullying. Homophobia impacted upon me so significantly because it was a sustained attack upon my *core identity*, upon something over which I had no choice (see Chapter 2, page 37). Our core identity is fundamental to our sense of self, but what does identity really mean and how are our identities constructed?

Identities and labels

Labels like 'lesbian' and 'gay' support a sense of definition or tribal categorisation. When we are young especially, labels can provide a sense of validation and belonging as we explore our personal and tribal identities and our roles within families. Once I had fully accepted myself as a gay man (outside of work), I became immersed in the gay scene. I drank in gay pubs, danced in gay clubs, shopped in gay shops and occasionally told people I was gay even before I had shared my own name. This once resulted in me getting punched. Having spent many years as a repressed teenager, finding my tribe was hugely significant and for a while my 'gay identity' overwhelmed my individual identity. Now aged 51, I am happy to be defined by my humanity and my name, letting people take me as they find me. My relationship to my identity has shifted over time, something we teachers experience as young people explore their identities.

Young people may value labels, but increasingly LGBT+ youth are finding that established labels such as gay, lesbian and bisexual are limited indicators of their complex selves. New labels such as 'genderqueer' have emerged; I find it joyous that young people are taking ownership of their identities but keeping up with evolving labels is challenging. Teachers increasingly express concern about evolving terminology such as asexual, pansexual and polysexual. Language relating to transgender and non-binary identities also evolves. Educators must be mindful of placing young people into rigid boxes or labels in order to make it easier for us to understand who they are. It helps to focus on the *individual*, not the label. As compassionate, non-judgemental listeners, we can gather relevant information about the identity of an individual from them. If we use a label incorrectly, we apologise, seek confirmation of the preferred label, correct ourselves and move on, as we would if we had mistakenly misgendered a transgender person.

Human identity is about making sense of our own uniqueness. Nursery children exhibit less obvious self-awareness around identity than do Year 6 children. Human identities are complex, being continually constructed and reconstructed from a range of extrinsic and intrinsic sources. We evolved to function as part of groups and identity can help or hinder this process.

Where do our identities stem from? There are multiple theories, but key factors influencing the construction of identity include:

- race
- ethnicity
- culture
- gender norms
- attraction
- physical sex
- geography
- nationality
- personal interests
- our comparing minds
- life experiences
- emotions
- parents or carers and families.

Additionally, the connections we form with other humans from birth enable us to develop a sense of authentic self. Increasingly young people especially are exploring a more fluid approach to emergent identities. Our selves are constructed in response to meeting different people and situations; interactions and relationships with different kinds of people result in shifts in our identity. We consciously and subconsciously sift through the options available to us, seeing what fits best. It may be we can never fully know who we really are, although my personal belief is that meditation helps us to connect with our core sense of self.

As teenagers we seek our tribe: a pop band, sports team, fashion craze, or religious, youth or political movement. We crave *belonging* that facilitates the affiliations we hope might nourish us. We experience pressure to conform with the majority, but in doing so we may compromise elements of our authentic selves. As a teenager I was a fan of electronic music, but at school it was labelled 'for gays and girls' by a majority of the heterosexual boys. As a result, I dumped my New Romantic headscarf and became a Mod, as they represented the cooler, straighter majority. I changed my hair, bought new clothes and listened to an awful lot of music I wasn't really into. The other Mods saw through me and I was nicknamed 'Shaun the poser'. As my bullying chances were already high, I thought fitting in with the cool group was a safer option. I was wrong!

In the case of LGBT+ youth, their sense of authentic LGBT+ identity may already be well defined by the time we teach them, but upon encountering prejudice from external sources at home and at school, as a survival tactic, they may be forced to hide or repress this core aspect of their identity, sometimes throughout childhood, with damaging effects upon mental health.

Take a pause

From where did your own sense of self arise? From where did your own sense of gender identity arise? Take a moment to consider these two questions.

For the sake of this activity, I might consider my own core identity to be:

- my physical characteristics
- my ethnicity (white British)
- my age (51)
- my gender identity (I was born physically male and I identify as male, which makes me a cisgender male)
- my sexuality (I'm gay).

When reflecting upon my own core identity in terms of bullying or prejudicial treatment, one aspect stands out – my identity as a gay man.

Now reflect upon your knowledge of yourself. Try to identify some key aspects of your core identity and write them down in your notebook. Reflect upon your personal journey through school, social life and employment. Have you been treated less favourably or been bullied for any of these core aspects? Which core aspects made you vulnerable?

Finally, reflect upon the young people in your own context. How might their own core identity render them vulnerable to prejudice?

Thinking about what we think

Whether we like to admit it or not, I believe we are all to some extent fearful, biased and prejudiced about certain things. Until we accept this honestly and non-judgementally, we can't begin to work towards noticing and negating the impact of fear, prejudice and bias upon our own lives and those of others. Read these three examples from my own life:

1. One afternoon whilst still living at home the doorbell rang. My four-year-old brother opened the front door to a cold caller. With a scream of fear, he ran into the living room shouting that the man at the door had a 'burnt face'. After apologising to the Nigerian man at the door, my mother talked to my brother about human diversity. The next time he saw a black person he didn't react.

2. At primary school aged six I was introduced to a child in a wheelchair with a significant facial disfigurement. No one had explained the condition and my reaction was to withdraw fearfully, potentially causing emotional trauma to the child in the wheelchair.

3. My grandparents lived in Leicester. I overheard racist language from my granddad when the first non-white families moved in. Over three decades the shifting demographic of Leicester resulted in it becoming the first British city not to have a white British majority. I recall this initial period of change as being often uneasy, marked by racist language and name-calling. There were regular fights between skinheads and new arrivals, and I would hear racial slurs and negative stereotypes. On a few occasions I observed these being challenged by teachers in school; students got wise and carried on using racist language, albeit more covertly to not get in trouble. Outside of learning about other faiths in religious education, nothing was done to challenge stereotypes or to address negative attitudes themselves. Education about the lives of our increasingly diverse neighbours, colleagues and classmates wasn't forthcoming, and fearful and negative attitudes were left to fester, often into adulthood.

These childhood experiences inform my approach to my work on diversity. I believe we view others through various 'filters' that have accumulated during our lives. My filters have been:

*   what my grandparents told me
*   what my parents told me
*   what my friends told me
*   what their parents told me
*   what my brothers told me
*   what their friends told me

- what pop stars told me
- what faith leaders told me
- what teachers told me
- what the TV told me
- what newspapers and magazines told me
- what the internet told me.

All of these factors had the potential to skew my perception of myself and other human beings.

Take a pause

What might your filters be? How might these filters affect your perception of LGBT+ identities?

Society grants privilege to human beings because of certain aspects of their identity. Privilege is a right or advantage that you have and others may not have, which you might not notice or even take for granted. As a result of our privileges we *may* receive preferential treatment. Humans can forget their privileges when making judgements about others. Some of my privileges might be that I'm:

- white
- male
- able to access education
- generally considered to be 'straight acting'
- cisgender
- middle class (so others tell me)
- living in a country with equal marriage
- living in a country where it is currently legal to be me
- able to live in my home country
- able to use my first language
- a homeowner
- not visibly disabled.

Examples of non-LGBT+ privilege *might* include:

- not having to face questioning over the 'normality' or 'naturalness' of your sexuality or being told it is a result of personal choice, poor mental health, trauma or abuse
- not fearing that family, friends or co-workers might uncover your sexual orientation, thus having negative or potentially fatal consequences for you

- never having to be accused of being perverted, mentally ill, psychologically confused or dysfunctional purely as a result of your sexual orientation
- not being sent for exorcism, conversion therapy or 'corrective rape' due to your sexual orientation.

Take a pause

What might your own privileges be? How might these mean that you are treated differently from someone who is LGBT+ (if you are not LGBT+ yourself)?

Be gentle with this. There is no need for judgement. Notice your reactions or responses to being asked to reflect upon your own privileges.

Bias

Historically, scientists thought that people might have negative perceptions or views towards different people. Stereotypes and prejudices were considered to work at the level of 'conscious prejudice'. However, many biases occur rapidly and are held at the subconscious level, meaning that instinctively we prefer people who are like us. According to Tajfel and Turner (1979), we place people into categories and subsequently attach certain values to these categories.

This is known as 'unconscious bias' and, however much we would like to think we are being fair, the reality is that our biases are influencing our behaviours. Very subtle forms of bias remain present, often playing an unconscious role in our recruitment and promotion decisions and dealings with parents, colleagues and young people. Whole-staff training on the different forms of bias is therefore crucial and will underpin and reinforce your LGBT+ work and wider work on equalities. Nurturing greater self-awareness in all school stakeholders will serve to disempower our bias and prejudice. Meditation can hasten this process as the mind becomes more finely calibrated to noticing thoughts and feelings and assumptions.

We make assumptions, often rapidly and based on limited information, leading to misunderstandings and sometimes a sense of unease.

Take a pause

Consider the following questions. Note down anything that arises.

- Are our first impressions always correct?
- What happens when we act on our first impressions?
- How can making assumptions subsequently lead to misunderstandings?
- What assumptions do you make about colleagues?
- What assumptions do you make about parents?

- What assumptions do you make about children?
- What assumptions do you make about LGBT+ people?

Our brains evolved to negotiate complex emotions, social structures and environments. One of the most primitive structures within our brains relates to emotions and fear and is called the amygdala. When human beings still resided in caves, there was a good chance of us becoming a wild animal's dinner. The amygdala helped us to react quickly to survive in dangerous environments by generating fear. This survival mechanism was less about stopping and thinking and more about taking rapid action to protect oneself from harm. When faced with a bear you might 'fight' your corner; you might take 'flight' – run away; or you might 'freeze', paralysed with fear, unable to do anything, like a rabbit in the headlights.

The amygdala still acts as our panic button; think how you react when the school bell sounds unexpectedly or when a child drops something, making you jump. When your panic button is pressed, your body undergoes physiological changes and hormones are released, sometimes leading to a feeling of being overwhelmed by anger, fear or anxiety. Unexplained differences can trigger the amygdala; recall the example of my brother and the Nigerian man.

When the amygdala 'hijacks' the brain, our thinking, rational brain shuts down and most of our physical and mental resources apply themselves to ensuring our immediate survival. In our busy 21st-century lives (depending upon where we live) our amygdala might not be triggered by a hungry tiger, but by a road rage incident, an abusive parent, a violent pupil or an individual or group of individuals whose identities, gender identities, culture, appearance or faith are very different to our own. Our reactions to these situations often arise from a place of fear as opposed to rational logic and we react, not respond. In these heightened moments we might say things or experience overwhelming emotions that we feel shameful about later. Unfortunately, by this time, we might have dehumanised someone or even committed a hate crime.

It was only by becoming a meditator that I was able to notice and disempower my own prejudices by, for example, using the PPOP method described in Chapter 2, page 36. I am a flawed human being too, who grew up amongst many prejudicial voices. I made a conscious choice to first explore and then let those voices go and it was meditation that empowered me to do so.

Using meditation, we can create more space between the amygdala firing up to warn us of perceived danger and our subsequent reactions and responses. Viktor E. Frankl (1959) famously said: 'Between stimulus and response there is a space. In that space is our power to choose our response. In our response lies our growth and our freedom.' Some studies into the impact of mindfulness indicate a reduction in the size of the amygdala over time (see Taren et al., 2013, for example). This increase in space supports us in pausing and responding.

Like the construction of identities, the construction of prejudice is also complex. Prejudice can stem from perceived economic or cultural injustices, and be perpetuated inter-generationally through families, propaganda, policy, media, religious beliefs or even our schools. Prejudice can be rooted in generalisation and stereotyping. One negative encounter with an individual can be interpreted as proof of the unworthiness of an entire community, whilst positive encounters with individuals from the same community can pass without comment. Our minds focus on the negatives, unless we make a conscious effort to shift our awareness. Meditation can support this shift, but so can education about human diversity in all its joyful forms and colours from the outset of our learning as children.

Understanding sexual orientation, gender identity and expression

As I have mentioned, our world is currently experiencing a significant shift in terms of the ways in which young people are identifying themselves. Gender is a complicated subject, with many different facets to consider. Expectations around gender vary from culture to culture and are informed by societal expectations, involving social status and legal status. Gender is a spectrum and should not be viewed as being a binary choice between being a boy or a girl or a man or a woman, for there exist transgender, non-binary and intersex human beings and they also exist on their own spectra.

My colleague and contributor to this book Dr Joseph Hall (see pages 86, 87, 209 and 232) is currently engaged in an ongoing project at the University of Leeds exploring understandings, experiences and practices of gender amongst young people aged 16 to 24 in contemporary Britain, as this intersects with sexualities, class, race, age and other social identities in families, intimate relationships, peer groups, leisure spaces, formal spaces of school and employment, and social media spaces. There will be a range of related academic presentations and publications available at https://living-gender.leeds.ac.uk/.

Attitudes and responses to LGBT+ identities and gender identity of course vary significantly according to global geographical location and social and political contexts; we may see some of these global attitudes reflected in our increasingly diverse school communities. It is not surprising that people often get confused about sex, sexuality and gender, and perceptions can vary. However, these are the basics:

- *Sexual orientation* is different from *gender identity* and *gender identity* is different from *gender expression.*
- *Sexual orientation* concerns who you're attracted to and who you want to have relationships with. It's about who you feel drawn to emotionally, physically and romantically.
- *Gender identity* relates to one's core sense of self as female or male, or perhaps as having elements of both male and female, or possibly neither (agender).

A person's gender identity may *differ* from the sex they were assigned at birth; for example, a child may be assigned 'male' at birth based upon physical sexual characteristics but subsequently identify as female. A person with significantly conflicted physical sex and gender identity may be termed *transgender*. A person whose physical sex and gender identity fully align is termed *cisgender*. It is important to note that transgender people, just like cisgender people, have a wide range of sexual orientations and we must remain mindful of making assumptions. An increasing number of transgender people define being transgender as 'when the gender you are assigned at birth does not match the gender you identify with'. As I am not trans myself, it is important that I listen to the experiences and perceptions of a range of people. *Gender variance* is an umbrella term and describes those individuals who don't fit into boxes we might label as male or female. Despite widespread talk of medical *transition*, not all trans people undergo surgery. We can view transition then as the beginning of a lasting change of gender role throughout all aspects of a person's life.

As children grow and increasingly express themselves, they also display a growing awareness of their physical differences. As they begin to read books, watch television, play with friends or go online, they are exposed to social situations where they internalise elements of identity that society labels as 'male' or 'female', often in the form of societal 'norms' or stereotypes.

But who decides what normal is? Is it schools, parents, toy companies or governments?

With a planet teeming with unique human beings, can there ever truly be a definition of normal at all? If we take the view that anything is 'normal' then this immediately implies one correct mode of being. Sally, aged nine and from a school in Liverpool, has this to say: 'I think normal is whatever is usual for you. We all have different lives so how can anyone tell someone else what normal is?'

Take a pause

Imagine, if you can, growing up in an environment in which *nothing* is classified by gender. Books, names, clothes, hairstyles, clubs, activities – they all are gender neutral. Apart from your physical sex, how would you know whether you identified as male, female or something else entirely?

Take time to think about this, noticing any charged thoughts, feelings and sensations that arise as you do so.

As a culture we are becoming more aware of unhelpful gender stereotyping of toys, sports, games and clothes, and an increasing number of families and schools are raising children in a gender-neutral environment. If society presents only one way to be a boy, let's say aggressive, sporting, muscular and wearing camouflage, then many boys will feel pressure to conform to this stereotype, despite it not always reflecting their core sense of self. If society only presents the stereotype of passive, stay-at-home, 'girly' girls, who like pink fluffy rabbits, glitter and hairspray, then young women will feel pressure to conform with the stereotype, even when it doesn't reflect their core sense of self.

Now there is nothing wrong with boys who like sport and there is nothing wrong with young women who like pink glittery rabbits, but children are individuals, not stereotypes. If society only presents and applies pressure to conform to stereotypes, then it is by default limiting the potential for individual expression – I suspect that is the whole point!

Breaking down the stereotypes allows children to express themselves without compromise. As I know only too well, when a child's interests and abilities are different from societal 'norms' they can be subjected to prejudice, discrimination and bullying. It is vital that schools avoid gender categorisation wherever possible and create safe, respectful spaces in which young people can authentically explore themselves. Who would we be, I wonder, had we grown up in a world without gender stereotypes?

Gender expression

Gender expression is different from either gender identity or sexual orientation. We express our gender through clothing, hairstyles, preferred titles, names, pronouns, voice, activities, social behaviour, physical or non-verbal presentation, and social relationships. Our gender expression might conform to behaviours and characteristics typically associated socially as being 'normal' for the binary categories of masculine or feminine. Or it might not.

Gender is a spectrum and humanity is non-binary, but in many cultures, binary remains the default, despite the fact that gender diverse and transgender people are woven throughout human history.

Language around gender identity rapidly evolves and it is important that in seeking to know more about an individual's identity we avoid making assumptions. Create a space in which individuals are able to tell you who they are and how they identify, noticing any resistance within yourself to their identity. Many of us have grown up in a highly stereotyped, binary world and as educators it's important to explore how this has shaped our lives both positively and negatively in order to inform our work with young people.

Intersex

Intersex is an umbrella term incorporating a range of conditions in which a baby is born with a reproductive or sexual anatomy that doesn't fit the 'typical' physical definitions of female or male. Intersex is *not* about sexual orientation. Intersex is *not* transgender. Intersex people have a diverse range of sexual orientations, just like non-intersex people. Neither are all intersex people the same person!

I meet educators who confuse sexual orientation with gender identity, or who make assumptions about a person's sexual orientation as they are transgender.

Transgender people vary from individual to individual; so do their preferences. It is only by taking the time to listen to individual stories that we can avoid assumption, stereotypes and false narratives. It is important that we allow people to self-identify and we bring compassion.

For young people living in the UK, non-discrimination is enshrined in the United Nations Convention on the Rights of the Child. I meet many young people who remain unaware of their fundamental human rights. UNICEF and Amnesty both produce resources to facilitate greater conversation and awareness around children's rights and I advocate teaching and learning about children's rights from nursery onwards.

Prejudice has absolutely no place in our noble profession, but it will inevitably arise within us; what changes the game is our ability to be self-aware, and to own and work with our own prejudices. It's not just LGBT+ identities that trigger prejudices; there are many other common triggers. An honest reflection amongst colleagues enabled me to compile this list of perhaps surprising things and people that might trigger prejudice:

- ginger hair
- piercings or tattoos
- 'obese' people.

Which of these (if any) resonate with you?

We sometimes find ourselves working with colleagues, parents and young people whose identities or life experiences are *vastly* different to our own, and anxiety or misunderstandings may arise. As educators, we share a collective duty of care to every diverse individual. They are all deserving of dignity and respect, even if at times this is a challenge.

In this first part of this book, I have recounted my own journey through education, highlighted some of the suffering of young people in our schools, and helped you to gain a greater sense of your relationship towards LGBT+ identities, whether or not you are LGBT+ yourself. Remember, effecting organisational change within education systems begins with changing hearts and minds at an individual level.

Time to reflect

Before turning the page, please take a moment to reflect.

Things to think about:

- Does your school community have a clear sense of what constitutes prejudice-related bullying? How might you begin to define and communicate your own definitions?

- Do your existing positive behaviour and teaching and learning strategies include any detailed examination of prejudice and why and how it occurs?
- How might you begin to facilitate more open and honest conversations within the school community that take into account our human potential for prejudice? Could these conversations be triggered by existing school behaviour data?
- How might your policies account for non-binary identities (i.e. the + in LGBT+)?

Things to do:

- Draft and share whole-school definitions of what constitutes homophobic, biphobic and transphobic bullying.
- Update key policies to ensure they make specific reference to homophobic, biphobic and transphobic bullying.
- Update parental, staff and pupil behaviour codes and contracts to ensure they make specific reference to homophobic, biphobic and transphobic bullying. These should be shared on the school website and with governors.

Tier 2
Focusing as a team

Chapter 4
Expectations and misconceptions

'Everyone has the right to education, without discrimination on the basis of, and taking into account, their sexual orientation and gender identity.'

The Yogyakarta Principles (2016)

Welcome to Tier 2, within which we bring our focus away from us as individuals towards our teams and staff in school. In doing so, it is important to keep your thinking and learning from Tier 1 foremost in your mind and consider how you might best cascade the activities and your new learning and reflections from Tier 1 to your staff in a way that best meets your needs. It is worth pointing out that some schools I visit have staff in them who are afraid to even speak the word 'gay' or 'lesbian' out loud and this is why a whole-school approach is so vital.

A whole-school approach to LGBT+ inclusion involves sustained organisational change. I meet headteachers who believe that celebrating LGBT History Month in February means their schools are fully LGBT+ inclusive. Positive LGBT+ inclusion isn't only about LGBT History Month or Anti-Bullying Week (although they are key parts of the puzzle); instead it encompasses every aspect of school life and must be visibly *lived* in every office, corridor and classroom before shining out of the school gates and into communities beyond!

A preventative approach starts with whole-staff training as a non-negotiable for all school stakeholders. Schools (I would hope) do not wait until a black, Asian or minority ethnic (BAME) student is on roll to teach that racism is wrong, but some school leaders hold the view that LGBT+ identities are unworthy of discussion *until* a problem with an LGBT+ student or teacher arises. How sad that schools tackle LGBT+ bullying, before addressing positive LGBT+ inclusion. This approach not only fails young people but it also violates the principles of UK equalities legislation.

In this chapter I will explore why we are on this journey towards LGBT+ inclusion, discussing the expectations of the UK Equality Act 2010 and the current English school review system (Ofsted), to help build an understanding of what is morally and legally required of schools as we begin to plan LGBT+ inclusion. I will also highlight barriers to LGBT+ inclusion work in schools. I don't encourage you to dwell on problems, but it is important to be informed as you start work. Our journey is defined by the needs of our young people, not adults who might attempt to bring their own prejudice to bear. I hope this chapter will help you clarify in your own minds what positive LGBT+ inclusion is and is not, and I hope it will help you confidently explain why you are on this journey.

Why should we undertake positive LGBT+ inclusion in schools?

Before I discuss our moral and statutory obligations towards LGBT+ inclusion, let me start with a very simple and practical argument. Time-consuming matters of interpersonal kindness might seem less important when faced with exam pressure, mountains of paperwork and playground duties, but when schools celebrate LGBT+ identities as part of daily life and engage in critical thinking around human responses to diversity, they create a culture in which homophobic bullying is less likely. Reflect upon this statistic from the Stonewall 'School report' (2017a): nearly half of all LGBT pupils experience bullying at school for being LGBT, and more than two in five trans young people have tried to take their own life.

Consider the amount of time (and thereby money) school stakeholders, parents, medical practitioners, police officers, the government and youth services spend listening to, reporting, managing and responding to incidents of LGBT+ bullying and hate crime. Via early education about human prejudice and our reactions to it, could we reduce human suffering and loss of life and free up more time and money for key services to do the core aspects of their jobs? Would this not then leave schools more time and energy to focus upon the exam pressure, mountains of paperwork, playground duties and, most importantly, keeping our brilliant young people safe?

If that's not enough to convince you, let me present the moral, human rights and statutory obligations we are under to commit ourselves to LGBT+ inclusion.

The moral obligation

If you are non-UK based, you may (or may not) have your own equality legislation. Now I don't advocate positive LGBT+ inclusion because laws or school inspectorates tell me to; I do it because I know that if I don't, the statistics show young people get hurt or hurt themselves. In some global territories school staff could be imprisoned or even killed for doing what I have done in UK schools; if this resonates with your own context you must consider personal safety, whilst taking whatever small steps you can to change attitudes and find allies.

The UK Department for Education statutory safeguarding guidance, 'Keeping children safe in education' (2018), states that governing bodies should consider how children may be taught about safeguarding, including covering relevant issues through PSHE education. Best practice LGBT+ inclusion does not, however, occur in one lesson, assembly, theme, strand or subject, but through all aspects of school life, all of the time. LGBT+ identities must be included and celebrated in the same ways that non-LGBT+ identities are throughout the life of the school. The most successful examples I have seen in the schools with whom I have worked are the schools who integrate teaching and learning about diverse families, LGBT+ identities and history into a wider diversity and inclusion curriculum offer. This approach has been particularly beneficial in getting faith schools on board. I endorse the view that sex and relationships education must be fully inclusive of LGBT+ identities (as a gay child I had no relevant sex education whatsoever), but my work is about a whole-school organisational approach to diversity, difference and inclusion.

This is where I stand, but where do you and your school community stand? Where do the parent community, government, trustees, governing body or diocese stand?

How would it feel if I said that as a headteacher, my core role is to ensure all children, *except* those who identify as LGBT+, feel safe, happy and included in my school? Writing that made me wince – but how does it *feel*? What happens if I replace 'those who identify as LGBT+' with 'those who identify as Christian, Traveller, Muslim', or 'those who are black, Asian and minority ethnic (BAME)', or 'those who are disabled'? Or 'those who identify as heterosexual'?

We are either committed and courageous enough to advocate on behalf of all our young people, or we are not. Diversity requires us to bring full awareness to the needs and preferences of other individuals whose lives, identities and experiences may be very different from our own. In this way we can treat them as they would wish to be treated, as opposed to how we think they want to be treated or how we like to be treated ourselves.

The human rights obligation

In Chapter 1, I invited you to explore the United Nations Convention on the Rights of the Child (UNCRC). Many young people I meet have no idea that they have inalienable human rights that must be upheld under the UNCRC. The UNCRC is the most globally ratified human rights treaty. All UN member states (except for the United States of America) ratified this treaty. The UNCRC came into force in the UK in 1992; four articles are especially significant and play a key role in realising all the rights in the UNCRC:

1. non-discrimination (Article 2)
2. best interests of the child (Article 3)

3. right to life, survival and development (Article 6)

4. right to be heard (Article 12).

Articles 28 and 29 afford a right to an education for all children, whilst Article 30 affords children of minorities a right to their customs, family, language and culture. LGBT+ young people (and those perceived to be) have a right to an education, a right to be safe and a right to be able to speak openly and without shame about their own identities or those of family and friends who might also be LGBT+. Under Article 30 young people who have same-sex parents have the same right to celebrate their family in school as those who do not. LGBT+ students attending a Pride event also have as much right to openly celebrate and talk about it as someone attending another kind of festival.

My last school was a 'UNICEF Rights Respecting School', which meant we worked with human rights from nursery onwards. Thus, by the time children arrived into formal education, they knew their basic rights. Starting early means that children progress through school knowing that whilst their own rights should not be taken away, they also have a duty to uphold the rights of other children. This structure provides an invaluable foundation for conversations around diverse families and identities; I strongly recommend it.

The UK statutory obligation

Diversity requires us to be proactive and compassionate in removing the barriers that exclude and disadvantage those who live within minority groups. We should *never* need to wait for parliamentary consent to do what we know is right for our young people, but supportive legislation can provide a key line of defence if challenge arises. In 2009 when I started my LGBT+ work, I was unaware of existing supportive legislation, apart from the UNCRC; this soon changed with the introduction of the UK Equality Act. The Act is not why I undertake my work, but it absolutely helps me 'sell' my vision for LGBT+ inclusive schools. I encounter education professionals, young people and parents whose knowledge of the Equality Act is very limited, if indeed they know about it at all. Provide dedicated Equality Act training for staff, young people and parents at the outset of your journey. The Act serves to protect them and therefore they should know about it alongside the UNCRC.

The Equality Act came into force in 2010 and drew together separate existing equality legislation into a single act, providing a legal framework to protect the rights of individuals and advance equality of opportunity for all. At the time of writing (in addition to the existing requirements of the Employment Equality Regulations Act 2003, the Human Rights Act 1998 and the Gender Recognition Act 2004), the Equality Act is the key piece of legislation pertinent to work in schools on positive LGBT+ inclusion. Section 153 of the Act enabled Welsh and Scottish ministers to impose specific duties on certain Welsh and Scottish public bodies through secondary legislation, resulting in local variation. Northern Ireland equality legislation remains unconsolidated under a single 'Equality Act' resulting in uneven implementation of equality law.

There are three key sections to the Equality Act 2010:

1. employment protections
2. goods, facilities and service protections
3. public sector equality duty.

Public sector organisations, including schools, are covered by the public sector equality duty. In England, the Act applies to all maintained and independent schools, as well as academies and free schools. The Act covers all aspects of school life to do with how a school treats pupils and prospective pupils, parents and carers, employees, and members of the community. All the actions of a school must be non-discriminatory and not put individuals or groups of people at a disadvantage, in terms of access to jobs, opportunities and services.

People who identify as gay, lesbian, bisexual or heterosexual are protected against four types of discrimination:

- **Direct discrimination** is, for example, refusing someone a job or service because of their sexual orientation.
- **Indirect discrimination** is making decisions, or a public body planning services, in a way that disadvantages lesbian, gay, bisexual or heterosexual people unless the policy can be objectively justified.
- **Discrimination by association** is about discrimination against a person because of their association with another person, for example as a family member or a carer.
- **Discrimination by perception** is about the discrimination of people based on the perception that they have a particular sexual orientation, even if that is not the case.

The Act (as it applies to schools) provides protection via the following 'protected characteristics':

- age (staff only)
- disability
- gender reassignment
- marriage and civil partnership (staff only)
- pregnancy and maternity
- race
- religion or belief
- sex
- sexual orientation.

Take a pause

Which of the 'protected characteristics' apply to you? Perhaps you fit into more than one characteristic: for example, you might be Muslim and black, have a disability and be transitioning. How do they apply to your students and colleagues?

How might these categories of identity result in different forms of prejudice? How might they intersect in terms of positive and negative experiences in and around school?

Consider how you might then deploy intersectional teaching and learning and training for all stakeholders based upon the Equality Act in order to support the range of complex identities in your own context.

Gender reassignment

Gender reassignment is defined in the Equality Act as applying to anyone who is proposing to undergo, is undergoing or has undergone a process (or part of a process) for the purpose of reassigning their sex by changing physiological or other attributes. In order to be protected by the Act, students don't have to be undergoing a medical procedure to change their *physical sex*, but they *must* be taking steps to live in the opposite gender or have plans to do so in future.

At the time of writing the law is yet to acknowledge non-binary students or staff or those who do not identify themselves as having a particular gender, but despite this, our duty of care and moral obligation remains unchanged.

'Due regard'

To have 'due regard' means that in making decisions and in other day-to-day activities a body must consciously consider the need to do the things set out in the general equality duty. Under the Act, schools must have 'due regard' to the need to:

- eliminate discrimination, harassment, victimisation and other conduct prohibited by the Act
- advance equality of opportunity between people who share a relevant protected characteristic and those who do not
- foster good relations between people who share a relevant protected characteristic and those who do not.

Schools must also ensure they do not treat students less favourably due to the protected characteristics of sexual orientation and gender reassignment.

The inclusion of sexual orientation and gender reassignment as protected characteristics requires us to adopt a critical approach to heteronormality (the view that promotes heterosexuality as the 'normal' or 'preferred' sexual orientation). The Equality Act and their global equivalents remove the hierarchy of value attached to

LGBT+ and non-LGBT+ identities, thus if teaching and learning centres around the view that 'heterosexual is best, normal or natural', there exists, I believe, conflict with the aims of the equality legislation. A critical approach to heteronormality is vital to laying foundations for all work on positive LGBT+ inclusion. I recognise that this may seem challenging to some non-LGBT+ people who have been privileged enough to have never had their own identity brought into question. Challenging heteronormativity is *not* about challenging or attempting to negatively judge heterosexuals; it is about challenging the view that heterosexuality is the 'normal' mode of being.

Some people view the 'protected characteristics' as 'political correctness' but, from experience, the opposite of 'political correctness' is cruelty, bullying, exclusion, discrimination, prejudice, violence and hate.

Working with the Equality Act

If we bring a positive 'can-do' attitude to the Act and don't regard it as a tick list of characteristics, the aims of the Act fully support the case for schools to be proactive in their journey towards full and celebratory LGBT+ inclusion.

On triggering my own school's journey towards positive LGBT+ inclusion, I revisited our existing 'Equal opportunities policy' and worked with staff, parents and pupils to bring it in line with the requirements of the Act. Rather than being a tedious task, this afforded a positive opportunity to revisit our core ethos and vision around inclusion and equality. It also enabled summarised versions of the core expectations of the Act to be disseminated across our school community, in turn facilitating discussion. In territories where equality legislation differs, the UNCRC might be deployed in a similar manner.

My starting point was posing to leadership the following questions:

1. How do we currently eliminate discrimination?
2. How do we advance equality of opportunity between people who share a protected characteristic and people who do not share it?
3. How do we foster good relations across all characteristics and between people who share a protected characteristic and people who do not share it?
4. What existing training, resources, skills and strengths do we have that support the above?
5. What barriers might we face in terms of eliminating discrimination, advancing equality of opportunity and fostering good relations?

This process required an honest and non-judgemental approach, enabling us to bring curiosity to areas of strength and development in order to strategically plan more effective provision. Our equality policy was then rewritten to reflect the needs of our school community, in addition to making us Act-compliant. The revised policy enabled us to represent and live the core aims of the Act in strategy, policy, behaviour expectations, home–school agreements and handbooks.

Undertaking this process also enabled the writing of our 'equalities action plan', part of which was to create a summary of our expectations around equalities, which was handed then to all visitors on arrival. This was printed on the reverse of our 'Safeguarding for visitors' booklet and no one crossed the door until they had read and agreed to it. The school website also bore a page dedicated to equalities, displaying our expectations for all stakeholders and visitors to the school.

Although it is no longer a legal requirement for schools to have an 'equalities action plan', I regard this approach as best practice, provided the plans are kept live and are informed by current data and experiences relevant to your own context. The effectiveness of policies and plans are significantly impacted by the attitudes and intentions we bring to them; therefore if we regard equalities work as 'another box to tick' or 'being politically correct' then the more likely it is our paper policies and plans will remain just that – paper – instead of fully blossoming in all aspects of school life.

To start working with the Equality Act in your own school, discuss the following as a staff team:

- What does 'equality' mean for you in your own context and how do you know?
- How does your vision of equality intersect with local laws and human rights law?
- Does your vision of equality leave any member of the school community vulnerable or unprotected? If yes, who are they?
- How do you communicate your vision for equality within your school context?
- How do you communicate your vision for equality beyond the school context?
- How do your stakeholders experience your vision of equality? How do you know?
- What is the impact on your vision of equality?
- How can training on and the use of human rights underpin your vision for equality in your own context?

Equality objectives

Schools should set equality objectives to tackle any issues of discrimination, inequality and disadvantage. These objectives should be informed by the need to pay 'due regard' as outlined in the Equality Act. Take into account data and challenges the school is already responding to within the school improvement plan or address issues and concerns identified through consultation with pupils, staff and parents.

Some areas for equality objectives might be:

- Ensuring data is collected on all incidents of prejudice-related bullying and that incidents are dealt with in a robust manner.
- Reducing prejudice-related bullying and the use of derogatory language.
- Using data gathered to identify underachieving groups or individuals and planning targeted intervention.
- Ensuring that equality and diversity are embedded across the curriculum and assemblies.
- Encouraging girls to consider non-stereotyped career options.

Objectives need to be specific, measurable and used as a tool to help improve the experiences of a range of different pupils. A school should set as many objectives as it believes are appropriate to its size and circumstances; the objectives should fit the school's needs and should be achievable. Remember when setting these objectives that your vision for equality should never be rooted in statute or inspection criteria; it must be rooted in compassion for human beings and a desire for all young people to do well. We can write wonderful policies and objectives, but unless they are lived and breathed in every aspect of school life then they are not worth the paper they are printed on.

Ofsted

In England schools are inspected by Ofsted; other territories, for example the Isle of Man, have their own inspection process. Back in 2011 I was phoned by Ofsted as they sought to understand how I was 'getting away' with undertaking LGBT+ work at primary level. This was the same line of enquiry that the Department for Education had used when they first contacted me.

Ofsted were gathering best practice examples of LGBT+ inclusion in order to upskill inspection teams and disseminate best practice. After long conversations with Ofsted they requested a visit to my school to spend a day looking solely at my work on positive LGBT+ inclusion. When Ofsted visited, they found our work to be an 'outstanding' element of practice. Having undertaken the journey from suicidal teenager growing up under Section 28 to a point in time where a school inspection team would actively seek out best practice in the primary school I was responsible for, I was moved to tears.

Ofsted (2013) would go on to produce guidance aimed at guiding their enquiries into LGBT+ inclusion in schools. These are the key areas lifted from the initial suite of guidance, which has now been subsumed into inspector induction. It is still a useful stimulus for reflection upon your own contexts.

With primary pupils inspectors were invited to explore whether:

- pupils ever heard anyone use the word 'gay' when describing something, or whether they have been told by teachers that using the word 'gay' to mean something is rubbish is wrong, scary or unpleasant and why it is wrong
- pupils ever got picked on by other children for not behaving like a 'typical girl' or a 'typical boy'
- pupils had any lessons about 'different' types of families (I prefer the word 'diverse' here)
- pupils thought if there was someone born a girl who would rather be a boy, or born a boy who would like to be a girl, they would feel safe at school and be included.

With secondary pupils inspectors were invited to explore the above and whether:

- there was any homophobic bullying, anti-gay derogatory language or name-calling in school or on social media sites
- if a gay pupil was 'out' in school, the pupil would feel safe from bullying
- pupils learned about homophobic and transphobic bullying and ways to stop it happening in school
- pupils learned in school about different types of families and whether anyone was, or would be, teased about having same-sex parents
- there was any homophobic bullying or derogatory language about staff
- someone – pupil or teacher – who thought of themselves as the opposite gender would feel safe and free from bullying at school.

With senior leaders, and when looking at documentary evidence, inspectors were invited to explore whether:

- they were aware of any instances of homophobic or transphobic language in school, whether this was recorded and how it was acted upon
- there was any homophobic language used against staff
- the school's bullying and safeguarding policies and equality objectives addressed gender identity and sexuality
- training had been provided for staff in how to tackle homophobic and transphobic bullying, including language
- the school had taken any action to ensure that provision met the needs of LGBT pupils, for example in sex and relationships education and other aspects of PSHE, including providing age-appropriate advice and guidance
- the school sought to support LGBT pupils and those from LGBT families, and how they did this

- policies promoted safety for all groups of pupils regardless of sexuality or gender identity, including the use of language
- there was specific mention of gender identity and sexuality in the equality, diversity, behaviour and bullying policies
- policies included reference to carers as well as parents.

Under the Education and Inspections Act 2006, governors also have a duty to promote the wellbeing of all children and young people, including any children who experience homophobic, biphobic or transphobic bullying. Therefore with governors inspectors were invited to explore:

- how the school met its statutory duty to prevent all forms of prejudice-based bullying, including homophobia and transphobia
- whether they were aware of any homophobic or transphobic bullying or language in school and whether incidents were followed up effectively
- how they ensured that sexuality and gender equality were covered within the school's behaviour guidelines and policies.

It can be very helpful to use this guidance to review your provision and formulate an action plan.

Take a pause

Reflect upon the Ofsted lines of enquiry in terms of your own context and make some notes on the following:

- How might you adapt and improve upon this guidance in order to audit your own school environment?
- How will you capture evidence and, when you have, with whom will it be shared?
- What will happen as a result?

Moving to misconceptions

I am sometimes contacted by colleagues in schools who are passionate about making their schools more inclusive for LGBT+ stakeholders but who are facing leadership or governance indifference at best and prejudice at worst. Some are trying to work with the same fear, anxieties, myths, misconceptions and prejudices that I have faced over the past ten years. However, these have never prevented me from helping schools to put the needs of all young people first.

When faced with challenge or prejudice, my first response is to bring compassion, which can admittedly sometimes be challenging. I keep a diagram nearby to ensure my awareness is drawn to the right place:

Me
Bring awareness to my
personal emotional response

Identify

My challenger
Visible emotion
Secondary emotion
Unmet needs
Work with unmet need where possible

My aim is to identify the unmet need of my challenger and work with it positively, whilst still highlighting current statutory expectations of UK schools. The needs of our students take precedence over our adult prejudices and misconceptions.

In the style of my favourite 1980s television music show *Top of the Pops*, I now offer you my 'Top Ten' of potential barriers to LGBT+ inclusion and my responses to them, in the hope that they will enable you to move forward confidently with your own work.

10. Primary school children are too young to know

Sometimes when I tell people that I helped spearhead LGBT+ inclusion training in UK primary schools, I get the following response: 'Are they not a bit young to know what being gay is?'

I recently undertook an anonymous online survey, asking three simple questions in order to explore at what age people became aware of their LGBT+ identities. 260 people responded as follows:

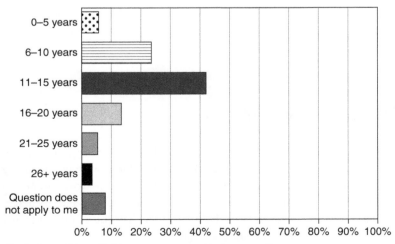

At what age did you first know you were not heterosexual?

These results reflect my own experiences and those of many of my LGBT+ friends.

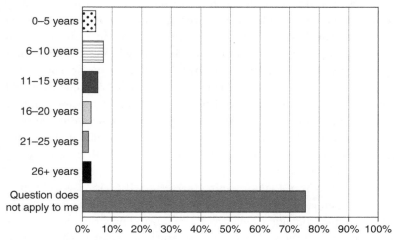

At what age were you first aware you were not cisgender?

The Gender Identity Development Service (2016) state that the earliest signs of transgender identities can begin to manifest themselves prior to the onset of formal education. The service, based at the Tavistock and Portman NHS Foundation Trust, is the only NHS-run clinic that specialises in helping young people experiencing difficulties with their gender identity. It is a highly specialised clinic for young people presenting with a mismatch of physical sex and gender identity (see Chapter 3, page 62). In 2016–17 there were 2,016 referrals received at the clinic, which represented a 42 per cent increase compared to the previous year. 2015–16 had a 104 per cent increase – from 697 to 1,419 referrals, compared to the previous year.

In light of these statistics and the findings of the Stonewall 'School report' (2017a) in relation to trans pupils' experiences of bullying (see Chapter 2, page 46), it is vital that we keep our compassionate focus upon the voices and needs of our young people. It is important to remind ourselves of the fact that transgender people fall into the protected characteristics of the UK Equality Act and have rights under the UNCRC.

Regardless of personal opinion or debate on transgender and non-binary identities, educators have a clear duty of care to non-cisgender young people who are clearly not 'too young to know'. Authentic identity is for us to decide as individuals. How could we ever be so conceited and self-absorbed to think that we hold the power to define the identity, the lived experience, of another? This is abusive.

Shockingly, I have been contacted over the years by a number of concerned trainee teachers who attempted to raise the issue of LGBT+ bullying at some teacher training faculties and in schools only to be told that LGBT+ bullying is 'not an issue for primary schools'.

The pupil data I gathered in my school in 2009 (see Chapter 1, page 15) is sufficient to illustrate that homophobic bullying and the pejorative use of the word 'gay' is just as much an issue for primary schools as it is for secondary schools. 'But they don't know what they are saying' is a common response. When I dug deeper into our data, I found that most homophobic incidents occurred at lunchtimes and would usually result in offenders being brought to the senior leadership team. In most cases, the pupil was told calling someone 'gay' wasn't 'a nice thing to say' (a problematic negative reinforcement) or students would claim they didn't know what the word meant, believing it was just another way of saying 'bad'. We unpicked the second scenario by asking more questions around intent and word choice. In the majority of cases, the children knew what being gay, and lesbian, meant. Knowing they were in trouble, they chose to say that they didn't understand the meaning.

Consider a child in Year 1 who is using 'nigger' or 'Paki' in class publicly – whether the intention is to hurt or not, teachers must address this situation sensitively but with authority. Children are never too young to know right from wrong.

Young children are surrounded by LGBT+ personalities, popstars, characters on TV, debates, news items and website articles. They may have LGBT+ parents, family friends or older siblings. Even if children are *not* exposed to LGBT+ people, we use the words 'marriage' and 'love' from a very early age. What is wrong with using the correct terms 'gay' and 'lesbian' to describe the parents of someone who has two mummies or daddies? Then there can be no doubt about the correct use of these words. We talk about heterosexual marriage and mummies and daddies with children of nursery age without resorting to the intimate details of the wedding night. Why then would we not be able to talk to a child in nursery who has simply asked why another child has two daddies or why a teacher is in a same-sex partnership without going into the details of their sex life?

9. Gay teachers shouldn't be out at work – it's private

Remember when you were at school and your heterosexual teacher brought their husband or wife to a school concert or leavers' assembly? Remember after the summer holiday in primary school when heterosexual teachers asked pupils to share 'what I did in the holidays' and proudly slipped a photo of themselves on honeymoon on their desks? Remember that lovely photo your heterosexual teachers or school leaders sometimes had of their family on their desks or noticeboards?

In all of these 'heterosexual scenarios', could you ever imagine the teacher being told that their husband, wife, partner or family represented an aspect of their life that was considered 'private' and was not to be shared publicly with young people or governors? Did any of these heterosexual teaching professionals ever go into the details of their sex lives in front of students? I sincerely hope not, for it would not only be wholly unprofessional but it would also be a serious cause for concern.

As soon as we start talking about LGBT+ teachers being 'out' at work (and by that, I mean being open and authentic and not being forced to tell lies), dissenting voices often emerge from the press and from within school communities, governing bodies or dioceses that staff's 'private lives' have no place in schools. Many LGBT+ teachers in same-sex relationships still face being told to keep their 'private lives' secret, which not only falls foul of the requirements of UK equality and employment acts but is also a prejudicial request based upon the limited and prejudicial classification of LGBT+ people by one aspect of their lives – and by that I mean their sex lives, a subject I am regrettably forced to return to repeatedly in this list.

No LGBT+ person should be forced to come out, or outed without consent, just as non-LGBT+ teachers should never be forced to share any aspect of themselves with the school community that they do not feel comfortable sharing. However, if heterosexual teachers being open about their relationships and families isn't considered 'private' then neither should it be when LGBT+ staff members do the same.

If school leadership is unwilling or unable to support LGBT+ staff choosing to come out in the workplace, then how on earth do they expect to be able to provide a diverse range of role models or fully include and celebrate LGBT+ identities with young people? LGBT+ school staff are entitled to the same freedoms as their non-LGBT+ colleagues; it is our job to facilitate a safe, respectful space in which this can happen.

From experience, some people also sadly equate being a gay man working in a primary school to being a paedophile. Being labelled as a paedophile purely for being gay is discriminatory. Being gay means showing sexual interest in and attraction to members of *one's own sex* whereas paedophiles are individuals who are sexually attracted to *children*. They are clearly different concepts and yet in a poll in 2005 run by Gallup in the USA, just 49 per cent of respondents thought gay people should be allowed to be clergy members, and 54 per cent said they should be primary school teachers.

Depicting gay men especially as a threat to children is a potent weapon for whipping up public fears about homosexuality. Gregory Herek (2005), a professor at the University of California, one of the leading researchers on prejudice against sexual minorities, reviewed a series of studies and found *no evidence* that gay men molest children at higher rates than heterosexual men. I have met many charismatic, talented and well-educated LGBT+ individuals who would dearly love to have had the privilege of educating young people, but who have been driven away from even entering the profession through fear of prejudice.

I was at a party recently when a fellow partygoer (a heterosexual mother of four) asked me whether I found it difficult not to 'look at the little boys when they are swimming'. I asked her whether she found it similarly problematic not to look lustfully at the children who shared her own children's paddling pool in the summer months. She looked offended but after a bit of processing time (which it is always important to allow) she said, 'I think I get it now; they are not the same thing.'

Three years after leading the first suite of LGBT+ inclusion training in my own school, I was approached by a member of support staff who appeared uncomfortable. When I asked her whether she was alright she referred back to my initial training day. She explained how, at the time, my training had conflicted not only with her Christian beliefs, but also her firmly held view that gay men working in primary schools were only doing the job as they were covert paedophiles. Once I had steadied the contents of my stomach, I brought compassion and thanked her for her honesty. I then asked her why she thought this to be the case. She explained that it was told to her by her grandfather, when she was in her twenties, a case of intergenerational prejudice and stereotyping. When I asked her why she was telling me, she said that she had seen the benefits and compassion that my work had brought to our school community and that she knew that she had been wrong to believe myths about gay people that were based on fear and prejudice. As she left she thanked me for my work and for allowing her to challenge her own beliefs. I wiped my eye and made a very sweet cup of tea.

8. Teachers will have to teach against their religious beliefs

There can be a misconception that LGBT+ identities and faith identities are completely at odds and exist in a state of permanent conflict. Whilst there remain many individuals and organisations who harbour very negative views of LGBT+ people, let us also remember that there are very many LGBT+ people of faith and many people of faith who have LGBT+ friends and family and who act as loving allies. At the other extreme we have recently seen reported on the news ISIS throwing LGBT+ people from rooftops and LGBT+ rights (or, as I would prefer to call them, 'human rights') being attacked aggressively by the leader of Chechnya and the President of the United States.

I have been privileged to have supported faith schools to instigate a range of inspiring work on positive LGBT+ inclusion in schools at primary and secondary level. The Equality Act applies to faith schools, but there can be some tension with certain members of school communities with strongly held beliefs. Strive to find intersections between faith and LGBT+ communities. Celebrating LGBT+ identities of faith during interfaith weeks and LGBT history months will provide relevant opportunities.

To honour the experience, safety and wellbeing of young people, I have never engaged in a prolonged debate around theology or been drawn into a verbal *tête-à-tête* with those few who quote sections of religious texts, for example the section in *Leviticus* that reads 'do not lie with a male as you would lie with women' – an apparent condemnation of sex between men.

I have seen LGBT+ activists offer spirited rebukes to these kinds of religious, text-based attacks, drawing upon different sections of biblical texts, for example *Leviticus 11:9–12*, but the role of a school leader (I believe) is not engaged in verbal sparring matches around faith, but in teaching young people about the diverse world in which we learn, play, live and work and in ensuring everyone in the school community is safe, happy, successful and authentic without exception. This is the profession, the privileged role that we chose to embrace. We teach about many things, to many people, every day in an objective manner without bringing our own beliefs into the conversation. Where we do deploy our own points of view this must be done in a manner that does not cause harm to young people, parents or colleagues.

I once observed a philosophy for children lesson in which Year 2 children were reading a book with their teacher called *King and King*, by Linda de Haan and Stern Nijland (2002), about a same-sex wedding between two 'kings'. Whilst discussing the text in the context of varied families, one pupil became a little upset. When the teacher asked the child why she was upset, she replied that although she had enjoyed the book, she was worried for the kings (and indeed me) as her parents had told her that men who loved other men would 'burn in hell' and she personally thought that was sad.

After validating her feelings, the teacher gently explored the child's own feelings towards same-sex relationships, which were, in fact, quite accepting. After some class discussion, another child (who openly said they were Muslim) posed the question: 'If someone who was a Christian or Muslim was told by someone who wasn't they would burn in hell for believing in Jesus or Muhammad, how would it feel? Would that be a kind thing to say?' This student-led line of questioning subsequently opened up another line of discussion about the need to express personal opinions and beliefs sensitively so as not to hurt other people. By the end of the lesson the student who had been upset was happily writing a 'congratulations on your wedding' message to one of the fictional kings.

A range of beliefs and points of view must of course be expressed and listened to in education contexts, but these must always take place within an established context of dignity, respect, compassion and ongoing explorations of the spectra of free speech to hate speech and banter to bullying. Ultimately as school leaders we must be respectful of those with faith and those with none, but if we allow our own strong beliefs or those within our school community to prevent us from talking about LGBT+ identities, you have already identified where that leads. It leads right back to the 'impact of LGBT+ bullying' activity from Chapter 2, page 40.

7. You teach it in PSHE only

Where and when in a school do we teach about respect and positive learning behaviours? Where and when do schools teach about racist or disablist behaviours? Where and when do schools celebrate heterosexual and cisgender identities? Why, everywhere and all of the time!

Dr Joseph Hall at the University of Leeds researched the impact my initial suite of work was having in my own school between 2011 and 2013. He said:

> *'Shaun's school stood out for the way LGBT+ equalities and inclusion were integrated throughout school policy and "whole-school" curricula. While themed topic weeks provided opportunities for concentrated work around (hetero)sexism, homo/bi/transphobia and anti-bullying, this was the beginning — rather than the end — of the school's engagement. I was struck by the inventive connects that teachers made to LGBT+ content and how learning was supported and extended across subjects, including literacy, maths, art, PSHE, and ICT. This meant that teachers did not have to divert from the National Curriculum and could fulfil these requirements while also exploring, for example, homo/bi/transphobic bullying statistics in maths or gender stereotypes in literacy.'*
>
> Dr Joseph Hall

Learning and celebration of LGBT+ identities is *not* something for one subject, one topic, one term or one day; it is an ongoing process integrated into every aspect of school life, from ethos and vision to recruitment and induction, from maths and history to provision of pastoral care. It is not something to be buried solely in sex and relationships education or PSHE or citizenship work. LGBT+ people are around us all the time, in all walks of life, whether we know it or not, or indeed whether we approve of it or not. Some of those young people who sit in our primary and secondary school halls and classrooms already know they are LGBT+ and many others already have LGBT+ friends and family. They deserve the very best we can give them, not just some of the time but all of the time.

6. It's against the law

Some of you may be reading in countries where laws differ from the context in which I write. In these contexts, you must keep yourselves and your young people safe, striving for human rights to be upheld and making small differences and adjustments in any way you can. Working in these kinds of contexts especially requires us to be courageous leaders on behalf of our children and you have my utmost respect. Here in the UK I do sometimes still meet education staff who cite and fear Section 28. In these cases, it is important to reassure them that the law was consigned to history in 2003. For now, this work is legal and long may it be so. Section 28 is in the trash and just maybe we all need to let it go, whilst remembering that it's still essential to teach young people that prejudicial legilsation has existed and could exist again.

5. Gay agenda

If we don't talk about and celebrate LGBT+ identities, young people get hurt or hurt themselves. The 'agenda' is human rights, kindness and compassion; everything else is merely propaganda.

As leaders in education we need to be able to communicate this message simply and passionately on behalf of our young people, over and over again if needs be. When we create an inclusive, safe school culture for our young people, more of them in time will reveal themselves as LGBT+ and this in turn will help us keep them safe and celebrated. When awareness was raised about left-handedness, there was an apparent increase in people identifying as left-handed. This didn't of course mean that people magically 'turned' left-handed or made a left-handed 'lifestyle choice'; it merely meant that, often for the first time, they could be authentic about a part of their core identity about which they had previously been forced to feel shameful. Creating an LGBT+ inclusive school has the potential to similarly reveal a core part of our identities, but this does not mean we have suddenly 'turned'. It just doesn't work like that.

Dr Joseph Hall has this to say on the subject:

> *'This sense of a "gay agenda" is partly a result of playing catch-up. It may seem like more attention is being given to LGBT+ equalities and inclusion, but this is to redress a historical imbalance in which LGBT+ equalities and inclusion have been largely, if not entirely, absent in UK primary and secondary schools.'*
>
> *Dr Joseph Hall*

4. Reprisals

Some school leaders fear reprisals if they undertake work on positive LGBT+ inclusion.

These might be from:

- parents
- faith groups
- the press
- the governing body
- the diocese
- management boards.

In ten years of work I have supported around 15 schools who faced moderate challenges to their LGBT+ inclusion work and three where the work has resulted in reprisals from parents and the press. In all of these cases there was a common theme: the press or parent groups involved were working on limited information and were bringing visible prejudice to the table.

I supported school leaders to be able to communicate their moral obligations in addition to their statutory and Ofsted expectations, as discussed earlier in the chapter. Underpinning this approach was the use of local data (for example: 'We have a large number of pupils hearing and using homophobic language') and national data (for example the Stonewall 'School report' (2017a) discussed in Chapter 2, page 42).

Where schools had clear expectations around the celebration of difference clearly represented in their school vision and ethos statements, it became easier to reduce anxiety in the individuals and groups taking issue. School leaders must seek support from relevant outside agencies, whether it be Stonewall or myself in the UK, or your education trade unions.

I led a headteacher and a small number of parents of faith through the same exercise as you undertook in Chapter 2, page 40, exploring the damage of prejudice-related bullying. This reframed the discussion and a Muslim parent thanked me for taking a stand that would make school safe for children of faith as well as LGBT+ pupils.

Ultimately, should a parent of faith or no faith wish to withdraw their child because of the LGBT+ inclusive ethos then that is their choice; our work to make all young people feel safe goes on and other schools are presumably available, although the same moral and statutory obligations may well apply.

3. You obviously don't care about other forms of bullying

If you 'focus' on LGBT+ bullying, you are making a fuss, singling it out and giving it preferential treatment. I get this one a lot on social media. I even had it recently from an education minister who really should have known better. The rationale for teaching and learning about LGBT+ identities and bullying are very simple and apologies if I am sounding like a broken record by this stage!

- Young people need to be safe, represented and fully included in order to succeed.
- In the UK it is the law.
- LGBT+ identities are 'singled out' not by LGBT+ people but by the people who choose bully them.
- Research shows a huge historical training deficit for educators in terms of knowing how to tackle LGBT+ bullying.

In any case, if an individual works in one branch of a hospital, such as maternity care, we do not assume that individual cares *nothing* about those with a terminal illness. It is no different for individuals and schools working to celebrate LGBT+ identities. We are responding to decades of untold misery and suffering. The joyous thing is that if, as a global community of educators, we can get this right in the present, we can change the future for so many young people.

2. My identity is being attacked

When I first started teaching in South London I noticed resistance from *some* parents to our work on non-white role models and topics such as Black History

Month. From *some* of the local white pupils I also noticed a tendency to negatively compare themselves to children of faith or those with very strong cultural identities. On several occasions pupils remarked that as they had no faith, they were 'not as good as' the children who talked in class about their weekly trip to the mosque, for example. When engaging in activities that encouraged us as a class to share aspects of our core identities, I also detected very quickly a lack of awareness, and in some cases confidence, in these pupils in expressing the factors they felt contributed to their core sense of self and identity. Thus, when the school engaged in activities around non-white identities, some of these young people experienced anxiety and a sense that by more visibly celebrating diversity, their own identities, opportunities and social standing would be reduced.

As my education journey has evolved, from class teacher to school leader to LGBT+ inclusion advocate, I have often been reminded of these pupils and the lack of secure awareness of their own uniqueness and identity that left them feeling vulnerable. When in 2009 I began speaking out on LGBT+ inclusion in education, a strong and common thread emerged in the online trolling and hate speech that would often be posted under my articles and it felt familiar to me. In striving to place LGBT+ identities on equal footing (as UK equality legislation to a great degree expects) there exist *some* individuals and groups who feel their own identities are being attacked and diminished in some way, perhaps in the same manner in which LGBT+ identities have been diminished before and during my lifetime.

It became clear to me that any work undertaken in education contexts and communities specifically around LGBT+ identities has the potential to create a sense of threat and anxiety in some of those who do not have LGBT+ identities and in particular those who may lack a strong sense of secure identity. In response to this I devised a whole-school topic and approach in order to underpin and bolster individual identity before proceeding to specific work on LGBT+ identities, and I trialled it in my own school with highly beneficial results. This initiative was called 'Our heritage' and I discuss it in more detail on page 155.

Positive LGBT+ inclusion is not an *attack*; it is a realignment based on equality of opportunity and compassion.

1. Sexualisation

I've been told that LGBT+ people are forced to 'recruit' others as we cannot have children of our own. I wonder whether those who express this factually incorrect view are aware that LGBT+ people can and do have families. LGBT+ people have never needed to 'recruit' as nature (and our parents) ensures that we exist.

My personal and professional experience is unequivocally this: underpinning the vast majority of disapproval with LGBT+ identities is the classification of LGBT+ people by non-LGBT+ people by one small aspect of our lives – our sex lives.

Some parents might complain about books featuring same-sex relationships at primary level and ask to view them, which is fine. I have on more than one occasion made a cup of tea for anxious or prejudiced parents and sat them in a room with a selection of the books about varied families, the kind I use in primary schools. After flicking through the books the parents invariably look disappointed, as they realise that the depiction of same-sex sexual acts they had previously been imagining exists solely in their minds and their own inherent tendency to define LGBT+ people by what they may or may not do in bed.

In our school nursery we had books about different families, diverse lives, festivals and faiths. A number of these books featured heterosexual weddings. Yet in none of these was to be found a depiction of wedding-night heterosexual sexual activity, for that would be age-inappropriate. Yet when primary schools stock classrooms and libraries with a book about same-sex parents, for many parents and some teachers, this triggers anxiety around same-sex activity because this is their limited prejudicial definition of the existence of LGBT+ human beings.

This pie chart, although intended as a bit of fun for my training slides, has proved to be very powerful indeed; take a look.

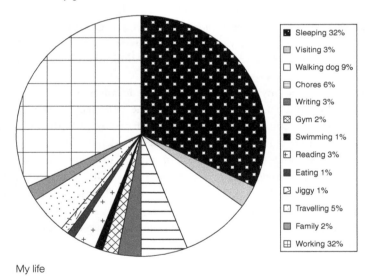

■	Sleeping 32%
□	Visiting 3%
□	Walking dog 9%
⊟	Chores 6%
■	Writing 3%
⊠	Gym 2%
■	Swimming 1%
⊡	Reading 3%
■	Eating 1%
⊠	Jiggy 1%
□	Travelling 5%
■	Family 2%
⊞	Working 32%

My life

For 'jiggy' read 'sexual activity'. Our role as educators is not to focus upon a sole aspect of the existence of other diverse human beings – one that is as private to them as they wish it to be. Human beings laugh, learn, smile, play, cry and love. This is our holistic, authentic self. This is where I choose to place my awareness. Do you?

In the next chapter I will explore the concept of authenticity in schools, not just for young people but for ourselves and our staff too.

Time to reflect

Before turning the page, please take a moment to reflect.

Things to think about:

- If a school governor or parent asked you why you are undertaking a journey towards positive LGBT+ inclusion, what might you now say by way of rationale?
- If a student asked you why you are undertaking a journey towards positive LGBT+ inclusion, what might you now say by way of rationale?
- How might you use the 'Top Ten' in this chapter to help you challenge LGBT+ stereotypes, myths and misconceptions with staff, students and parents?

Things to do:

- Communicate the requirements of the Equality Act to the whole school community, via training, policies, handbooks and the website.
- Begin to identity with staff opportunities to make LGBT+ identities more visible around school and to openly share your expectations around LGBT+ bullying and language.
- Plan a staff meeting in which you explore current terminology and acceptable language around LGBT+ identities. Disseminate summarised learning and activities from Chapters 1 to 3 of this book. Explore with staff LGBT+ historical figures, such as Alan Turing, bringing awareness to the non-sexual aspects of their lives.
- Identify the members of your steering group. Ask them to undertake research using the Ofsted questions as a prompt to gather evidence of existing culture within school.

Chapter 5
Empowering authentic schools

'In my first teaching job I told my head I wanted to be open about the fact that I was in a long-term relationship with another woman and that we had three children. I was told that the school governors wouldn't approve and that if anything went wrong the school couldn't support me. From then on, the head hardly looked me in the eye and so at the end of my first year I left and went back to banking.'

Paula, secondary school teacher from Devon

In this chapter I will explore what defines an 'authentic school', in addition to exploring the link between supporting LGBT+ staff and LGBT+ young people. Tier 2 requires your school community to reflect upon its existing ethos and culture, not just in terms of visibility of LGBT+ identities but also in the current capacity of your organisation to empower all stakeholders to be their authentic selves, should they choose to be.

Building an 'authentic school' requires respectful use of language, effective inclusive leadership, creating a representative workforce and developing an inclusive vision and ethos. This chapter will look at each of those aspects in turn.

Use of language

Using language respectfully and with confidence is an important building block for any school wishing to become fully authentic, so let's start this chapter with a quick challenge.

Can you say the word 'gay' out loud in front of children or colleagues without:

- going a bit red
- feeling slightly awkward
- feeling a bit worried
- wanting to look down

- wanting to laugh
- avoiding eye contact?

Sometimes when school leaders call me up to enquire about staff training on positive LGBT+ inclusion, they will drop the volume of their voices, adopting a rather furtive tone to inform me that their school has a staff member, parent or perhaps a pupil who is 'lesbian', 'gay' or even 'transgender'. On some occasions colleagues almost 'hiss' these identities like a stage whisper, taking me back to Leicester in the 1970s, when my grandparents would point at the house next door but one and whisper that a 'coloured' family had moved in.

Reflect honestly on your own confidence in using words to describe LGBT+ identities out loud in front of colleagues. Try saying the words out loud in a range of different contexts. Notice whether it is any easier, for example, to use the words at home or socially when not with colleagues and professionals in school. What do you observe in the faces of colleagues, parents or service providers when they use these words or when you openly use them? This reflection is not intended to patronise, judge or shame. I too recall a time at secondary school when I factually referred to black people in a hushed voice, as if I feared causing offence or being accused of racism.

It is important that school communities (including school leaders and governors) are made aware of and given permission to confidently use *appropriate* language describing LGBT+ identities, whilst being open to new learning, as these can shift over time. If a school leader or class teacher is visibly embarrassed or balks at even using the word 'gay', 'lesbian' or 'bisexual', young people who are very intuitive will pick up on it, leading some who may already be aware of their own LGBT+ identity (or those with LGBT+ friends and family) to begin suspecting that there is something shameful about their selves.

Effective inclusive leadership

The subject of positive LGBT+ inclusion in education still retains the potential to cause a range of reactions, on a broad spectrum from respectful debate to parent or media outcry or occasionally even threats of reprisals. Recently I attended a number of events centred upon transgender inclusion in education, during which social media views were expressed that were so deeply unpleasant and prejudicial that they fall into the category of hate speech. If then, even in the 21st century, the inclusion, representation and celebration of LGBT+ identities in schools remains contentious, outrageous or blasphemous for some individuals and groups of individuals, where school leadership teams display compassion and courage on behalf of all the young people in their care by openly celebrating LGBT+ identities in schools, what message does this send about their integrity as a professional body? If an organisation gets things right for a specifically vulnerable group of people, what does this say about the quality and courage of its leadership?

After training staff at St Gabriel's School in Lambeth I was pleased to find that their leadership team were setting an example. They said:

> 'When we discuss LGBT+ inclusivity as a school, we make a point to ensure that staff know that this also includes them too. While sustaining a safe space for our LGBT+ students, our staff know that the school is a safe space for them too. Our principal is very clear that if our teachers experience any LGBT+ prejudice from anybody who visits our school, including parents, then they will be supported and those being prejudiced will be challenged. We are not afraid to call out prejudice of any kind.'

Yet in 2015 a poll summary by the UK teachers' trade union NASUWT found that 30 per cent of teachers felt it necessary to hide their LGBT+ identities at work, with nearly 40 per cent having experienced bullying, discrimination, harassment or victimisation related to their LGBT+ identities in school. Almost 60 per cent reported having experienced colleagues making stereotypical assumptions about them and worryingly nearly half said they would not recommend family or friends take up teaching as a career. The subsequent NASUWT conference asserted the need for recognition that raising standards in education for all young people requires diversity and inclusivity. The conference also called for urgent action in terms of:

- tackling prejudice-driven bullying and harassment
- making explicit reference to addressing LGBT+ bullying in policy statements and anti-bullying policies
- promoting school systems, policies and training that enable all staff to identify and deal appropriately with reported incidents of LGBT+ bullying.

I absolutely concur, but how do we achieve this?

Firstly, school leaders must strive to be self-aware about their own motivators, experiences, beliefs, prejudices and bias (whether conscious or unconscious) whilst bringing awareness to their preferred style of leadership and how this adapts itself to make meaningful connections with different individuals in different contexts and indeed of varying diverse identities. Any school leadership team that undertakes a journey towards the full inclusion and celebration of LGBT+ identities is steadfastly refusing to let any dissenting voices or viewpoints, whether they be stemming from personal, political, faith-based or any other form of prejudice, interfere with their core purpose of making all children feel safe and included. Children who feel excluded (for whatever reason) are less likely to do well at school and are less likely to want to stay in formal education. Some of them tragically will even feel that they no longer wish to be alive, a view I can unfortunately vouch for with authenticity. By placing the safety and wellbeing of young people above those harboring prejudice towards LGBT+ identities, these highly effective school leadership teams send a robust message that they are driven by a strong moral imperative, one that enables them to proactively tackle concepts that may be deemed by some to be 'sensitive' or 'controversial'.

I ask you, which discussion is more 'sensitive': explaining to a group of parents why you are undertaking teaching and learning about LGBT+ identities or explaining to a grieving parent why their child has committed suicide?

The role of an education leader is not to empower younger generations to merely repeat beliefs or values based upon our own fears of human diversity and evolution. At its purest, the role of education leadership must be free of ego, and education leaders must aspire to equip all authentically diverse young people with skills for life that enable them to think, feel and learn, whilst responding to the changing world and social landscape of interpersonal relationships with compassion, self-awareness and emotional intelligence.

Creating a representative workforce and an inclusive workplace

What kind of schools do we want? Schools in which we all look, think, talk and act the same or schools that represent the joyous diversity of human existence?

One of the core privileges of my journey has been to visit and support a broad range of schools, ranging from tiny rural village schools in Yorkshire to faith schools in the home counties, schools for those excluded from mainstream provision in the Midlands, gleaming inner-city academies and dust-covered playgrounds in the Arizona desert. In every school I met a diverse range of human beings, working, playing and learning together, every one worthy of respect and of being nurtured and treasured in order to fulfil their full potential during their limited time on Earth. Global business brands often boast visible and successful LGBT+, BAME, faith, disability and gender networks. This is an area within the education system that currently needs further development.

It can be challenging when educators lack the self-awareness and commitment to ongoing life learning in order to recognise when their own fears around human difference and diversity preclude them from doing what is right by their school communities. It can also be very challenging when educators fail to acknowledge the diversity within their school communities, especially where a school intake might be mainly limited to one socio-economic background or geographical area. When exploring diversity and heritage with school leaders in the north of England, one school leader said, 'The problem in our schools is that we are all white working class; we don't have any diversity' – to which I replied, 'Do you all have the same family groupings, history, beliefs, likes and dislikes, love stories, looks and opinions?' The school leader reddened slightly and said, 'I thought diversity meant different skin colour.'

In schools with ethnically diverse intakes it is vital that school leaders are able to fully represent a range of experiences and role models within the workforce that reflect young people's existence. It is no different with any other 'protected characteristic' (see Chapter 4, page 73). Even if school demographics suggest parity of experience and identity, look deeper; one of the privileges of our technologically advanced world is that we can bring the whole world into our classrooms, so let's get broadening those minds at every opportunity. I grew up in a small town full of predominantly white faces, but there was more to life than white British and there was more to relationships than boy meets girl.

Take a pause

What does the word 'diversity' mean to you?

Write down your definition of diversity in your notebook and then write a list of ten factors that contribute to a diverse set of human beings or a society.

All done? Below I have made a list of some of my own. How do our lists intersect?

- Colour of skin
- Gender expression
- Physical appearance and abilities
- Heritage
- Race
- Personality
- Age
- Ethnicity
- Wealth
- Skills
- Cultural background
- Faith
- Social standing
- General perspective on life
- Geographical location
- Neurodiversity
- Preferred learning and thinking styles
- Job or role in society
- Beliefs
- Language(s) spoken
- Education background
- Life story and experiences
- Political views and beliefs
- Status of family
- View of self
- View of others
- Personal relationship with 'difference'
- Gender identity
- Sexual orientation

Now combine the two lists and divide the factors into three categories:

- Never visible
- Partly visible
- Always visible

I hope by completing this activity you might have gained a clearer sense not only of your own view of diversity but also of how some factors are immediately obvious, but many others are not always apparent for all of the time. We must strive to look beyond our human propensity for generalisation, assumptions, stereotyping and judgement to fully embrace the complexity and diversity of every individual we represent, whilst ensuring that individuals have the freedom and safety to express their own identities. It is also important to realise that different individuals will have to adapt or compromise their identities in different contexts based upon a number of social and cultural factors, leading to multiple identities.

As human beings, we simply have no choice as to whether or not we experience the diversity of life, for we are not only an integral part of it ourselves but diversity also surrounds us and enriches all aspects of our lives – this is an unchangeable fact. What can shift and change is our relationship to diversity and our reactions and responses to it. In education contexts, the emotional and physical energy some parties expend upon fearing 'difference' would be spent far more productively upon teaching and learning. Diversity is inalienable but inclusion is not, and it is the role of effective leadership teams to ensure this is the case, not just to facilitate an inclusive and safe school environment, but also to prepare young people for living, playing and working in a diverse world.

Getting the best out of yourself and other people

As educators we give an awful lot of ourselves to other people, for much of the time. If we are an LGBT+ school leader, teacher or teaching assistant, we may be forced to strategically select which aspects of our selves we reveal to avoid criticism or simply to stay safe.

In Chapter 1 I described how until 2009 much of my professional life in schools saw me hiding the fact that I was in a long-term relationship with my partner David. This was a direct result of experiencing homophobia in school as a child and from experiencing unchallenged homophobic language and attitudes from staff and pupils in a variety of school contexts as a newly qualified teaching professional and into my teaching career. This meant that for a large portion of my working life I was investing emotional and physical energy (believe me, it can get very wearing indeed) into lying and covering up my relationship and a core aspect of who I am. I was being inauthentic purely to survive.

As a result, in addition to all of the normal stress of being a teacher, I spent much of my early teaching career feeling depressed, anxious, tired, ashamed and therefore unable to reach my own potential on behalf of the children in my care. I was also by default modelling how to lie and be inauthentic. On the day I finally 'came out' to my whole school community I felt as if my life had finally started. It was in that moment, at the age of 40, that I became fully authentic and finally all of my energies could be applied to my role as an educator. I became far more productive and happier in work as a result.

How would you define authenticity in the workplace? This could be a sentence of two or a list of attributes.

My own definition of authenticity looks like this:

- Able to show compassion before judgement.
- Able to bring self-compassion.
- Keeps an open mind; doesn't remain in a 'fixed' state.
- Present and listening.
- Regularly steps out of 'doing mode' into 'being mode'.
- Able to express true feelings, thoughts and views in a manner that doesn't diminish the humanity of others.
- Avoids assumption.
- Listens to their gut.
- Not 'people pleasers'.
- Able to acknowledge own strengths and bring non-judgemental curiosity to areas for development.
- Takes responsibility for forging own path based upon informed choices.
- Notices and avoids a comparing mind.
- Starts with people not policies.
- Manages a whole person, not just one aspect.
- Doesn't conceal or pretend to be someone they are not.
- Is aware of their own bias or prejudice.

In the case of the penultimate factor, in some global contexts the decision not to conceal LGBT+ identity may either be taken out of an individual's hands or even be a matter of personal safety. I once heard from a teaching colleague in Arizona who had been outed by a pupil and who was physically assaulted in a local grocery store by the pupil's family, who repeatedly called him a paedophile based purely on the fact that he was in a same-sex relationship.

LGBT+ people don't just come out once; they are repeatedly forced to come out each and every time they enter a new context, in some cases forcing them to evaluate and re-evaluate every single day the safety of the context in which they are working. In the online teacher surveys I undertook in preparation for this book, I was moved to read of a number of gay, bisexual and lesbian teachers working under concealment in faith schools who were asked to sign a contract stating they were in a 'heterosexual relationship', a clear indicator that faith schools bring their own set of challenges in terms of authenticity. Some reading this book may sadly recognise these experiences, but others will not, so let us then bring some curiosity to these experiences.

Take a pause

With a colleague, friend or family member try to find out some of the following information about one another's lives, without planning or preparation; give yourself a time limit of around ten minutes each and only share as much as you feel comfortable with:

- full name
- age and date of birth
- address
- whether you have a faith or no faith
- place of birth
- number of people in your family
- where you went to school
- what you like doing at the weekends
- where you like going on holiday
- what makes you happy
- what makes you sad
- the kinds of people you feel more comfortable with.

How was it? Easy? Maybe keeping to time isn't so easy once you have warmed up!

Now repeat this exercise, once again with no time for planning or preparation. Again, set a time limit and try to keep to it. The key difference this time, however, is that you both must *lie* throughout and make up answers as you go. Try to notice any thoughts or feelings that arise as you do.

How was it? Easy? Not so easy? Fun? Frustrating?

The above is a version of an activity that I have been using in training with school leadership and governors for several years. Their responses to the activity range from a minority who say it was 'fun' to those who state that it is hard to keep thinking of false information and those who express deep unease at being asked to tell untruths. What the majority of participants realise is the amount of effort and energy one puts into concealment in the space of just ten brief minutes. Extrapolating this activity out to a lifetime might just give you a sense of how some LGBT+ people are forced to live their lives at home, in society and at work.

The energy many LGBT+ educators are forced to expend in concealment would be better spent on teaching young people. Any school leader who takes on the role must be brave enough to value and celebrate their whole school community without exception and compromise. If school leaders expect fellow professionals to lie about core aspects of themselves in order to keep the peace, young LGBT+ people are being denied openly LGBT+ role models, who could make a positive impact upon young people purely by being their authentic selves at work. This is not to say, however, that being LGBT+ automatically brings role model status, as this must be earned. Nor must any member of staff be pressured into coming out.

When young people witness staff being able to be authentic in the school community and being shown respect and acceptance, these expectations are then modelled to young people, setting a standard not only for how they should be treated but for how they should treat others. I am often asked what might have made a difference to my feelings of shame growing up gay in primary school and my answer is always this: 'A teacher who just happened to be LGBT+ and just got on with their job.'

If we don't aspire to facilitate an authentic school community, whether by intention or purely through weakness or lack of training, we are condoning prejudice in our schools. We all deserve to bring our whole selves to work (should we choose to), as do our young people, and it is for us to model our core standards in all we do.

Schools without shame: supporting LGBT+ staff

In order to facilitate an environment in which LGBT+ staff can feel safe and included, all teachers should feel empowered and comfortable to be open and educate openly about LGBT+ identities, just as they would teach about heterosexual, disabled or black and ethnic minority identities.

Policies, school rules, home–school agreements and codes of conduct should clearly express expectations on the use of homophobic, biphobic and transphobic language and bullying whilst being seen to proactively address the use of 'banter'. There must be a visible commitment to celebrating LGBT+ lives, history and experiences, not merely in one aspect of school life, but in every aspect, from teacher recruitment to policy, from assemblies to curriculum and from school trips to inspirational speakers.

Nevertheless, our LGBT+ colleagues are still experiencing bullying and discrimination in schools. In my 2018 online survey of 238 UK teachers I asked the question: 'Have you experienced bullying or prejudice from colleagues whilst working in schools?' Eighteen per cent said that they had. Their experiences ranged from 'offensive comments', 'micro aggressions' and 'casual homophobia' to being 'denied promotion' due to their sexuality.

In February 2018 I was speaking at the NASUWT LGBTI Teachers' Consultation Conference when they undertook a live poll of delegates. It showed that a third of LGBT teachers stay in the closet at school and nearly half said they would not recommend teaching as a career to family or friends. In a profession struggling to recruit and retain high-quality teacher staff, this is especially worrying. In my own online survey, 84 per cent of respondents were out as LGBT+ at work and 16 per cent were not. However, only 34 per cent were out to students and a quarter had been targeted by students with bullying or abuse in school. Only 61 per cent felt that their leadership teams were able to support staff to be authentically LGBT+ at work and only 42 per cent felt their leadership teams were fully equipped to support students in being openly LGBT+.

The respondents' experiences of 'coming out' at school naturally divide into five categories:

1. Those who were authentic at the point of entry, when they first joined the school

These respondents report talking about their partners and their lives openly right from the start or speaking about their sexuality during the application process. One respondent explained, 'When I saw LGBT posters in the classrooms on my interview I knew it was somewhere I would be happy working.' Another said, 'I personally see it as a selling point as embracing differences and being understanding.'

2. Those who have full authenticity

Respondents who have full authenticity talk about receiving 'great support and acceptance from both staff and students' and becoming 'positive role models they could look up to'.

3. Those who have limited or compromised authenticity

Several respondents report only being 'out' to 'close friends' or 'allies'. One respondent said they 'have only opened up to one member of staff in my school [...] I only felt comfortable speaking to him once I had heard him challenge a student on their use of homophobic language.' Another comment really stood out: 'To some close colleagues when it felt relevant.' I can't help but wonder whether a heterosexual or cisgender member of staff has ever had to question when simply being who they are is 'relevant'.

4. Those whose authenticity is denied

The reasons why respondents do not 'come out' at school range from being 'too afraid' to it not feeling 'safe to do so' and having 'little confidence to confide in the leadership team'. Two respondents report being obliged to keep their sexuality private, saying, 'My contract explicitly states that I must be engaged in a heterosexual relationship' and 'We are told to keep it private and not make a fuss [...] generally it is clearly considered to be transgressive to mention that I am in a same-sex relationship.' A number of these respondents work in faith schools.

5. Those who were outed

Two respondents say they were outed, one by a student.

Stonewall's (2017c) 'Workplace equality index survey' found that 'out' employees were more likely to experience job satisfaction, security and a sense of achievement when supported by their managers, showing the essential role school leaders play here.

The question of confidentiality for LGBT+ staff and pupils is vital. As my survey results show, being out at work is a very personal decision based upon personal safety. In the 'National LGBT survey' in July 2018, 21 per cent of respondents had experienced someone disclosing their LGBT+ identity without permission, which classes as a breach of confidentiality and harass-ment (Government Equalities Office, 2018). Young people increasingly may feel pressured by more confident LGBT+ peers to come out whilst still at school or whilst working through their own personal journey in terms of who they are. Being forced to come out early renders them vulnerable and this can also in fact apply to LGBT+ staff in schools where there might be other out teachers.

Staff as a whole must be made fully aware that outing or disclosing an LGBT+ staff member or student's identity without consent is a breach of confidentiality. Provided this is clear in school policies (as it should be) outing without consent must be treated as harassment. Staff surveys and wellbeing surveys are a useful tool for gaining insight into experiences, behaviours and attitudes, with anonymous surveys affording staff or students who don't want to out themselves a safe means of raising concerns. If we invest in staff over a period of time and they leave because they don't feel included, we have not met their needs.

It is vital that students and staff are able to talk through their problems or concerns, report bullying or discriminatory behaviours or offer feedback both openly and anonymously. It is crucial not only that young people know how and when to report negative behaviours, but that their confidence in the behaviour and disciplinary procedures in place is maintained; otherwise they cease to be effective as a protective factor. Effective and specific recording and reporting of incidents of homophobic, biphobic and transphobic bullying is a must, but it means nothing unless the data gathered informs ongoing practice.

If students, parents or staff disclose to us that they are LGBT+ it is important for their mental wellbeing and performance that we bring compassion and validation. It must be made clear that this information will not be shared any further without their consent, unless a safeguarding issue is involved.

Vision and ethos

Vision and ethos are essential to facilitating an LGBT+ inclusive school environ-ment. A school that is able to openly support staff who are LGBT+ is, by default, setting out its stall in terms of LGBT+ acceptance for young people. The reality of working in leadership within any organisation is that to lead effectively, we must be able to inspire change and bring people with us.

The unapologetically inclusive nature of our vision must be central to school ethos and communicated within publicly shared school rules, vision statements and aims. In my own South London school, when faced with homophobic bullying, we immediately added an additional objective to our strategic school action plan with specific aspirational expectations around a numerical reduction of homophobic language and bullying incidents, auditing of LGBT+ representative resources, models and images, and support for staff and pupils to be openly LGBT+ if they choose. We revisited our ethos statement as a whole-school exercise to ensure it established our expectations publicly, resulting in a final version that read:

'Building strong relationships, and celebrating difference and creativity today.
Inspiring individuals who will fulfil their potential as world citizens of tomorrow.'

The key words in this context are 'celebrating difference' and 'individuals'. We ensured that this ethos was shared widely and publicly with existing and potential parents, pupils, staff, governors and visitors to the school via handbooks, annual reports, governor minutes, induction packs, postcards, job adverts, letterheads, the school website and Twitter feed, posters, home–school agreements and in every policy. Alongside the ethos statement we made certain that there was specific reference to welcoming LGBT+ identities. In addition to being supportive to existing LGBT+ students and staff, this also extended a welcoming ethos to potential LGBT+ staff, students and parents or those with LGBT+ parents and family members.

The statement also formed the basis for an interview question and presentation activity for potential new staff to assess their own commitment to and strategic view of equality and diversity. It expressed what we as a school community robustly and unapologetically stood for. Any individual or group hoping to attend our school was requested to read and reflect upon the context of our vision statement prior to entry. From this point on, if complaints were made by mid-term admissions or new arrivals that the school was celebrating LGBT+ role models or marking the annual International Day Against Homophobia, Biphobia and Transphobia on 17 May or LGBT History Month in February, the conversation was led swiftly and directly back to the vision statement and went something like this:

'Thank you for coming and sharing your perspective. I can see you have some anxiety.
This month we are celebrating LGBT History Month, in the same way we celebrate Diversity Week and Black History Month. Our ethos statement was shared with you when you first expressed an interest in coming to our school. It clearly states that we build strong relationships and that we celebrate difference. If this ethos is not to your liking please feel free to find alternative provision, although of course we would be sorry to see you go.'

Fear of complaints or actual complaints about LGBT+ content or openly LGBT+ staff based purely upon representations of LGBT+ identities should never force school leaders into compromising their vision for inclusivity and equality. It is also important that to avoid causing offence to our LGBT+ colleagues we do not enter into open debate with complainers about the validity of LGBT+ identities. They are a protected characteristic under equality law.

A number of staff in my online survey of 2018 raised concerns about fear and parental attitudes. Typical comments included:

- 'There is no prejudice amongst staff, and I am one of three gay staff members. However, I'm not sure how well I would be supported if parents were aware and unhappy.'
- 'Colleagues feel apprehensive about the parents' views – even though we have discussed the Equality Act and the importance of diversity.'
- 'I think there is still a "fear" amongst senior managers. Lots of positive words following training but a real reluctance to take positive action.'

LGBT+ staff need to feel that school leadership will resolutely support them as they would a member of staff who was experiencing racism. It is never appropriate, kind or compassionate to ask or direct a member of staff to not disclose their authentic LGBT+ identity in the workplace. Apart from being hugely distressing, can you ever imagine a scenario in which a heterosexual teacher would be asked to deny their husband or wife? School leaders must also avoid making stereotypical assumptions about family groups of staff, parents, carers and students or the pronouns and titles individuals use to identify themselves. If we make a mistake (and we will) we apologise immediately, validate feelings, seek to rectify our error and move on respectfully.

Take a pause

This is a very simple but very powerful activity that I use with all audiences, from parents and governors to staff and students. If possible obtain a large roll of paper that traverses your school hall or classroom floor. It is best done as a whole class or staff, in your initial staff training or in a follow-up staff meeting.

Begin by reflecting upon your own family group as a child and as an adult and write these reflections down. Mine would be, for example:

Mum and Stepdad, two brothers

Dad and Stepmum

My husband, myself and the dog!

Now with children, parents or colleagues spend ten to 15 minutes brainstorming as many different types of family groups as you can. When you are done, write them using large handwriting in a list on the roll of paper. When you have your long list, please roll it out over the full length of the hall or classroom floor and invite participants to walk around the roll in a slow circle, reading and processing what is written there.

Following this, set participants on a 'treasure hunt' with the treasure being books, images, models and resources that fully represent and include the full range of family groups listed on the floor.

It without fail proves to be a sobering experience due to the lack of diverse representation in schools. However, please invest no time and energy in shame, blame or judgement; instead invest time and money in resolving the issues of representation.

Moving on

The more proactive and upfront an organisation can be in terms of its visible commitment to equality from the outset, the more unwavering its approach can be and the more confident it becomes in managing detractors. Once ethos, aims and expectations are aligned to explicitly celebrate LGBT+ identities, any discussion with those who may choose to deploy their own prejudices to compromise the school's vision can take place in a depersonalised and factual manner based upon expectations clearly enshrined in vision, policy or equality law.

It is important that you now reflect upon your own context in order to establish a robust foundation for the change you want to make, not as one passionate, motivated individual, but as a passionate, motivated leadership team, whole-school community and governing body.

Take a pause

Consider your commitment to this journey in your own context under the following headings:

- Establishing your current position via data gathering.
- Selling your initiative to leadership or governance.
- Defining and communicating your moral rationale.
- Defining and communicating your statutory and legal foundation.
- Defining and communicating your intended outcomes.
- Refining and communicating ethos and vision.
- A schedule of revisiting key policies.
- Exploring training options.
- Identifying key players and existing strengths.
- Realigning behaviour management strategies.
- Realigning curriculum.
- Realigning resources.
- Working with staff, parents and governors.
- Seeking outside links and support.

- Developing student welfare and pastoral support systems.
- Inspiring, creating and communicating change.

In the next chapter we begin to explore how to establish and communicate a robust and inspiring strategic vision, whilst considering what needs to be taught in order to facilitate that vision in practice.

Time to reflect

Before turning the page, please take a moment to reflect.

Things to do:

- Research and contact local LGBT+ youth and family support providers and ask to meet with them to explore their provision and services. How will you ensure stakeholders (including parents) know about their services?
- Contact teacher trade unions for their official guidance on supporting LGBT+ staff in the workplace.
- Offer an open door to all staff who may want to talk to you confidentially about being LGBT+ or about matters pertaining to LGBT+ identities and bullying in the workplace.
- Share your whole-school expectations and definitions with young people in assemblies and classrooms.
- Share your new learning and reflections from the last two chapters with staff in INSET and engage them in some of the 'Take a pause' activities presented thus far.
- Contact local police or hate crime support services.
- Consider pastoral provision for children who have already been bullied.

Tier 3
Strategic development for organisational change

Chapter 6
Auditing current provision

'The discrimination and persecution of people because of their sexual orientation is as unjust as the crime of racism.'

Archbishop Desmond Tutu

Tier 3 is concerned with the informed emergence and development of a strategic vision. It involves the application of the individual and team reflection and new learning from Tiers 1 and 2, as well as whole-school auditing using a variety of sources to drive the development of a robust strategic vision for school improvement and a realignment of school ethos and culture. The plan will include short-, medium- and long-term aims and objectives and resourcing for its implementation, and can often be built from existing good practice.

Take a pause

Consider the following and write your thoughts in your notebook:

- What existing skills and strengths do you bring to work on positive LGBT+ inclusion?
- What existing skills and strengths do you have in your own context to support work on positive LGBT+ inclusion?
- What resources exist to support your journey, whether they be human, physical or structural?
- How might you apply the skills, strengths and resources you have identified to work on positive LGBT+ inclusion?

This is an exercise that I myself undertook back in 2009 prior to writing my first suite of Inclusion For All staff training, at a time when I was faced with a problem but a lack of training and confidence to deal with it. In reflecting on these questions, I was rapidly able to bring my awareness back to existing support mechanisms for the work we were about to do, including my own skillset. Repeating the exercise with my entire staff meant they were able to draw a line between teaching and learning about LGBT+ identities and existing work on bullying, families, history, faith, race, role models, PSHE, philosophy for children and circle time. Rather than feel pressured, staff felt empowered and could identify their own starting points.

The entry point for schools will differ based on responses to these questions, but my preferred option is training for staff, and assemblies and workshops for young people, as was the case at Victoria Road Primary School on the Isle of Man.

Victoria Road Primary School, Isle of Man

The first step was to get Shaun to speak with our Year 5 and 6 pupils. This session was extremely powerful and had an immediate impact on the pupils, and we did see a reduction in the use of the word 'gay' being used as an insult. However when we audited for this work as part of our school development plan, it became apparent that there had not been a sustained change in behaviour, which confirmed our suspicion that a more robust and long-term approach was required, as Shaun had stated earlier in our planning for improvement.

The overarching feeling was that 'permission' had been given by Shaun to talk about LGBT+ issues and information openly in school. It has been great to see that some displays in school depicting families have already changed to include examples of same-sex and 'different' family units. Texts depicting LGBT+ characters have been purchased and have been located in the library and in classrooms as part of reading schemes so that they get into the homes of our families also. This is as a direct result of Shaun's INSET training day and it is changes like these that show me that the training has reached my staff's mental models and belief systems. There is a real sense that this work is important and it really does matter, which is wonderful to see.

I was impressed by how Victoria Road embedded their journey within school improvement and headteacher appraisal, lending the work the gravitas it deserves. When I revisited the school in January 2019, I found that the school was seeing the benefits of their strategic action plan.

Starting conversations with staff and governors

One passionate advocate will not make for a sustainable model that can, as far as possible, withstand personnel, societal and political change; the best strategic models ride the waves of change and this is what we must all aspire to. I must stress again the importance of sourcing high-quality whole-school training for all staff and governors, without exception and as a non-negotiable. Identify your needs and preferred training styles. It is vital however to identify a model for training that is open ended, as the initial training should serve as a starting point, not a tick-box or once-in-a-lifetime event. In my own school, after I led the initial one-day training event, I timetabled additional training (for example around transgender identities and the use of diverse texts) into ongoing staff meetings and phase meetings rotas. These were supplemented by dedicated time in staff meetings, parent meetings, leadership team meetings, school assemblies and governor meetings in which to assess and share findings of emergent good practice, progress and impact, and identify evolving training needs. In this manner schools ensure a visible, sustainable, long-term view of the work, so that when an incident of LGBT+ bullying or language occurs, every member of the school community knows how to manage it firmly and consistently.

If you are operating as a group of schools, for example a multi-academy trust, consider facilitating training as a cluster. Also contact local LGBT+ youth support services and invite them along to forge greater awareness and links with them. Colleagues struggling with LGBT+ bullying or supporting LGBT+ young people will often find a resource they require in close proximity. Also consider asking pupils themselves to share their own experiences, as this can be very powerful. I took a number of Key Stage 2 children to Millwall football ground, where I was due to give a short presentation on my life and work. Once I had finished, our amazing young people gave their own presentation on the use of the word 'gay' as a pejorative term. As they spoke I could see a number of jaws dropping. At the coffee break the children were swamped by educators praising them for their sensitivity and maturity, with several seasoned primary and secondary school leaders remarking they had not only been moved to tears, but that they also felt somewhat shameful that their own fear of parental complaint meant that they had blocked similar work in their own schools, something having now seen our students speak they intended to address immediately. I think often, for the staff of faith schools particularly, seeing young people speak and listening to their own views and life stories can be hugely supportive in terms of reducing the anxieties and, dare I say it, prejudices of adults.

Only recently I was reading the results of Year 5 and 6 student questionnaires on the Isle of Man, where I think it is fair to say from some parties there is still a significant amount of anxiety around positive LGBT+ inclusion in schools. The responses to the questionnaires flagged up a generational shift in terms of acceptance towards LGBT+ identities and I repeatedly see this when working with young people. Many of them have far more knowledge than adults think they have (gleaned from friends, the media and online) and just can't see what all the fuss is about. 'I think having to talk about homophobic bullying is boring,' wrote one Year 4 student in one of my surveys in a Liverpool school last year. 'Why can't we stop making a fuss and just love people for who they are?'

I have found there to be several key themes in terms of challenges that might arise when schools try to represent LGBT+ identities and history. Many of the schools I work with are somewhat nervous or overwhelmed when I arrive to lead INSET sessions, either because they view the forthcoming work as 'above and beyond' their already significant workloads or because they feel they have no existing skills to apply to work on LGBT+ inclusion. In Chapter 4, page 80, I explored the 'Top Ten' barriers to LGBT+ inclusion in schools, but it is also important to bear in mind issues of patriarchy, sexism, gender 'norms' and gender stereotyping.

We live on a planet in which men hold much of the power and women are often either excluded from it or forced into subservience. Young people are exposed to viewpoints, role models and attitudes that reinforce this status quo. The model in which 'man is strong, man is best' places women and girls at a disadvantage from the outset and fuels sexist attitudes and gender stereotyping. This is complicated by exclusive and hypermasculine views of what constitutes a 'man', leading to familiar expressions, such as 'man up', that have no place in our schools. It is vital that schools champion gender equality (at all levels) and challenge negative and stereo-typical views of women and the roles they play in our lives and societies. It is also vital that children are exposed to multiple modes of existence in order to show that there is no 'correct' way in which to be a human being. It is not enough to merely base any discourse on gender around binary identities; gender is a spectrum and our discussions should reflect this from the outset. The human race is not simply male and female; that is a fact of nature and there should be nothing threatening about it whatsoever.

Take a pause

Consider this scenario. A primary school teacher begins a lesson by holding up a poster featuring images of a range of families, but no same-sex families are represented. What is the possible impact of this teaching upon a child in the class who has same-sex parents? How might the views of children about themselves and their own families change as a result of this teaching?

If a child with same-sex parents is taught in a school where visible models, images and reading materials only represent heterosexual families, what might be the impact of this?

Stereotyping of LGBT+ people and communities

Stereotypes of LGBT+ people exist and are passed down through schools, family and the media. Individuals are grouped together, and often negative judgements are made about them without knowing them personally. Minority groups are especially subject to stereotypes, which may then be used to 'other' or scapegoat them. Media misrepresentation of what LGBT+ inclusion work entails is often rooted in these stereotypes.

A few common examples are:

- Gay men are limp wristed.
- Lesbians all look like men.
- Which one of you is the man and which is the woman?
- Bisexuals are greedy.
- Gay men are all camp.
- Transgender people all have surgery.
- Bisexuals can't make their minds up.
- Gay men can't do sports.
- Black men can't be gay.

I see great work around stereotypes in schools, utilising the increasing range of stereotype-breaking role models and celebrities that many young people have access to via social media. I will often cite the example of Olympic diver Tom Daley, as many young people know who he is and what he does. I will start by making an apparently provocative statement such as, 'All gay people are rubbish at sport' and then allow young people to lead me backwards from there, resulting in evidence and examples of any number of successful LGBT+ sporting heroes. Breaking down stereotypes is actually a lot of fun and young people respond very well at all ages to these kinds of important discussions, the point being that, in the end, we are all unique individuals with human rights, worthy of love and respect.

Auditing current provision and attitudes

Having been through any number of audits as part of school inspections, subject leader duties and quality mark applications, I know that auditing can seem daunting or even dull, yet in ten years I am still to find a school who found their initial LGBT+ auditing process anything less than enlightening.

Effective auditing has a dual purpose as a confidence builder but also as a diagnostic process in order to baseline and establish strategic direction. Therefore it's important to adopt an attitude of non-judgement and celebrate being on the journey. In identifying what we have not been doing, we gain a very strong sense of what we need to do. It's also important that even prior to auditing you are considering how your analysis will ultimately inform changes to practice. I would also stress the need for a top-down *and* ground-up approach. Yes, the journey needs leadership buy-in, but there may well be passionate staff and existing good practice to draw upon, as you hopefully discovered in the activity on page 111.

It is the case that many of the organisations I work with at the very start of their journey have policies, home–school agreements, school rules, websites and handbooks that only imply that everyone is welcome or state that *some* forms of bullying are unacceptable. At this early stage a critical eye must be passed over *every* aspect of school life, starting with ethos, vision and policy.

An LGBT+ inclusive school must, as a bare minimum, be fully committed to:

- Tackling and preventing LGBT+ bullying.
- Ensuring they are fully trained in order to support LGBT+ pupils.
- Supporting LGBT+ staff to be authentic.
- Ensuring support for victims of bullying or hate crime.

Some years ago I met a headteacher who told me that his school was 'some way behind' with LGBT+ awareness, but that he had recently had a strong sense that one of his male students might be gay and struggling with it. Compassionately he had spoken to the student in order to advise him that if anything 'was wrong' his door was always open. The head seemed a little put out that following this the young man never sought his counsel, but went on struggling. I first asked the head to reflect upon how the term 'wrong' might be interpreted by a young person questioning their identity, before asking him in what other ways his school environment visibly celebrated LGBT+ identities, thereby sending a message that in school being LGBT+ is nothing 'wrong' but everything to be celebrated. The head was unable to identify one image, book or poster that validated LGBT+ identities.

With this in mind, please then let me introduce my magic LGBT+ glasses activity.

If you have never lived your life as anything other than heterosexual it can be hard, I think, to fully understand what all the fuss is about LGBT+ inclusion. If you are not LGBT+, please imagine I have gifted you a pair of 'magic' LGBT+ glasses. Now please put them on (if a real pair of glasses makes this exercise more tangible for you then please by all means go for it). Don't worry, they won't make you permanently LGBT+, I don't think.

Now you are sporting your lovely glasses imagine you are one of the following:

- an LGBT+ child
- a young person with same-sex parents
- a parent in a same-sex relationship who wishes to send their child to
  your school.

Decided? Okay, let's begin. Remember, be gentle with these activities, bringing curiosity and an open heart, not judgement.

Firstly, visit your school website and look for evidence of where you might find protective factors for your own identity mentioned explicitly. By this I mean in headteacher welcome statements, policies, and school behaviour and equality statements. I don't mean general cover-all statements; I mean the use of the words lesbian, gay, bisexual, transgender, and homophobic, biphobic and transphobic bullying. Do you see images of families, school work or activities on the school website that suggest that a range of family groups are welcome and accepted? Do you see any evidence of work to celebrate diversity, difference and specifically LGBT+ identities? Is there any evidence of signposting for support if you were covertly being bullied for being LGBT+ but you didn't want to tell anyone? In short, do you feel you would be welcome and safe at this school? If not, why not?

The second half of this activity involves an early start, I'm afraid. After a preferably hearty breakfast please go to work earlier than usual and stand at the school gates. Please bring a notepad and something to write with.

Once there please put on your magic LGBT+ glasses and explore your school building, classrooms, corridors, books and resources, displays, work in books, shared areas, libraries, sports areas, playgrounds, changing areas and halls. Look for evidence of where you might find protective factors or your own identity represented or celebrated specifically. Is it clear from walking around that homophobic, biphobic and transphobic bullying is unacceptable but that LGBT+ stakeholders are welcome and included? Do you see images of families, school work or activities that suggest a range of family groups are welcome and accepted? Do you see any evidence of work to celebrate diversity, difference and specifically LGBT+ identities? Is there any evidence of signposting for support if you were covertly being bullied for being LGBT+ but you didn't want to tell anyone? Is there evidence of safe spaces or gay–straight alliances? Can you see visible representations of specific whole-school themes and topics such as anti-bullying week or LGBT History Month?

You may also like to imagine you are a transgender or non-binary student seeking to use a bathroom or changing room that aligns to your gender identity. What challenges might you face? Would you be asked, for example, to use a disabled toilet solely for being trans? How does the school uniform and PE kit policy support you in terms of transition? Or doesn't it?

From experience, this activity, when undertaken robustly, can change everything in a school. I undertook this learning walk with a headteacher in a large faith school. We saw nothing in the way of specific or visible LGBT+ or varied family representation. Afterwards, over tea in his office, he admitted that the school had two sets of same-sex parents and he now felt shameful for having let them down. Rather than sit in a negative space, he wrote a memo asking all of his leadership team to meet him at the end of the day and that afternoon they trotted around school, all wearing their magic LGBT+ glasses. The following week they did a similar walk with all staff and then set about ordering resources and writing a strategic action plan.

Key factors for auditing

After conducting this initial activity, it is important to run a full audit of your current provision. Key factors for auditing are listed on the next page. Whilst all of these are relevant you will need to prioritise based upon knowledge of your own context. It may be that for the sake of manageability you build a short-, medium- and long-term schedule of the factors you consider to be most relevant. Most schools I work with already have a general sense of what their existing problems are and use this information to guide their initial auditing process. You could consider:

- Existing attitudes towards LGBT+ identities and varied families amongst pupils, staff, leadership, management and governors.
- Existing resources, models, images, and whole-school or classroom-based teaching and learning representing LGBT+ identities and varied families.
- Confidence of staff in terms of discussing LGBT+ identities and varied families.
- Your own diversity as a school community and your current freedom to be authentic.
- Existing pastoral strategies for developing good emotional health and wellbeing and resilience in relation to those with LGBT+ identities and varied families or those perceived to have them.
- Whether existing school vision, ethos, behaviour expectations, guidelines and policies are supportive of LGBT+ identities and varied families.
- Existing induction and staff training resources representing LGBT+ identities and varied families.
- Previous continuing professional development (CPD) with any relevance to LGBT+ identities and varied families.
- Existing curriculum areas in which LGBT+ identities and varied families might already be discussed or that lend themselves readily to the concepts.
- Protective factors and threats for those with perceived 'non-conforming' identities, inducing pastoral and welfare support and links to outside agencies.
- Pupil, staff, parent and governor needs and attitudes in terms of securing safe inclusion of actual or perceived LGBT+ identities and varied families.
- Existing signposting and support in terms of securing safe inclusion of actual or perceived LGBT+ identities and varied families.
- Existing local and national knowledge around potential for partnerships and collaborative working.
- Opportunities for external celebration of work undertaken in school around LGBT+ identities and varied families.
- The current diversity of role models and speakers invited to speak to young people in school.
- Existing strategies to ensure high-level accountability for all staff working with due regard to the core ethos of the Equality Act (see Chapter 4, page 72).
- Existing lines of communication that could be strategically deployed to share intentions and celebrate work around LGBT+ identities and varied families that align with the core ethos of the Equality Act and reduce opportunities for 'backlash'.

The Ofsted questions in Chapter 4, page 78, can also form part of your auditing stage. Remember, it is important that in doing all of the above we do not treat transgender as a sexual orientation. Transgender and non-binary identities are specific with specific needs.

Initiating discussion in order to gauge attitudes and opinions

Recalling my own entry point back in 2009, it was important (bearing in mind that no obvious previous work had been undertaken around LGBT+ in our school) to gauge attitudes at the start of the process, partly due to personal safety (the far right organisation the National Front were not too far removed from my context) and partly to ensure that the introduction of what might be considered new and potentially 'sensitive' work be smooth and without challenge or reprisal. I was careful in my initial suite of training with staff to include an activity based upon short films that explored LGBT+ identities and soap opera clips that featured LGBT+ characters to open up conversations with staff around their existing experiences of and attitudes towards LGBT+ people. By applying structures of respectful and dignified discussion I had gained from philosophy for children to an adult activity, staff felt comfortable in voicing some highly disparate views about LGBT+ identities (some based upon stereotypes or faith-based and intergenerational prejudices), which I could then explore and debunk as I progressed through the training. Knowing the context within which I was working enabled me to support people as individuals as they went on the journey, in addition to supporting staff to identify consistency of approach in tackling prejudicial behaviours in the playground.

Staff feedback gave a clear sense of permission gained, and in some cases a sense of letting go of long-held concerns, leading to a strong sense of relief. As with low academic aspiration, prejudicial attitudes can be passed down through families, and we need to be able to identify and work positively with this. A key strategy was to use posters representing a range of varied families in prominent positions around the school, including by the nursery entrance, the main reception area and main corridors. I downloaded an application to my phone that enabled me to make slogan-style posters that could be cheaply and easily printed off. I made a number of these posters, including:

- 'Families are all different, but all special.'
- 'Homophobic bullying has no place in our school.'
- 'Transphobic bullying has no place in our school.'
- 'Biphobic bullying has no place in our school.'
- 'Say the word "gay" in a respectful way.'

The posters were deployed without fanfare and I recruited a number of Year 5 and 6 pupils to act as 'poster monitors'. These kind souls spent some of their free time in breaks and lunches in the vicinities of the posters, either recording reactions and comments made about their themes or engaging other students and staff in conversations about them. This immediately enabled a window into the existing knowledge, thinking and attitudes of the school community. My monitors would report back their findings to me over a number of weeks, noting their own reactions and responses not only to the posters themselves, but as a result of their interactions with others.

Monitors' findings included:

- Many children across the school had a good idea of what homophobic bullying was, but not so much biphobic and even less so transphobic.
- Some children said they had gay friends or family members, but that because they heard homophobic language such as 'That's so gay' they deliberately chose to keep this information private or mostly private.
- Older children were sometimes conflating transgender identity with drag or sexual fetish.
- Children were unsure as to whether saying 'gay' was homophobic or not.
- Many children thought 'gay' was not a nice thing to say.
- Some children expressed prejudicial views. In the majority of cases these related to intergenerational or faith-based prejudice or misconceptions about LGBT+ identities.
- Many children could name LGBT+ celebrities, especially soap opera characters and pop stars.

My poster monitor responses were very insightful too, and I was sure to hold regular opportunities to 'touch base' and of course a final debrief:

- Some reported challenging their peers when they expressed openly prejudicial views using their own knowledge of LGBT+ identities to counter them.
- Some reported hearing staff members and parents expressing openly prejudicial views.
- The majority of children had noticed an increase in conversations in the playground about LGBT+ people, stating that they felt this was a good thing.

After this initial process of gauging general attitudes (during which, by the way, no parent complained) the posters were also placed in classrooms for teachers. There was no initial requirement to use them in discussions or teaching as I was interested to assess initial teacher confidence and enthusiasm. A number of teachers, evenly split across the school, elected to use the posters as initial stimuli for circle time or philosophy sessions. I gathered some written feedback afterwards and was heartened by the responses:

- 'In nursery we talked in simple terms about people who love and take care of us, and from this we introduced the poster. All the children readily accepted the varied families represented, with one child stating, "I have two Mums" when we reached that image.' (Nursery teacher)

- 'The prevailing message from children was that families love each other and look after each other regardless of their make-up in terms of what are considered societal family "norms". The ongoing discussion is proving to be a valuable and important tool to gain greater understanding of children's ideas and attitudes.' (Year 1 teacher)
- 'I quickly learned how accepting my class are of difference and how mature and understanding they can be when they are seeking new information about subjects that adults might sometimes feel awkward about.' (Year 2 teacher)

The general feeling from staff was that they, as adult professionals, had more anxiety about exploring these concepts with children than the children themselves did. Once they had initiated the conversation for the first time and actually referred to same-sex parents or used words like 'gay' and 'lesbian' out loud for the first time in the presence of children, young people's responses afforded them a sense of permission. In the relatively few cases where giggling or negative opinions or comments had been shared, teachers already felt that they had the existing skills to manage these situations, which meant that rights, dignity and respect were upheld for all present. In other words, they had recognised the potential for a wide range of existing knowledge and attitudes and brought compassion to them.

Even before our strategic plan was formulated and disseminated, I already had a number of teachers who shared openly in staff meetings their experiences and increased confidence and enthusiasm for taking the work to the next level. Over time these teachers became invaluable in driving forward the work by inspiring colleagues who were feeling less confident. In fact one of the staff in the school who was stereotyped as a bit of a negative or 'rock' thinker I involved very early on and they became a wonderful ally for the journey. Find your allies, deploy them well and, of course, share, celebrate and praise their work.

Surveys and questionnaires

Surveys and questionnaires can provide an important baseline in terms of assessing current experiences, knowledge and attitudes. Schools sometimes want 'off-the-peg' surveys and questionnaires and a quick internet search will throw up ideas or versions to download or purchase. I would argue, however, that designing your own surveys and questionnaires is actually part of the process itself. You know your own context and you as a leadership team should be able to explore what information you wish to gain and from whom. In terms of LGBT+ concepts it is useful to consider a balance of teacher-led, independent and anonymous online surveys with staff and pupils. This can also be extended to parents and governors. Ask questions around:

- Existing staff and governor training and confidence on LGBT+ issues in education contexts.
- Behavioural experiences of LGBT+ pupils and non-LGBT+ pupils in school at structured times, unstructured times and coming to and from school.
- Types of negative language being heard by pupils and staff in school and online.
- Types of unwanted behaviours being experienced by pupils and staff in school and online.
- General attitudes towards LGBT+ education and LGBT+ members of the school community.
- Intersections between the experiences of those who identify as LGBT+ but who may also be free school meals, be disabled, have faith, be non-white or have English as an additional language.
- Staff and pupil confidence in school behaviour strategies.

Some primary schools fear that asking young children about LGBT+ identities might confuse them, lead them somehow or cause reprisal. No one questions teaching and learning about non-LGBT+ identities from an early age, provided we are being age-appropriate. So please, get surveying as soon as possible, in a differentiated way, across the whole school.

Next steps

The time you allocate to auditing and surveying attitudes will differ from context to context and depends upon other priorities. Remember though, that even in the hours, days and months we might take to gather information and assess our current position, some young people sat in our classrooms may already be suffering.

It is vital that we adopt a robust timeline to this process and, having gathered our evidence in all its variations, we must apply an analytical view in order to gain an accurate sense of priorities that in turn will feed into our whole-school improvement plan; thus, we need to be pre-visualising our emergent strategic action plan in terms of:

- short-term priorities
- mid-term priorities
- long-term priorities.

We must take into account:

- development
- implementation
- monitoring, reviewing and evaluation
- recalibration: how will your ongoing analysis and scrutiny inform changes to practice?

In this way, we can hope to achieve bigger wins on behalf of all our young people to avoid those who experience suffering at the hands of bullies also experiencing suffering as a result of our school systems and processes. In the next chapter I will continue to explore Tier 3 and develop further how we can drive forward meaningful organisational change. Oh and please do be sure to bring your magic LGBT+ glasses and keep them somewhere safe, for I am sure during your years in education, you will need them again, for yourself and to share with others.

Time to reflect

Before turning the page, please take a moment to reflect.

Things to think about:

- In what ways (if any) does teaching and learning currently lend itself to critical discussion of heteronormativity?
- How might you realign your provision based upon your 'magic glasses' learning walk?

Things to do:

- Give students an opportunity to describe what is most concerning them at a personal, school-wide, local, national and global level. This information should feed into your curriculum, and whole-school themes, topics and assemblies.
- Undertake surveys and questionnaires to find out what is *really* going on. Schedule opportunities to repeat them to monitor impact.
- Give staff and governors the 'magic glasses' learning walk activity with time for reflection afterwards.
- Begin formulating a long-term CPD plan on equality, diversity and inclusion that positions your LGBT+ focus alongside that of other protected characteristics and explores intersections between them.
- Revisit your school vision, aims, goals and mission statements in order to realign them around your journey towards full inclusion and celebration of all identities in school.

Chapter 7
Developing a strategic vision and action plan

'It is important for schools to tackle LGBT+ issues because then you'll be able
to expand your knowledge and gain greater respect whilst you are learning about
their lives and struggles.'

Miya, aged 14, London

In this chapter I will explore how the information gathered from your various
forms of auditing in Chapter 6, page 115, once carefully analysed, can be deployed
to formulate an effective strategic action plan – intended to be kept live as opposed
to sat gathering dust in a folder!

Aim to gather ideas, potential actions and advocates for your action plan from
the moment you begin your journey and don't wait for the fully formed finished
plan, which should evolve over time anyway. Keep your intended outcomes at the
forefront of your mind and communicate your vision and intent often. Remember,
the intent of our journey is to safeguard the happiness, safety and success of all
young people, without exception; please be prepared to robustly defend this vision,
for there will be challenges ahead. Your resilience and moral imperative support you
in this journey, as will a smile and a well-developed sense of humour!

The commitment to your journey towards LGBT+ inclusion involves a robust
plan, just as if this was any other type of school improvement. Targets should be set
by governors or trustees to the headteacher, who in turn builds this into a strategic
vision and action plan to cascade targeted priorities to all staff via performance
management. This includes senior leaders, middle leaders, class teachers and non-
teaching staff. It is important that everyone is involved and made accountable for
the action plan to be a success. How might this look? The model on the following
page is just one example; there are many more!

In this chapter, we will then look at how to develop an ambitious vision for
LGBT+ inclusion and how to draw up an action plan to make this vision a reality.

Headteacher
Develop a strategic vision and action plan to shift the culture and ethos of the school, raising visibility and awareness at whole-school and strategic level. Establish a steering group. Improve outcomes and attendance for those experiencing LGBT+ bullying.
Senior leadership
Reduce incidents of LGBT+ bullying and pejorative language. Record and report incidents and ensure policy compliance.
Middle leadership
Provide teaching and learning opportunities and oversee focus groups. Review the curriculum and establish long-term whole-school teaching and assembly rotas.
Class teachers
Deliver lessons. Undertake peer observations. Provide feedback on LGBT+ themed sessions.
Non-teaching staff
Support focus groups and reduction of playground incidents. Source models, images and texts.

Developing an ambitious vision

In order to achieve sustainable and expansive change that will continue to embed and evolve over time, schools must be precise in identifying what their shared commitment to LGBT+ inclusion looks and feels like in daily practice and at a strategic level, and this must be lived and modelled by the leadership team, board and governing body. Key to this process is the development of clear values, an ethos and a strategic vision that are subsequently shared, modelled and lived by all members of the school community.

Take a pause

Identify the following:

- In ten words or short phrases what does your school stand for? What is your overarching vision for all members of your learning organisation?
- How does this vision manifest itself?
- Is this merely the view of leadership or is it a shared vision?
- How do you communicate your vision to all stakeholders?
- How much of your vision are you prepared to compromise if faced with challenge from either internal or external sources? (Hopefully none!)
- Could this list of factors be used to redefine your own school vision statement or ethos?

- How will you ensure these are not just aspirational words in a book or policy?
- How do you currently judge the success of this ethos? What data and evidence are collected?

With the above in mind, it's important to now think about what you want your *inclusive* school to look and feel like, and what might change in your school's vision accordingly. Consider access to the physical school, the curriculum, classroom culture, whole-school culture and authenticity at work. Take into account the perspectives of staff and newly qualified staff and those in training, parents and carers, students, visitors (including external assessors), and the community beyond the school gates. You can use data gathered from your questionnaires and surveys in Chapter 6, page 121, to help with this.

Setting out your stall

Strong, resilient vision and strategic direction are paramount to ensure buy-in. In any organisation there will be any number of individuals at any number of levels within school who have passion, skills and knowledge that can be hugely impactful; our role as leaders is to enable a space into which these individuals can offer forth their skillset and wisdom, knowing that this will be welcomed and supported by senior leadership, without fear of reprisal from parents or the press. To ensure buy-in, once you have undertaken your auditing, whether it be attitudinal or numerical, it is vital that you share findings with all stakeholders via staff meetings, memos and bulletins and with parents via newsletters and websites. Once you are clear on your vision for an inclusive school, it is then essential you set out your stall to key stakeholders as soon as possible. This involves amending school policies and documentation, targeting immediate need in your school, and starting conversations with pupils, parents and outside agencies.

Many of us will also be able to picture energy drainers amongst our school community, or those who sit in fixed, unmoving space like a limpet on a rock, unwilling or unable to change. Aim to draw these kinds of colleagues along on the journey by bringing compassion to their professional anxieties around change and being very clear as to the damage unchallenged LGBT+ prejudice can do to children.

Policies

In the previous chapter I asked you to deploy your 'magic LGBT+ glasses' to the physical environment and to consider attitudes, resources and training; now turn a critical gaze to your existing policies, especially those concerned with anti-bullying, equality and behaviour. Policies must make *explicit* mention of your statutory expectations under the UK Equality Act, with evidence of your expectations around tackling and preventing homophobic, biphobic and transphobic bullying and language, whether it be at staff, parent, governor or student level.

Research undertaken by NatCen in 2014 (Mitchell et al.) found that the reporting and recording of homophobic bullying was seen to work better by school staff where there were *clear policies* for reporting and recording different types and levels of bullying, including homophobic, biphobic and transphobic bullying. Schools must remember to take into account the 'plus' in LGBT+, in addition to those who are targeted with LGBT+ bullying despite not actually identifying as LGBT+.

Picture a prospective same-sex parent or a parent with an LGBT+ child who has heard great things about your provision; they then explore your policies online in order to ascertain how welcome, included and safe they and their child will be. If policies make no reference to positive LGBT+ inclusion and anti-bullying, how will your 'customers' know that your school is a safe place to be? It is vital then that all relevant policies are compliant in terms of equality legislation and inspection frameworks and robustly centred around the needs of your customers. We must send an unequivocal message that they serve as a protective factor and they actively celebrate LGBT+ identities equally along with everyone else.

Now pin your knowledge of your moral and statutory obligations to the mast and make it explicitly clear in all policies, home–school agreements, school rules, websites and handbooks that not only are LGBT+ identities welcome and celebrated but they will be protected from homophobic, biphobic and transphobic bullying and sanctions *will* be implemented, alongside restorative approaches. State in policies that you are aware that LGBT+ bullying can potentially be targeted at any school stakeholder, whether they identify as LGBT+ or not; parents often need reminding of this.

Using the 'protected characteristics' (see Chapter 4, page 73) as a structure makes this easier for those in UK school contexts. This is a short section of text from the ethos section of one of the London faith schools I work with. LGBT identities and varied families are explicitly mentioned.

> *'Saint Gabriel's College is a Church of England school, serving our local community. Our inclusive Christian ethos is rooted in our faith that we are all made in God's image, and put into practice through our school's Christian values, which help us learn and live well together, becoming the people God calls us to be. We are a joyful and diverse school. We strive to be a community that is hospitable to students and staff of all languages, ethnicities and nationalities, those with special educational needs and disabilities, those who are LGBT, those of all family structures, of all socio-economic backgrounds, of all body types, of all faiths and none.'*

Reflect upon this example from the point of view of being a young LGBT+ person, a young person with same-sex parents, or same-sex parents wishing to send their child to the school for the first time.

Now consider what message this sends to any parents who might harbour prejudicial views.

In order to foster confidence, all stakeholders must be aware of your policies, of their expectations and of their intent. School stakeholders, including parents and governors, must be made aware of the implications of *not* adhering to school policy around LGBT+ inclusion, whether this be through appraisal or the disciplinary process. Policies must reflect the aspirational strategic direction described within your strategic school improvement plan, with aims and objectives being cascaded via staff appraisal and, where relevant and needed, whole-school targets. Policies must be robust, be accessible for stakeholders (including pupils and parents) to understand, be widely shared and reflect the voices and experiences of those at every level within your organisation. They should be directive — but in an aspirational way. Too often I see policies written in a negative or punitive style; effective leadership requires the power to take people with you, to inspire!

Setting out your stall from the outset means that all prospective parents and young people know what you stand for, prior to coming to your organisation. If these stakeholders subsequently attend your school, they know from the outset your school values. You can then deploy the school values should any parental challenge arise (for example if you invite an LGBT+ speaker into assembly) and use them as a way in which to depersonalise the challenge from parents whilst acknowledging the fact that they were clearly visible from the outset. The importance of a clearly communicated vision cannot be overstated.

Targeting immediate need

To make diverse young people feel safer and more included in your school, it is vital to start tackling unwelcome behaviours and negative language associated with perceived or actual LGBT+ identities immediately. Do not delay on this whilst you develop your strategic direction; this should be part and parcel of setting out your stall to stakeholders. Word use changes over time; at school in the 1980s I was called 'poof', 'bender', 'queer' and 'shirt-lifter' and you may be familiar with more contemporary pejorative terms such as 'batty boy', 'faggot' and 'tranny'. In Chapter 9, page 175, I will explore the use of pejorative language, but as of *now* please start gathering examples of current playground and online vernacular around LGBT+ identities in your context.

What is being said in a small rural school in Cornwall, England, may differ from the language being deployed in Brooklyn, USA. Strong relationships with students can enable honest and non-judgemental discussions with young people (who may or may not be LGBT+ themselves) in which contemporary prejudicial slurs can be revealed, discussed, defined and shared with staff. In this way we can explore them respectfully in lessons and assemblies with students in order to set boundaries and minimise their use and impact. When we create a space of open and honest reflective dialogue, young people often tell us what we need to know. They will also often tell you when teachers are deploying prejudicial language themselves and they need to see this challenged. LGBT+ organisations can also provide guidance about acceptable terminology.

Explore LGBT+ related bullying and language through the lens of LGBT+ and non LGBT+ members of the school community; unwanted behaviours can be targeted at anyone who does not comply with social stereotypes or anyone who is 'different' and, as we are all different, this makes us all potential targets.

Starting conversations with pupils

'Shaun's work has been groundbreaking in terms of open discussion and acceptance of the use of language and issues which may have been previously taboo for some children in terms of the climatic norm.'

Barnston Primary School, Wirral

When children arrive at nursery or primary school, they need to be able to speak about and feel pride in their own family group or network of affection. Some young people have same-sex or transgender parents and family members; that's a fact. If we are unable to validate and celebrate this fact (even if the nature of their parental structure is at odds with our personal beliefs) then we are simply in the wrong job.

Take a pause

Reflect on this (true) scenario:

I was observing in a school nursery on the first day of a new term. Child A arrived with two mums who were invited to stay and ease the child into this overwhelming new context. They seated themselves at a table and began making a fine old mess with a hand-painting activity. After a short time, another child, Child B (who had been dropped off at nursery by his mum and dad), approached the nursery leader and asked her audibly in front of the class why Child A had two mums and not a mummy and a daddy. I glanced up at the nursery leader and for a moment I could see that time had stopped for her (at this point the school had not initiated any staff LGBT+ inclusion training) and she visibly reddened around the face and neck. I could see that one of Child A's mums was looking and waiting for a response from the nursery leader. After an awkward silence the nursery leader physically escorted Child B away from Child A and his two mums to another activity. As she did so, she said, 'We are not going to talk about that right now.'

Now consider the following questions:

1) What did Child B wish to understand and why do you think this is?
2) What emotions might Child B have been feeling as he asked the question?
3) What emotions might Child A have been feeling as he heard Child B ask the question?
4) What might the parents of Child A have been thinking and feeling as Child B asked his question?
5) What might the nursery leader have been thinking and feeling as Child B asked his question?
6) What might Child B have been feeling as he was led away?
7) What might Child A have thought and felt as Child B was led away?
8) What might the parents of Child A have thought and felt as the nursery leader responded to Child B's question?
9) What could the school have done in order to prepare the nursery leader for this situation and other similar situations?
10) What might the impact of this scenario have been upon all parties involved?
11) What would your answer to Child B's question have been?

As a result of witnessing the scenario above, it became very clear to me that in situations where education professionals shy away from, balk at or speak with obvious hesitation or shame about same-sex families and LGBT+ identities we immediately (and often without knowing it) become part of the perpetuation of the problem between generations. Even very young children can be highly intuitive and know when an adult is concealing, fudging or being awkward; children instinctively know when something is wrong. A teacher or indeed nursery leader who avoids or balks at acknowledging or explaining that some children have two mums or two dads, and that is called being lesbian or gay, may unknowingly be triggering a sense of shame within the child who has same-sex parents.

Some children (as I did) know very early in their lives that they are attracted to people of the same sex; others might have LGBT+ brothers and sisters. How do these young people feel if they are raised in a home where LGBT+ is a simple fact of life, but in school LGBT+ identities are left unspoken or are spoken about with shame? Visible first steps, such as posters in public places making it clear that LGBT+ people and same-sex families are welcome, can start conversations and make an immediate difference as you set out your vision for inclusivity.

Nevertheless, be mindful of casually using the term 'LGBT+' before staff have been given clear and simple explanations for these terms and are made aware that there is an expectation of them to teach and refer to them in class.

These conversations become easier when teachers find regular ways of referring to LGBT+ celebrities or historical figures throughout the curriculum and in assemblies, such as:

- 'Alan Turing, who is known as the father of modern computing, also happened to be gay. That means he was attracted to or fell in love with other men.'
- 'Billie Jean King was a famous tennis player. She is also a lesbian, which means she has relationships with women.'
- 'Caitlyn Jenner you might know as one of the parents of the Kardashians. Caitlyn identifies as female but was born physically male and was named at birth Bruce Jenner. This meant that Caitlyn spent much of her life feeling unhappy and that the sex assigned to her by doctors at birth did not match her own gender identity. Caitlyn was trapped inside Bruce's body. Now Caitlyn has affirmed her female identity, which means she is living a life as the person she always knew she was. This is called being transgender or trans.'

Keep it simple and speak without shame or embarrassment. Start by asking the children what they already know (usually quite a lot) and use this to reframe and plug knowledge gaps. You might be thinking, 'When I talk about heterosexual celebrities or historical figures, I *don't* point out the fact that they were straight' (although you may refer to their opposite-sex spouse without registering it), but there is no accumulation of evidence that heterosexual human beings are persecuted or legislated against for *just being heterosexual*. LGBT+ are a minority group targeted with prejudice on a global scale; education, visibility and representation are vital.

Marking the International Day Against Homophobia, Biphobia and Transphobia (17 May) or LGBT History Month with an assembly makes an immediate impact upon young people who need to know they deserve their time and place on Earth. In doing so you set out your stall and lead from the top, whilst giving a public indication that positive change is in the air. I have been contacted by ex-pupils on social media wanting to thank me, not only for coming out at school but also for leading assemblies around the country on LGBT+ identities. It is not an exaggeration to report that for some of them, it saved their lives. Such is the power of validation of authentic identity.

Do not, however, assume that all pupils have a clear grasp of what LGBT+ human beings are and what LGBT+ bullying is. An assembly can sometimes lead to confusion amongst pupils and staff if you do so. It is important to embed understanding and usage of these terms. Children are far less likely to snigger their way through an assembly when the words 'lesbian' and 'gay' have been in their lexicon and general awareness since starting school. There is no shame in using these words, so use them well and make them 'usual'. Ultimately, we should aim to move beyond 'giving permission' and involve young people in taking responsibility as participants within a shared vision of positive LGBT+ inclusion, as is the case at Barnston School in Wirral:

'The older children have led the way, preparing assemblies, displays and workshops for the younger children – teaching them about issues and how to discuss and support people. The openness and honesty of the children has been amazing and they now comfortably use language that previously would not have been commonly used. The older children carry out homophobia surveys before teaching and then a few weeks after teaching to review changes in attitudes and learning acquired. They do this on the playground at playtimes. The results looked great. It is clear that after the teaching, the children understand the teaching and how it applies to everyday life.'

Starting conversations with parents

Starting conversations with parents is an important part of setting out our vision for LGBT+ inclusion. Parents have approached me in schools (having been prompted by visible first steps such as LGBT+ posters and books) asking for help explaining the term 'LGBT+' to children at home, stating they have LGBT+ family members and lack confidence and knowledge in defining these terms to their children. These parents require a simple sheet of definitions or a book about two mums or two dads to read at home and again that sense of permission. It was fascinating to learn just how many parents avoided these simple explanations because they perceived it to be a conversation that would involve a discussion of same-sex physical activity. Books in primary schools featuring LGBT+ characters are not the same as pornography, despite what some people might think!

When books featuring models, images and stories of LGBT+ lives and achievements are embedded throughout school and class libraries from the outset, children emerge knowing what and who LGBT+ people are; many will also have seen their own life experiences validated. If these books are also deployed at home, they stimulate discussion and new learning in family homes and, over time, in wider society. Make it about human diversity; make it about history; make it about compassion; make it about love.

There exists a generational link between the lack of education about LGBT+ identities and levels of LGBT+ bullying and prejudice around the world. Russia, currently under the leadership of Vladimir Putin, has introduced stringent laws against so-called 'gay propaganda' aimed at restricting 'the characteristics of propaganda of homosexual relations'. This law was ruled discriminatory and likely to encourage homophobia by the European Court of Human Rights in 2017. What underpins laws like this, and similar laws around the world, and indeed in our own history (Section 28), is the fallacy that even talking about LGBT+ will somehow 'turn' our young people into LGBT+ people, when all education and information really do is make those who are LGBT+ feel they are worthwhile and valid human beings. It doesn't take a university degree to work out why such laws are introduced at any point in time or place on Earth – it's called fear and prejudice, and we tackle this through education.

As LGBT+ inclusive education is a relatively new introduction in UK schools, especially at primary stage, many grandparents and parents of our current school intakes were never afforded the opportunity of learning about LGBT+ history, identity, prejudice and suffering. Despite this, it is important to note that over ten years of my work, my positive experiences with parents far outweigh the infrequent challenges or complaints.

Please never be afraid of challenge. Our work at its core is about stimulating conversations and then bringing curiosity, patience and compassion to what is revealed. After first writing press articles and being interviewed about my work in schools, I received many messages from colleagues, friends and family who were appalled by the resulting negative and sometimes hateful comments. As a result of these challenges, I soon found myself with a strong and supportive team of allies (in school and out) wishing to help me progress my work. I am grateful to those who shared negative points of view about my work; it taught me not to be afraid of revealing the prejudice of other human beings. When prejudice is revealed one can hope to work with it, if one has the time, the energy and the resources. If prejudice (and all the insecurity, fear and anxiety that goes with it) stays unspoken, it accumulates over time and when the lid finally pops off this can place individuals at significant risk of bullying and hate.

When schools provide books featuring LGBT+ families, lead LGBT History Month assemblies and teach lessons as to the respectful use of the word 'gay', they *will* trigger conversations in school, in the playground, online and at home. Be aware and mindful as you open Pandora's 'rainbow' box for the first time. Most of all (and I am aware this is a big ask) aspire to be non-judgemental; otherwise you might unintentionally shut the conversations back down again and with it any chance of forward motion. The all-important awareness training you provide for staff, parents and students at the outset of your LGBT+ inclusion journey on human rights and the Equality Act 2010 will support you in facilitating a respectful space into which conversations can be held with stakeholders who are aware not only of their own rights and protected characteristics but also of the need to uphold the rights of and foster good relationships with those whose identities and beliefs may differ from their own.

Ultimately, whether you inform parents about your LGBT+ inclusion work is a decision that must be yours and one I would strongly advise you to think through very carefully before taking action. When I am invited to train a whole-school staff body on LGBT+ inclusion I am sometimes asked whether the school needs to inform the parents that I am coming. My response is: 'That is your choice, but can I just check, do you normally inform parents when a trainer comes in to train staff about non-LGBT+ related matters?' If the answer is 'Yes, every time', there is no problem. If the answer is 'No' or silent red-faced embarrassment (it happens a lot!), I then ask: 'Why do you feel it is necessary to inform parents about this particular suite of training but not any others? What message might that send to parents?'

Another recent scenario occurred on the Isle of Man, wherein a primary school asked me to lead them in whole-staff training that would then lead on to LGBT+ inclusion work across the school for the first time. The question was this: 'After you have trained staff, before we actually do any work, do you think we need to call a parent meeting and have you explain what we are going to be doing?' My answer was this: 'When you undertook teaching and learning about racism did you first call a parent meeting to explain yourself? How about when you covered the inclusion of children with additional needs or disabilities within the school community?' In ten years, no one has answered 'Yes' to this question. Every school I have supported has simply got on with work around racial inclusion and representation of the diversity of human history and existence *without* feeling the need to call in the parents first to explain themselves. Parent meetings are held about school trips, exams, transition and the content of sexual education programmes, but I question why there should be a need for a special parent meeting at the outset of the journey towards LGBT+ inclusion when our primary customers are our young people. These meetings can also put up a red flag that a school is about to undertake something that is up for negotiation; I don't aim to negotiate over something so vital as children's well-being. Sexual orientation and gender reassignment are protected characteristics under the UK Equality Act. Schools therefore have a legal duty to eliminate discrimination towards LGBT+ people. If a school is seen to hold parent meetings before LGBT+ training, speakers and initiatives when this practice is not consistently applied to non-LGBT+ identities or those identities that fall within other protected characteristics, such as race and disability, I would question whether this could be viewed as 'othering' and prejudicial and a practice that reinforces the sense that LGBT+ is a 'sensitive' or 'controversial' subject in school. Society and education systems must undertake a significant and lasting shift away from this default position, as these views are deeply damaging to the mental health of young people.

There *is* absolutely a place for supportive education and awareness sessions for parents around equality legislation and LGBT+ awareness. Other LGBT+ training organisations may take a different view on parent meetings. I know of one that provides a standard letter for parents, inviting them along to an LGBT+ meeting in the school hall upfront. Sending home a more generalised newsletter can be effective, making reference to any data gathered on LGBT+ bullying and the school's intention to prevent it. Make it clear that such behaviour is not welcome from any stakeholder on site. This could also contain information about a range of other anti-bullying events and strategies, therefore not singling out the specific LGBT+ issue on its own.

You can also lead parent workshops on bullying prevention, during which bullying data and aims to make the school LGBT+ inclusive can be shared alongside a broader discussion of behaviour in school, in order to avoid singling out LGBT+ work as something 'other' or particularly worthy of parental concern. Present it as the right thing to do and something you legally have to do (in the UK) to keep the children safe.

'Shaun's visits to our school have been celebrated through social media channels and parents have made appointments with the headteacher to discuss some of the home conversations his work has prompted. All such meetings have been positive, and parents have expressed gratitude for the work we are undertaking.'

Representative from Dhoon/Laxey Federation,
Isle of Man, July 2018

Of course, when you have been on the journey for some time and you have good news stories to share then please do so via the school website and special events. Just be very careful about inadvertently causing a parental flashpoint; you know your own contexts, so own it and make it work for your children.

Take a pause

Imagine for a moment you are an emergent LGBT+ child in a primary or secondary school and at the end of the school day your parents sit you outside a school hall full of parents discussing (or perhaps disagreeing) with teachers about the fact that the school will from now on be simply representing you in all aspects of its work.

What positive and negative messages might you gain from this experience?

Ultimately it is entirely your decision how you present your vision and intentions to parents and carers, but I would implore you to be resilient and forthright in the knowledge that you are doing nothing wrong. Learning about and celebrating heterosexual identities in schools are never questioned. If we act apologetically in terms of LGBT+ identities, then we become part of the problem (often without even meaning to) and we compound a sense of unease in a potentially already judgemental number of stakeholders.

Take the time to broaden your knowledge base around LGBT+ identities to keep it current and to pre-empt challenge that might arise as a result of negative reporting in the press. Parents will sometimes challenge LGBT+ work based upon negative press representation and we need to be prepared, whilst being resolute in our strategic vision.

Finally, without wishing to stereotype LGBT+ staff as being saddled with emotional damage, we must be mindful that increased awareness, teaching and LGBT+ role-modelling may result in a variety of emotional responses from some LGBT+ staff. LGBT+ staff may also be exposed to prejudicial views from other staff, parents and students, thus emotional and pastoral support, open doors and robust wellbeing strategies are vital from the outset in order to create a safe, trusting collegiate space.

Starting conversations with outside agencies

It is vital to reach out to other organisations and agencies when setting out your vision for LGBT+ inclusion for a number of reasons:

- To see what training and support is already out there.
- To gain information that would inform your strategic vision.
- To facilitate links between your own school and other local and national services working to support LGBT+ students, teachers and families.
- To create a proud, shame-free and transparent public 'buzz' about your work, to inspire not only your own school stakeholders but also other schools.
- To forge links with services providing support for children with additional needs and their parents to ensure that they are represented and included.
- To forge links with local LGBT+ faith groups.
- To broker support and therapy for those within the school community who have already experienced LGBT+ prejudice or bullying.
- To attract LGBT+ speakers and role models.
- To form a supportive best practice network with other schools undertaking similar work.

When my own school reached out in this way, we found ourselves a focal point for LGBT+ inclusion in education and as a result a number of global banks and businesses sent high-profile LGBT+ speakers and network groups to undertake work in and around the school, often accompanied by a nice amount of money for improvements to the school site or our resources!

Get searching, emailing and calling; not only will you add to your support network and knowledge base but you also never know what additional benefits might come your way for simply taking a positive stand on behalf of your young people. Good luck!

Developing a strategic action plan

Once you have clearly established a vision for LGBT+ inclusion in your school and have set out your stall to key stakeholders, it is important to draw up a robust, written action plan as to how you are going to achieve this vision.

Your action plan must reflect:

- auditing and ongoing evaluation
- new learning
- fostering acceptance
- celebration and reframing
- dissemination beyond the school gates to educate the wider community.

You should also consider carefully your impact measures to ensure they are relevant to your own context. What is most important within your own organisation? How will you ensure that you measure diversity (demographic information) and inclusion itself – in other words whether all individuals are treated fairly and respectfully, have equal access to opportunities and resources, and are able to fully contribute to the life of the school whilst reaching their full potential? Governors must also be primed to seek the views of pupils, parents, carers and school staff on an independent and ongoing basis in order to assess progress and the effectiveness of the leadership team's actions to foster a positive school culture for all. Establishing a steering group (including stakeholders at all levels, including the school council and parents) and building focus and research groups into your strategic plan will ensure accountability and avoid nasty surprises when governors or inspectors come calling! Your strategy should not exist in a bubble, a bolt-on or aside to existing ongoing practice.

To write your action plan, first make sure you are absolutely clear on your strategic vision:

- Why are you undertaking this work – what is your key rationale and vision?
- How will you communicate your key rationale and vision to all stakeholders and beyond the school gates?
- How might you gain and communicate a whole-school vision in terms of what 'due regard' means in your particular context, whilst remaining compliant with the requirements of equality legislation?
- How will you ensure your vision stays resilient in the wake of staff and leadership mobility, student mobility and shifts in societal attitudes or education policy and governmental leadership?
- How will you minimise or remove disadvantages?
- How will you encourage participation in your strategic action plan?

Now write your action plan, making sure you include:

- Your overarching vision.
- Your aims and objectives.
- The high aspirations you would like to introduce to eliminate discrimination, harassment and victimisation, to further equality and to foster positive relationships.
- Equality Act-compliant policies, procedures and practice in relation to children, staff, governors and parents.
- Care, guidance and support in place for children, staff, governors and parents.
- Delivery of services and curriculum.
- Teaching and learning strategies.
- Rolling programme of whole-school events, topics and themes.

- How practice relates to pupils' progress and outcomes, admissions, attendance and behaviour.
- Partnership-working and outside support.
- Relationships and learning opportunities with the wider community.
- An assessment and review strategy.

Example objectives you might include in the plan are:

- Establishing your equality steering group and impact focus groups.
- Identifying groups of children in order to monitor progress in terms of changing behaviours and attitudes.
- Involving the school council.
- Reviewing key policies, handbooks, induction and anti-bullying guidance.
- Targets and actions for tackling unwelcome behaviours and attitudes.
- Ordering new resources.
- Curriculum, whole-school and assembly foci review.
- Review of uniform, toilets and changing provision.
- Implementation of robust recording and reporting of unwelcome behaviours using UK protected characteristics.
- Attendance and behaviour targets.
- Ensuring robust and rapid progress using staff induction and appraisal to set targets and expectations.
- Reducing exclusions triggered by unwelcome and prejudicial behaviours.
- Increasing engagement in learning and school activities.
- Improving staff wellbeing and retention.
- Establishing an LGBT+ youth group or gay–straight alliance.

Once a draft of the plan is completed, it is vital to revisit it as a leadership team and identify as many links as possible with other aspects of curriculum, school structures, management, learning and development. The rainbow doesn't shine in isolation above or around the school; instead, its colours inhabit every aspect of school life. In this way we are most likely to make our work sustainable and embedded, with the widest possible reach and thereby the greatest impact. What a privilege it is to be on this journey for our young people!

Once operational the plan must also be regularly revisited alongside the recording and reporting of data on incidents of LGBT+ related bullying and language. A detailed breakdown of the themes emerging from the recording of unwelcome behaviours, categorised specifically around LGBT+ categories, plays a core role in assessing the impact of your action plan and will inform future targets and priorities. Many schools include an initial target to reduce the use of the word 'gay' as a negative term and a high-profile school-wide campaign can reduce these incidents very quickly; however, what often happens as a result is that young people seek out other pejorative terms that are also derogatory to LGBT+ identities, such as 'faggot'. The maintenance and analysis of behaviour logs, alongside pupil voice and interviews, enables you to refresh and reframe your action plan as the inclusive culture of your school evolves over time, making you fully accountable to school governors (bullying data should be reported at every governors' meeting to an identified inclusion governor) and to external inspection agencies.

Reflective strategic planning activity

To help you formulate your strategic action plan, I would like to introduce you to a reflective activity. Below are reproduced the first and last sections of a whole-school self-review audit tool first written back in 2010 to help a number of schools experiencing LGBT+ bullying. Schools used the tool to ascertain at what level of the journey towards LGBT+ inclusion they were on and what they needed to do to move forwards. The tool has four stages:

- **Stage 1: Focusing.** Represents schools at an emergent stage in their journey.
- **Stage 2: Developing.** Represents schools who have authored and are beginning to implement an effective whole-school training action plan and who are beginning to work towards sustained and strategic organisational change.
- **Stage 3: Embedding.** Represents schools who are embedding the various aspects of their strategic plan, looking for evidence of impact.
- **Stage 4: Advanced.** Represents schools who have well-developed practice and whole-school vision. The schools are also working proactively beyond the school community itself.

Please read the first stage:

Stage 1: Focusing
- The wide majority of LGBT+ bullying is going unchallenged with detrimental impact upon pupils, staff and parents.
- Gender stereotyping is going unchallenged with detrimental impact upon pupils, staff and parents.
- Students, staff and parents are unclear about the nature and impact of LGBT+ bullying.
- Staff perceive LGBT+ bullying as something of low priority or as something that only affects children who are LGBT+.
- Some staff express negative views of LGBT+ identities in front of young people or colleagues.
- Some staff believe there can't be any LGBT+ members of the school community as children are 'too young'.

- Staff and students may believe that LGBT+ bullying does not occur.
- Staff may believe that the use of the pejorative form of the word 'gay' is not harmful or homophobic.
- LGBT+ incidents are not reported or recorded.
- The school places low emphasis upon PSHE development.
- No explicit link is made between LGBT+ bullying and other forms of discrimination.
- There is no intention to adopt a zero-tolerance approach to LGBT+ bullying.
- Leadership lack understanding as to how representation and visibility of LGBT+ people can improve wellbeing, pupil outcomes and attendance.
- There is little or no community involvement or links with local and national LGBT+ support groups.
- There is little or no pupil participation; pupils' experiences are not being heard and reviewed.
- Fear of adverse reaction from parents or the views and beliefs of school staff limit the school's actions in preventing LGBT+ bullying.
- Governors and parents have not been made aware of the requirement by UK equality legislation and Ofsted for schools to be proactively tackling LGBT+ bullying and for fostering good relations between protected groups.
- The pejorative use of the word 'gay' or 'tranny' may be acceptable in staff room conversations.
- LGBT+ staff feel unable to be authentic about their identity in the workplace.
- There are no discussions that challenge heteronormativity or cisgender privilege.
- Resources and displays do not reflect a range of family groups or positive images of LGBT+ people.
- The anti-bullying, equality and behaviour policies, home–school agreement, behaviour charter, code of conduct, school and class rules make no explicit mention of LGBT+ bullying and language.
- There are no opportunities for inspirational role models from a range of diverse careers and backgrounds to meet and speak to pupils.
- Some school staff regard the tackling of LGBT+ bullying as something only to be tackled within sex and relationships education, creating anxiety that they will be required to discuss homosexual sexual activity; as a result the work may remain untaught.
- The school has no effective strategies for supporting victims of LGBT+ bullying.
- Staff have limited knowledge or misconceptions of the issues surrounding LGBT+ people.
- Resources and the school's approach to some subject areas and clubs reinforce gender and other forms of stereotyping.
- Staff feel unsure what to do if a child makes a disclosure about their sexuality.

- There is little or no pastoral support for pupils or parents of pupils who are questioning or who wish to come out.
- There is no equality policy in place and staff may be unsure of the implications of the Equality Act and protected characteristics.
- The school has done little or no work on the rights of children (UN Convention, Rights Respecting, etc.).
- The school has nothing in the way of visual, text or resource material depicting LGBT+ people or a range of different families.
- People do little to acknowledge and support people who don't follow traditional gender roles or stereotypes.
- The rights, respect and dignity of transgender pupils are not upheld through the provision of gender-neutral facilities; they are instead being asked to use disabled toilets.
- The majority of LGBT+ stakeholders are not tolerated.
- Staff fail to model expectations of positive attitudes, intentions, behaviours and language towards LGBT+ stakeholders.

Now read the fourth stage:

Stage 4: Advanced
- The school deploys as standard practice highly effective preventive strategies for ensuring LGBT+ bullying rarely occurs, and these are clearly understood by and modelled to the wider community.
- All staff have undergone LGBT+ inclusion training and expectations form part of staff, parent, governor and pupil induction.
- All stakeholders understand they have human rights and they have a duty to uphold those of others.
- All stakeholders can communicate that LGBT+ bullying is unacceptable and the reasons why.
- All stakeholders monitor use of prejudicial language and are able to express an understanding of the commonality between all forms of prejudice and discrimination and the reasons behind it.
- Stakeholders are mindfully self-aware and able to recognise and work positively with their own bias and prejudice; the school nurtures a culture in which these discussions are part of daily life.
- Pupils and staff understand that bias and prejudice can be based upon stereotypes.
- Pupils can give examples of where they have refrained from using LGBT+ bullying and language outside of school and/or encouraged others to do so.

- All stakeholders are involved in work to promote equality and human rights outside of the school.
- Stakeholders will understand and be able to communicate with clarity the shared vision and understanding of the school and the impact and rationale of the work.
- Uniform, PE kit and changing facilities are gender neutral, and there is consistency with residential trip provision.
- The work is discussed and revisited regularly at staff meetings and provision continues to strengthen.
- The school fully complies with Ofsted requirements and the Equality Act 2010.
- The school ensures that LGBT+ bullying is minimised and that other forms of prejudice-based bullying are significantly reduced.
- There is a strong emphasis upon celebrating the diverse nature of individuals within the school and a visible commitment to avoiding labelling and stereotyping.
- The school shares their journey with outside agencies and other educational establishments.
- The impact of the work is celebrated with all stakeholders including parents.
- Subject knowledge is excellent and takes a wider voice of the nature of prejudice.
- Induction for new staff, NQTs and supply teachers makes the school equalities stance explicit.
- The school vision, aims and ethos clearly celebrate diversity with specific mention of LGBT+ and are shared via the school website, prospectus and promotions. These are shared and explained to all prospective stakeholders from first point of contact. School policies robustly underpin the aims, vision and ethos, again with specific reference to LGBT+ identities.
- Best practice teaching and learning strategies and teacher knowledge and experience are shared across the school.
- A reduction in LGBT+ bullying incidents means there is a greater focus on standards and achievement, based on high expectations that all pupils can fulfil their full potential in a fully inclusive environment.
- Across the year teachers adopt a strategic plan of LGBT+ inclusive one-off lessons, teaching units and topics. Assemblies and initiatives are delivered; this is underpinned by 'everyday' LGBT+ visibility in a range of subject areas and framed by a three- to five-year whole-school foci schedule.
- Learning and discussions on LGBT+ bullying and prejudice are taught with reference to other forms of prejudice. Stakeholders understand the links and intersections with clarity.
- Pupils take ownership for developing new strategies for ensuring LGBT+ bullying and language are not used.

- All stakeholders are open and confident when talking about LGBT+ identities and the protective and negative factors that impact upon them.
- All stakeholders are open and confident when talking about their own identity and those of friends and family members (where they wish to be).
- The school boasts a rich and diverse ongoing programme of inspirational role models who are utilised within lessons, assemblies and teaching units.
- The LGBT+ and Allies group are actively involved in local hate crime, LGBT+ forums and youth support services.
- Pupils, staff and parents are given opportunities to celebrate those within the school community who may act as role models and have inspiring stories to tell.
- The school has well-established and highly effective provision for supporting victims of bullying using a restorative approach.
- The school has well-established and highly effective provision for supporting children who are questioning their own identities.
- The school provides a suite of training and support materials for parents, via the school website, leaflets, meetings, working parties, etc.
- Equality policy is agreed and having significant impact upon workplace practice.
- Pupils are able to represent LGBT+ people and different families in their discussion and written work, drama, etc.
- Students feel empowered to act as allies and are involved in activities to uphold the human rights of others in and out of the school context.
- All stakeholders are included and celebrated, including those who do not adhere to accepted gender 'norms'.
- The rights respect and dignity of transgender pupils are robustly upheld through the provision of gender-neutral facilities.
- LGBT+ parents, students and staff are visible, and feel comfortable and safe being open and out (if they wish to be).
- Difference is seen as a unifying factor, not one to cause discrimination. This is highlighted and shared at best practice events.
- Ex-students who are LGBT+ or allies return to the school to share experiences with students.
- The inclusive ethos of the school itself is maintained throughout school trips, residentials and choices made in terms of external contractors.
- Heteronormative attitudes are openly discussed and challenged, as is cisgender privilege.
- Staff and governors proactively model a pro-social approach to LGBT+ inclusion and all stakeholders are supported and encouraged to do the same.
- Relationships between those who share a protected characteristic and those who do not are strong and respectful.
- LGBT+ stakeholders are not merely accepted; they are celebrated.

After reading Stages 1 and 4, please reflect upon the *strategic journey* that would need to take place between these two developmental stages. What might Stages 2 and 3 of this journey involve? Try to write at least ten bullet points for each stage in your notepad. Revisit these earlier sections of the book and any accompanying reflective notes you have made before you do so:

- 'The impact of LGBT+ bullying' and 'The reality of LGBT+ bullying' (Chapter 2, pages 39 and 42)
- 'Defining prejudice-related bullying' (Chapter 3, page 54)
- 'Working with the Equality Act' and 'Ofsted' (Chapter 4, pages 75 and 77)
- 'Moving on' (Chapter 5, page 106)
- 'Auditing current provision and attitudes' (Chapter 6, page 115)

Before starting, also take a moment to notice your attitude and intentions towards this activity. Take your time and enjoy it!

Once you're finished, reflect upon what went well, what was challenging and why this was. As an extension activity, if you were to write a Stage 5, how would it look?

I hope this activity afforded you a focused opportunity to consider strategic planning in your own context, as well as an opportunity to apply and consolidate some learning from earlier chapters.

Finally, let's hear from a school who have worked with me through the process up to this stage (Tiers 1 to 3) and the impact it has had for them so far.

Kewaigue Primary School, Isle of Man

We act with greater awareness, understanding and compassion than we otherwise would have. We are very much at the beginning of our journey. Curriculum development will feature heavily in the coming months. However, teachers have all said that they now have 'permission' to bring this to the fore and not shy away from LGBT+ inclusion.

Staff have reported that they have changed their way of thinking as a result of the input Shaun has had. Their outlook and perceptions around the issues have been challenged and a greater appreciation of the issues facing individuals within and across the LGBT+ community has resulted in their desire to challenge prejudice and promote positive messages around diversity and inclusion.

Staff were inspired, and their appreciation of why action needs to be taken and their knowledge of this aspect of diversity have been developed enormously. There is complete buy-in to ensure we develop our approach to fostering inclusion for all within our school community. There is a strength of commitment to ensure diversity is actively promoted throughout the school. Nearly all parents have been very appreciative of the work we have undertaken.

In the next chapter we will shift our focus from planning onto implementation.

Tier 4
Implementation

Chapter 8
Celebrating diversity

'Authenticity is your most precious commodity as a leader.'

Marcus Buckingham

Welcome to Tier 4! This tier is concerned with the implementation of your strategic action plan. Although this may look different from setting to setting according to the aims and objectives you have planned in your own context, I would like to focus on three key areas that will be universal in our LGBT+ inclusion work. The following three chapters will therefore focus specifically on embedding diversity in our teaching and learning, nurturing an accepting culture by tackling bullying and pejorative language, and helping a school community to speak out with pride and resilience about LGBT+ identities.

This first chapter will look at using teaching and learning to celebrate diversity through whole-school foci, curriculum and assemblies. I will offer example projects, activities, topics and resources.

However, before we go into the specifics, there are seven underlying 'steps to success' in teaching about LGBT+ identities that I would like to establish first; these ensure focus and resilience, and you and your staff should have a secure grasp of them before running any teaching and learning projects.

Steps to success

Step 1: Teaching and learning about varied families, heritage and difference of all kinds is a non-negotiable from the outset.

It is essential to provide regular opportunities to identify, explore and celebrate the similarities and differences between diverse human beings, the resulting reactions arising within us and the potentially damaging impact of our reactions and responses upon others.

Step 1 is where the PPOP technique (see Chapter 2, page 36) really comes into play. The existence of LGBT+ human beings is a *fact of life*. That the human race is non-gender binary is a *fact of life*. To make a school (or education system) LGBT+ inclusive, in which we foster individuals capable of compassionate acceptance as opposed to prejudice and hate, we must teach, learn about and role-model LGBT+ lives from the outset. As we've established, children entering nursery might have same-sex parents or LGBT+ siblings. This is the reality of their everyday lives. If they arrive at nursery and see no validation of their lives, the 'othering' and sense of shame have already begun.

Equally crucial in the Early Years is what I think of as the historical 'missing link' in many education systems: an exploration of our individual reactions and responses to difference and diversity. Earlier in this book (page 58) I cited the example of my younger brother, who upon meeting a black person for the first time exhibited fear. His reaction meant that additional teaching and learning was necessary for him to understand what a black person was, in turn enabling him to *respond* rather than *react* when meeting non-white human beings in future.

As my work has increasingly taken me around the world to a wide variety of school contexts, I pay close attention to how human diversity is taught, at least where it *is* being taught! Out of this scrutiny two key themes emerge with clarity. The first is a noticeable emphasis upon teaching about the 'differences' stemming from schools' admirable intention to explore human diversity, but very limited space given in conversations to subsequently explore what factors human beings have in common – our unifying factors.

Secondly, whilst observing lessons where primary teachers introduced LGBT+ identities for the first time, I have from time to time observed a few children who were uneasy with the conversations. Listening to pupil conversation it became clear that some children had already assimilated intergenerational or religious prejudice. Some voiced concern that the school and their own trusted adults at home were sending apparently contradictory messages about LGBT+ people. I have witnessed children responding in a similar manner when schools have undertaken work on non-white identities, where children came from homes where racist views were expressed. Bringing compassion, I could see there was doubt. Even simple discussions about LGBT+ identities, when filtered through layers of anxiety, fear, lack of information or prejudice, can result in a sense for some people that their own identity or beliefs are being challenged or diminished. It is important to explore autonomy of thought in our schools whilst being robust in school expectations around understanding of diversity. Reflecting upon my own education throughout the 1970s and 1980s, I can recall incidents when teachers had told us 'not to be racist' but I can recall not one single conversation about *why* racism or prejudice arises. Reflecting upon my own practice and that of my colleagues, I noticed we too had a strong tendency to direct children to 'not be unkind' or prejudiced towards those they perceived as different, without any robust explanation or exploration of *why* these feelings arose in the first place, let alone how these feelings and reactions might be tempered in a more considered and humanitarian response.

These two observations have led me to advise preceding any LGBT+ inclusion work in schools with a whole-school topic entitled 'Our heritage', exploring personal, familial and tribal identities at the outset of the school year in order to foster more secure identities and cohesive relationships throughout the school and with the world beyond the school gates. 'Our heritage' has a core teaching and learning component that involves exploring our human responses to difference. I will return to 'Our heritage' in more detail on page 155.

Step 2: Adopt a proactive approach to the activities that develop cognitive empathy from the outset of education.

We must never assume that other individuals experience empathy in the same way as we do. Some research shows that individuals who exhibit unwelcome behaviours lack empathy; other findings suggest that bullies *can* experience empathy but may (for a number of reasons) dissociate from it. It is important that we find ongoing ways of teaching and talking about empathy and the effects of our words and actions from the start.

Developing empathy for those we perceive to be very different from us can be challenging if time isn't taken to explore a variety of human emotions and experiences. I travel far and wide in order to speak to staff and young people of all ages in schools, some of whom come from backgrounds in which they have learned to be prejudiced towards LGBT+ people.

Personal testimony and life stories can elicit strong feelings and greater empathy in children as well as adults and it is important that they remain a core and ongoing feature of any work around human diversity, especially for humans who fit under the umbrella of the repressed minorities, including of course women. An ongoing programme of diverse speakers in schools can really help with fostering empathy. The use of social stories, life stories, and theatre and drama plays a key role in developing cognitive empathy.

Step 3: Teach without shame about LGBT+ identities.

Can you really use the words 'lesbian' and 'transgender' in front of colleagues with confidence? Do you avoid eye contact when a student tells you they are lesbian or non-binary? A shameful approach perpetuates shame in LGBT+ people and those with LGBT+ friends and family. There is no shame in talking about heterosexual relationships in schools, so why then should there be any shame related to exploring LGBT+ identities? If you, a colleague, a child or a parent looks embarrassed or shameful when (for example) using the word 'gay' or 'black person', bring non-judgemental curiosity and work through it.

I have observed that this is often because non-LGBT+ people oddly seem to define LGBT+ people by making assumptions about what they may or may not do 'in the bedroom'. The obsession with man-on-man sodomy culturally and legally throughout history spectacularly fails to take into account that not all gay men participate in this act anyway, whilst some men who do not identify as gay do enjoy the act with other men or indeed with women. Many of my heterosexual friends also claim to enjoy sodomy from time to time but no one seems to judge them negatively for it. In terms of making a school positively LGBT+ inclusive, outside of a positively LGBT+ inclusive sexual health education and relationships programme, why should this sexualised discussion even be relevant to teaching and learning about LGBT+ identities? We are actually teaching about diverse identities in all their richness, social history, human rights and justice.

The widespread focus on sex when defining LGBT+ identities has resulted in the erroneous and widespread view that learning about LGBT+ people is somehow 'sexualising children' or 'robbing them of their childhood'. I have significantly more concerns about young people being sexualised by social media and end-of-year proms than lessons featuring a diverse range of role models or the history of the rainbow flag. Detractors of LGBT+ inclusion work often claim that LGBT+ education 'confuses' young children. In ten years, I have yet to meet a young person who was 'confused' by LGBT+ education. Yes, they are curious and interested, as they are when learning about different faiths or animal diversity. I grew up in an overwhelmingly heteronormative education system. It didn't confuse me; I just instinctively knew it didn't represent or include me. I would surmise that 'confusion' is often used as a cover for parental prejudice.

Notice and work through these assumptions and misconceptions, first within yourself and then with your whole-school community. LGBT+ people are people and there is no shame in talking openly and confidently about us.

Step 4: Always maintain a child- or young person-centred approach

We undertake LGBT+ inclusion work to make children and young people safer and happier. Be resolute and unwavering in *regularly* communicating this to all stakeholders.

We should never assume (especially when we are specifically focused upon LGBT+ inclusion) that all adults with a stake in our schools place the needs of young people before their own. I once 'defused' a colleague in a small rural school who raised objections to children being taught about LGBT+ identities (stemming from their own generational prejudice) by stating that it wasn't about their needs but about the *children*. We knew of one child in the school who identified as transgender and another had same-sex parents. These children had a right to be represented and to feel valued, by UK and human rights law.

By keeping the wellbeing of young people front and centre, we can allow our adult anxieties or prejudices to soften as we refocus around the child. We can also learn much from young people in terms of accepting attitudes and curiosity towards human diversity from young people themselves, such as in this example:

> 'Near a display in school depicting families, including examples of same-sex and "different" family units, one picture shows Tom Daley, who the Year 6 children have been learning about in the Jigsaw programme, with his husband and baby. My deputy was stopped by a couple of children in the corridor and was asked if it was Tom Daley. She told them it was and that he was a father now. As she walked away, one child said to the other, "He's gay" and the other just said, "Yes", and they carried on. It was clearly no major issue for them.'
>
> Representative from Victoria Road Primary School, Isle of Man

Step 5: Clarify with all stakeholders how a curriculum that supports positive LGBT+ inclusion raises standards, improves attendance and nurtures positive mental health and emotional and physical wellbeing.

When schools move to a preventative state in terms of LGBT+ bullying we can improve outcomes by raising standards, improving attendance and nurturing positive mental health and emotional and physical wellbeing. Establish a strong connection in the minds of all school stakeholders between the negative impact of LGBT+ bullying and academic, attendance and wellbeing outcomes. Revisit Chapters 1 and 2 to help build your confidence first if needed.

In 2012 I spoke to school leaders at a National College event in Birmingham; it was one of the first occasions when I had addressed school leaders specifically. What struck me was a strong sense that working to prevent LGBT+ bullying was seen as an additional time pressure for overloaded school leaders. I was also surprised by the number of leaders who failed to link LGBT+ bullying and prejudice with impaired education and life chances.

After recounting my experiences and pointing out that bullying makes young people disengage, skip school and become emotionally and sometimes physically scarred, realisation dawned. Exploring and strategically deploying case studies and Stonewall's school and teacher reports will support you in making this case.

Step 6: Foster authentic learning communities in which all stakeholders can take their full selves to work, in order to learn and socialise without fear of reprisal.

Every member of a school community should be able to bring their true selves to working, learning and playing, without feeling targeted, diminished or that they have to lie about their core sense of self or relationship.

School leaders must facilitate a culture within which young people's energies are focused upon learning, not surviving. Sexual orientation and gender reassignment are protected characteristics under the UK Equality Act; therefore expecting individuals to hide away core aspects of their LGBT+ identity is a prejudicial act. I sometimes hear of LGBT+ teachers and pupils who have been told to act 'less gay' in the workplace. Consider for a moment a school leader asking a colleague or child to be 'less black', 'less Christian' or 'less disabled'. Not only would that be shocking, it would also be illegal.

We must respect the fact that LGBT+ staff may not wish to come out publicly or may wish to do so on their terms, as these honest words remind us:

'Being aware that they can be their authentic selves in their professional life as well as in their personal life: this was an aspect for me that felt a little uncomfortable as although I do not hide my sexuality I don't believe it is a defining part of my life and as such it does not feel important for me to "come out" in the school. I suppose everyone is different and the training did make it clear that it is about being authentic and sincere. For me it is about recognising that staff have this choice, and that is what we want life to be like for LGBT+ children in our school. They must just have the freedom to be themselves and know that is okay.'

Headteacher, Isle of Man

Step 7: Teach about LGBT+ lives and history whilst making strong links with the experiences and suffering of human beings from other protected characteristics and also those who are not LGBT+.

This step represents another strategy for developing empathy between those who have shared a life experience and those who do not, focusing on the commonality of our existences.

Intersectionality is a sociological theory that describes multiple discrimination, when an individual's identities overlap with a number of minority characteristics, for example race, gender, age, class, ethnicity and disability. A black female student may face sexism in addition to racism. Someone who is Muslim, transgender and also a lesbian might experience racial prejudice, transphobia and prejudice towards their faith as well as sexism, classism and so on. After coming out in my own school I was approached by a number of Muslim parents who thanked me for creating a safe space in school for everyone to be their authentic selves, as they felt this made it a safer place in which they too could speak about their faith and culture; we found our commonality. Deploy an intersectional approach to facilitating positive LGBT+ inclusion and look at prejudice across the full range of protected characteristics.

One accessible way into discussions around intersectionality is the use of a diverse range of role models, whether these be online, in books or in person. Harvey Milk, the American politician and first openly gay elected official in the history of California (who was later assassinated), is a popular classroom focus. Work can be based upon the book *Pride: The Story of Harvey Milk and the Rainbow Flag*, written by Rob Sanders (2018). Explore the themes and history of the book, make rainbow flags or cakes and explore the challenges and prejudice faced by Harvey and the LGBT+ community. Compare then the lives of other key civil rights heroes or figures who have faced adversity as a result of a core element of their identities, such as Martin Luther King, Rosa Parks, Caitlyn Jenner or Paralympian Claire Harvey. A *Doctor Who* episode on Rosa Parks is proving a popular way into discussions around civil rights.

This enables young people to find intersections between their lives and the challenges or prejudices LGBT+ people may face. Instead of students merely gaining knowledge of LGBT+ lives and challenges to their rights, they instead develop a broader sense of the core nature of prejudice as a consistent theme in the human condition – a much bigger win, surely?

From my experience in schools, children and staff initially exhibiting homophobic behaviour due to cultural or faith-based backgrounds can subsequently display greater empathy with people of LGBT+ identities as a result of having had the opportunity to explore the intersections of prejudice.

Ideas for teaching and learning

I would now like to present to you a selection of ideas that you and your staff can use to teach about LGBT+ identities in your school. Remember to implement them alongside the best practice discussed in the seven steps above.

'Our heritage'

This is a key teaching and learning opportunity that usually precedes my work on LGBT+ identities in schools. It is particularly important where no work has previously been undertaken.

When first undertaking LGBT+ inclusion work in schools some individuals feel frightened that the increased visibility of LGBT+ people and history somehow diminishes their own identity, which it most certainly does not. If this is the case at your school, try using this whole-school topic at the start of every school year. 'Our heritage' promotes greater empathy and cohesion and serves as an opportunity for *every* stakeholder to gain a secure sense of their own identity *before* moving on to more specific work on LGBT+ inclusion. In this way we can pre-empt negative reactions to LGBT+ work. 'Our heritage' also affords the whole school community a rich opportunity to explore and celebrate their authentic identities from the beginning.

The topic is split into two sections:

1. **Unveiling and exploring:** Identification and celebration of authentic identity

2. **Reactions and responses:** Exploring responses to human diversity

Let's look at each in turn.

Unveiling and exploring: Identification and celebration of authentic identity

During the first phase, pupils, staff and parents volunteer to gather, present and disseminate information about their unique lives, values, beliefs (whether faith-based or not), heritage and how they perceive their own personality and identity. It is best to prep them to do so prior to the summer break.

The resulting podcasts, heraldic shields, quilts, displays, culture boxes and bags, autobiographies, family trees, geography, and cultural, historical and faith studies imbue young people with a keen sense of pride in their authentic identity, enabling them not only to more confidently learn and socialise, but also to offer resistance to the increasingly dangerous forces that seek to embroil some of our more vulnerable young people in substance abuse, gang lives or terrorism.

Associated work by students should be completed, displayed and revisited throughout the school year, within subjects, assemblies and annual celebrations like Black and LGBT History Months and Anti-Bullying Week.

Reactions and responses: Exploring responses to human diversity

Phase 2 is very much underpinned by philosophy for children approaches, circle time, mindfulness skills, and school and class rules about respectful debate. It does require teachers to be able to facilitate sometimes sensitive discussions, in which the thoughts and physical feelings we experience when faced with human diversity are explored in a safe and respectful environment.

In this phase pupils reflect upon their individual and family identities before contrasting them with lives different to their own. Teachers facilitate structured discussions (with a clear emphasis upon respect for the feelings of others) to explore individual and group responses to our similarities and differences. I once recorded an 'Our heritage' lesson conversation in a London school during Year 2 circle time. I have included it here as an example of how this project might work in practice.

Example class discussion

Child A

(Holding up a photo of their parents to the class) I have a mum and a dad, but Simon has two mums.

Teacher

That's interesting. Have you met anyone with two mums before?

Child A

No.

Teacher

Some people don't have a mum or dad. They have two mums or two dads, like Simon.

Child A

Oh, I never knew that.

Teacher

What are you thinking or feeling just now?

Child A

Hmm, not sure. Is that true?

Teacher

Is what true?

Child A

That some people have two dads?

Teacher

Yes and some people have two mums. Some people might only have one mum or dad or live with someone else, like a carer or grandparent. There are lots of different kinds of families. What are you thinking just now?

Child A

I am not sure. I wouldn't like to have two dads, maybe two mums.

Child B

(Shouts out) My friend has two aunties who live together.

Teacher

Thank you for sharing. How do you know that you wouldn't like to have two dads?

Child A

Um, it just makes me feel funny.

Teacher

Thanks for sharing! That's really interesting. Can you tell me a bit more about feeling funny? Is it a funny thought or a funny feeling?

Child A

Feeling.

Teacher

Well done! Where can you feel the feeling?

Child A

(Pauses) In my head and on the back of my head.

Teacher

Is it a nice or a not so nice feeling?

Child A

Hmm, kind of not nice. It's a bit weird.

Teacher

That's really interesting. In our library we have a book about a little boy with two daddies. It might have a dog in it too. Would you like to read that and find out more about children who have families different to you?

Child A

Can I read it with a friend?

Teacher

Yes, of course. *(To class)* Does anyone else get a funny feeling when they meet or hear about people who are very different from themselves? *(Cries of yes)* That's really interesting. It happens to me sometimes. I meet someone I haven't really met before and I get a nervous or funny feeling, usually in my tummy, a bit like butterflies. It is important that we feel we can talk about these things in circle time because if someone is very different and we feel funny about it, it is not their fault for being different and it's for us to have a think about.

I really appreciate the honesty of the teacher's approach in this exchange and the gentle way she places the responsibility of working through our own prejudices upon us, not the person or group of people we are reacting to.

Over time 'Our heritage' can enable whole school communities to gain a profound sense of what lies at the very core of prejudice itself. Repeated and adjusted with a slightly different focus each year, the impact and coverage of 'Our heritage' deepens and is joyous to behold. Children become able to identify when and why prejudices arise within themselves and make positive behavioural changes.

Staff and parents should be involved in this project too in order to become more confident in externalising and processing their own fears, misconceptions and prejudices, safe in the knowledge that these are being gently revealed in order to work through them, not to shame.

Strategies such as philosophy for children, the UN Declaration of Human Rights, and texts about refugees and diverse families all enable discussions on the basic roots of prejudice and are accessible right to nursery level. Fears about difference can be externalised, valued, explored and rationalised in a safe, respectful space, not suppressed and allowed to fester.

In January 2018 I began supporting schools on the Isle of Man to become more fully LGBT+ inclusive. After spending some time talking to adults on the island I sensed that the introduction of teaching and learning about LGBT+ lives could, for some islanders, feel like a challenge to their identities. Thus, I suggested introducing 'Our heritage' prior to any LGBT+ work:

> 'The "heritage day" that Shaun helped staff lead discussed diversity in general. The message of everyone being different and how that should be celebrated resonated with a child who has a medical condition in the school. He has struggled for quite some time to come to terms with the fact that he has a condition that can sometimes inhibit him. During a review session at the end of the day, he spoke with pride that he was different – something he had not done before.'
>
> Representative from Kewaigue School, Isle of Man

Each school makes this project their own but below is a brief overview of some of the activities this particular school planned as part of their 'Our heritage' project. This will give you some ideas to plan a similar topic or theme to run before your more specific LGBT+ content.

- Drawing family trees and discussing the history of family groups.
- Creating 'people passports' that highlight personal histories and key aspects of self.
- Reading or writing autobiographies and memoirs.
- Sharing or creating personal crests or family shields.
- Reading *We Are Britain!* by Benjamin Zephaniah (2002).

- Using elements of individual identity to create a superhero for a graphic novel or comic. This helps factors that mark us out as different, such as dyslexia, being left-handed or ginger, become part of our superpowers.
- Reading and studying the structure and intention of the poem 'What Makes Me... Me' by Michael J. Burt (2005) and creating personal versions of this poem.
- Creating drawings, flags, quilts, charts and infographics illustrating multinational or mixed-race identities – for example, 'I am a quarter Scottish, a quarter Irish…'.
- Listening to stories of those who have overcome adversity or experienced prejudice whether they be students, staff or parents (drawing out role models from within the school community).
- Creating culture bags or boxes containing photos and valued and meaningful artefacts of family or cultural significance to the individual.
- Making displays of the geographical pathways families have taken to reach the Isle of Man.
- Contrasting island identities with those from around the world.
- Running a whole-school art project called 'One community – many individuals'.
- Holding philosophy, circle time and PSHE sessions exploring student reactions to ways of being that are very similar to themselves and those that are so very different they might prove challenging in some way; exploring how this manifests itself and what it might cause us to do.
- Exploring local cultural stereotypes.
- Comparing and contrasting crafts, customs and festivals from the Isle of Man with those from other countries represented on the school roll.
- 'Taking Pride In Our Diverse Heritage' songs/poems/podcasts.
- Exploring how cultural diversity enriches our communities, diets and economies.
- Listening to talks from parents, students and staff on their own lives and journeys, including worship and customs, aspects of festivals, food, language and national dress.
- Holding a 'Diversity Day' or 'Week' in the summer during which children make costumes, hats, banners or props that they feel represent their authentic identities and use them for a 'walk of pride' or carnival; parents are invited too.
- Celebrating work on social media, in newsletters, on art displays and at special events in order to disseminate the diverse lives and experiences within the school to the wider community.
- Holding whole-school celebration events at the end of the topic with galleries, work shared on websites, a cultural evening and pride-type events to celebrate all identities.

I have seen the topic run in many different ways and contexts, so please let your imagination run wild! The greater sense of self-awareness children develop about prejudice through this project enables teachers to build upon conversations about our reactions and responses to difference and diversity throughout the life of the school. If you include staff and parent identities, the whole school becomes more authentic.

'The teaching tent poles'

All around the year there are many themed days and weeks that provide useful access points into work around LGBT+ inclusion and human rights. When observed in isolation, schools are again merely ticking boxes, but if used as part of a long-term plan for teaching about LGBT+ identities across the curriculum, these events can be very powerful opportunities for teaching and learning. The timing of these events often varies year by year and according to global territory, but I have listed a few examples here to pique your curiosity and get you researching what is available:

LGBT+ inclusion events calendar

September

- International Day of Peace
- International Day of Democracy
- Bi Visibility Day

October

- World Mental Health Day
- Intersex Awareness Day
- Hate Crime Awareness Week
- National Coming Out Day
- Black History Month
- Asexual Awareness Week

November

- Anti-Bullying Week
- Transgender Day of Remembrance
- Transgender Awareness Week
- Universal Children's Day
- Interfaith Week

December

- World AIDS Day
- International Human Rights Day
- Pansexual/Panromantic Pride

January

- Holocaust Memorial Day

February

- LGBT History Month
- Safer Internet Day
- World Day of Social Justice

March

- International Women's Day
- International Transgender Day of Visibility

April

- Lesbian Visibility Day

May

- International Day Against Homophobia, Biphobia, Intersexism and Transphobia (IDAHOBIT)
- World Day for Cultural Diversity

June

- World Refugee Day
- LGBT Pride Month

Teaching ideas across the curriculum

Our aim is to make *all* stakeholders feel included, safe and visible *every* day of the school year. In order to achieve this, teaching and learning about LGBT+ inclusion needs to be embedded across our curriculum right from the Early Years. It must never wait until secondary school. Here are some ideas to help you achieve this in every key stage. Remember that throughout your curriculum planning at all stages it is important to make strong links throughout to:

- PSHE
- citizenship
- British values
- human rights
- history
- equality and democracy
- global citizenship

- school vision, rules and behaviour charters
- visible models and images
- young people (including of course LGBT+ members of the school community)
- protected characteristics in the Equality Act (see page 73)
- self-care and resilience.

Nursery and Early Years Foundation Stage

- Plan an 'Our heritage' topic to start the school year.
- Establish clear behaviour expectations and induction to the school vision for inclusion and equality.
- Explore children's wants and needs (linking to the UN Convention on the Rights of the Child).
- Become a 'UNICEF Rights Respecting School'.
- Discuss and represent diverse families and identities from the outset via models, images, texts and use of role models.
- Study different faiths and festivals to model human diversity.
- Discuss the role of adults in keeping us safe and use this to debunk gender stereotypes.
- Discuss taking responsibility for our actions.
- Consider social and emotional development.
- Look at similarities and differences and how they make us feel.
- Look at how we can be unkind and how people can be unkind to us.
- Discuss how and when to tell an adult when we don't feel happy or safe.
- Establish the use of Worry Eaters (soft toys with a pouch in their stomach) and Worry Boxes as a way to embed from the outset good habits in terms of reporting unwelcome behaviours and concerns. Children write down their worries, zip them away in the Worry Eater's pouch or put them in the Worry Box, and forget about them. A member of staff can then read them and address any issues arising as appropriate. This process is not only informative for staff but it also establishes good habits in children in terms of externalising and reporting factors that might be causing stress or anxiety. There is a clear through line to be made in terms of seeking (if needed) anonymous support for bullying later in school and adult life.
- Study diversity and variation in nature.
- Introduce a range of diverse role models.
- Introduce national dress from around the world as a means of debunking gender clothing stereotypes.
- Introduce strategies for self-care and resilience.

Key Stage 1

- All of the above, with more specific use of LGBT+ terminology, with simple, unfussy explanations and new learning that some people use words to hurt.

- Study reactions and responses to human difference.
- Introduce the concept of bullying, prejudice-related bullying and name-calling.
- Consider gender roles and stereotyping, using role models.
- Discuss the importance of speaking out when being bullied.
- Develop pride in core aspects of their identity whilst recognising and celebrating their potential for change.
- Discuss and run activities designed to develop empathy.
- Teach helping others in need, even when they are different to us.
- Use texts that feature characters considered to be 'different' or those who are not always accepted.
- Encourage talk about feelings, friendships and relationships.
- Teach self-noticing via mindfulness.
- Use lessons about the spectrum of light and radio waves to lead into learning about the spectrum of human diversity.

Key Stage 2

- All of the above with more sophisticated stimuli and activities exploring identity and culture.
- Hold assemblies with diverse speakers who have overcome adversity.
- Teach being an ally not a bystander, and identifying and managing unwelcome behaviours positively.
- Explore managing strong emotions.
- Discuss the causes and impact of prejudice-related bullying.
- Talk about emergent identity and feeling empowered to seek counsel or advice.
- Introduce learning diaries as a way to reflect upon thoughts, feelings and choices, including when prejudices are triggered.
- Study diversity and variation in human beings and how we are received in the world as a result.
- Study fairness, bullying and equality in sport.
- Explore assumptions and stereotyping.
- Explore bias in the press.
- Help students learn about neuroscience via mindfulness.
- Teach strategies for spotting fake news.
- Teach about the spectrum of human diversity, including identity, ability and needs.

Secondary school: whole-school ideas

- Designate safe spaces for LGBT+ youth and allies.
- Form gay–straight alliances.
- Improve visibility of LGBT+ allies using rainbow lanyards for staff.
- Buy a recording and reporting programme such as Tootoot.

- Plan diversity days and respect weeks.
- Establish LGBT+ and allies buddy systems.
- Seek work experience for students in LGBT+ organisations.
- Use a diverse range of role models.
- Use rainbow bookmarks.

Secondary school: ideas for individual subjects

Animal management and studies

- Consider the prevalence of homosexuality in the animal kingdom.
- Draw links between stereotypical representations of animals and human beings.
- Look at gender stereotyping of career paths, for example veterinary and zoological pathways.

Art, fashion and design

- Study the historical and cultural influences on fashion and how they change over time and geographically.
- Look at how expectations around gender 'norms' and conformity vary and what happens when they are challenged.
- Compare national dress, linking to explorations of gendered clothing and make-up.
- Use LGBT+ symbols such as the rainbow flag and inclusive variations of this.
- Consider the disruption of gender roles and stereotypes using clothing.
- Look at de-gendering clothing.
- Consider inequalities in clothing and textile suppliers, particularly in countries hostile to LGBT+ people and workers.
- Look at visible and hidden representations of LGBT+ lives through art over history, including hieroglyphics.
- Study the legacies of non-conformist artists, such as Leigh Bowery, David Hockney, Grayson Perry and Tracey Emin.
- Explore art as activism and its role in activism, including artists such as Keith Haring.
- Study LGBT+ stereotypes in fashion and the reality of LGBT+ lives and poverty.
- Study LGBT+ performance art and fashion, including drag and drag kings.
- Think about where LGBT+ fashion and culture have influenced and been absorbed into mainstream culture.
- Study tribalism and tattoo design.
- Study LGBT+ fashion design and designers, such as Alexander McQueen, Tom Ford, Jonathan Ive and Adrienne Wu.
- Run LGBT+ themed art competitions.
- Study Tove Jansson, a Finnish author famous for creating the Moomins.

Beauty and hairdressing

- Think about stereotyping and meeting the requirements of equality legislation.
- Discuss working respectfully with LGBT+ customers and staff.
- Study LGBT+ influences on styling and fashion throughout history.
- Ensure a range of visible LGBT+ models and images in salons.

Business and workforce development

- Discuss the benefits of a diverse workforce.
- Discuss barriers to LGBT+ inclusion in the workplace.
- Talk about working with and supporting LGBT+ staff and customers.
- Discuss recruitment and retention of LGBT+ staff.
- Consider how to avoid accusations of prejudice and discrimination at work.
- Consider how to prevent and tackle workplace bullying.
- Look at the role of LGBT+, disabled, gender and BAME networks and how they work together.
- Explore gender pay gaps and inequalities of promotion opportunities for LGBT+ people.
- Talk about how to work with global territories who are more hostile to LGBT+ identities whilst maintaining integrity of our own inclusive vision.
- Discuss how to empower and deploy a diverse range of authentic role models across the organisation and acting as ambassadors for the organisation.
- Raise awareness of the 'pink pound': the amount of money spent by those of gay or lesbian orientation and how companies target that sector.
- Discuss responding to shifting demographics.
- Consider mindfulness and wellbeing in the workplace.

Childcare

- Discuss how to ensure respect and visibility for LGBT+ families and young people.
- Raise awareness of the support agencies for LGBT+ families and young people.
- Raise awareness of the prejudice and bullying faced by many LGBT+ families and young people.
- Look at moral development.
- Discuss early exposure to a range of varied family groups using texts.
- Raise awareness of learned prejudicial behaviours and attitudes.

Computing

- Explore the work and life of pioneers such as Alan Turing and Tim Cook.
- Run a project to make apps to report bullying and hate crime.
- Discuss working with LGBT+ colleagues, customers and clients.
- Break down stereotypes.

- Look at how apps are used to protect but also track and arrest LGBT+ people across the world.
- Discuss the use of technology and social media to bully, spread 'fake news' and stereotype LGBT+ people.

Construction and engineering

- Discuss equality legislation.
- Talk about working with LGBT+ colleagues and customers, and the increasing diversity of the workforce.
- Run activities to break down stereotypes.
- Study the image and perception of LGBT+ people in the construction industry.
- Discuss workplace conduct and 'banter'.
- Look at barriers to recruitment.

English and literacy

- Study poetry, novels and other works by LGBT+ writers, such as Marguerite Radclyffe Hall, Wilfred Owen, Virginia Woolf, Sappho, Audre Lorde and James Baldwin.
- Study LGBT+ literature and its history.
- Using *Good Night Stories for Rebel Girls* as a model, ask students to create an equivalent LGBT+ storybook.
- Explore evidence to challenge assumptions that all human beings and fictional characters are heterosexual.
- Consider how LGBT+ books and writing have been suppressed throughout history and around the world.
- Talk about judging human beings by their 'cover'.
- Explore Polari – the 'secret' gay language and its legacy.
- Discuss covert and more clearly presented LGBT+ characters in books and stories.
- Look at stereotypical, sympathetic and allegorical representations of LGBT+ people.
- Study changing terminology and street slang for LGBT+ identities.
- Consider the erasure of LGBT+ identities from film adaptations of novels with LGBT+ characters.
- Explore inclusive and exclusive language and themes.
- Study bias and prejudicial attitudes in press and online reporting about LGBT+ people.
- Look at how poetry and books are used as activism.
- Encourage entries to the Amnesty Young Writers Competition.

- Study the use of LGBT+ related 'labels' and how 'slurs' have been reclaimed, for example the different perceptions of the word 'queer' and the intentions of those using the word.
- Hold public speaking competitions on LGBT+ themes.
- Run an LGBT+ icons competition. This might include, for example, Harvey Milk, Peter Tatchell and Marsha P. Johnson.

Food and catering

- Explore stereotypes.
- Encourage rainbow baking and hold cake sales.
- Cover the health and wellbeing of LGBT+ people.
- Discuss catering for same-sex ceremonies and celebrations.
- Discuss providing respectful services for customers.
- Talk about working with LGBT+ colleagues.
- Discuss ensuring workplace visibility and authenticity.

Health

- Explore the impact of social and educational exclusion upon physical and mental health.
- Discuss the links between bullying and prejudice and the use of alcohol and drugs to cope with rejection.
- Talk about threats to wellbeing and life for LGBT+ people.
- Discuss working with LGBT+ staff and customers.
- Teach about equality legislation.
- Teach the use of appropriate and respectful terminology.
- Discuss respecting individual identity and choice.
- Consider the importance of visibility.
- Study the history of the emergence of HIV/AIDS in the early 1980s and the initial response by UK/USA governments, including the work of Lord Norman Fowler.
- Discuss signposting support for those seeking to transition.
- Study poor mental health as a result of LGBT+ bullying and prejudice.
- Raise awareness of the shocking statistics around depression, anxiety, self-harm and suicide within the LGBT+ community.
- Raise awareness that the experiences of LGBT+ people differ as to how they identify.
- Ensure awareness that LGBT+ people may have already experienced negative reactions from medical practitioners so it's important to work to build trust.
- Study mindfulness, neuroscience and self-care.
- Study the emergence of HIV and AIDS, the political response to it and stories of those affected by it, such as John Curry and Freddie Mercury.

History and politics

- Study the impact of social and educational exclusion of LGBT+ history upon LGBT+ visibility and social attitudes towards LGBT+ identities (LGBT+ erasure).
- Look at the presence of LGBT+ people through history and their contributions to human existence.
- Discuss the shifting definitions of LGBT+ identities through history and across cultures.
- Explore the relationship between religion and LGBT+ identities.
- Discuss how legislation can be used to protect or diminish the human rights of LGBT+ people.
- Study the emergence of human rights and equality legislation for LGBT+ people and how this varies globally.
- Study LGBT+ monarchs and politicians, such as King William Rufus, King James I of England, Harvey Milk, Leo Varadkar and Ruth Davidson.
- Explore the Stonewall riots and the civil rights movement.
- Teach about the fight for same-sex marriage, equal age of consent and adoption rights.
- Study the Wolfenden Report and the decriminalisation of homosexuality in the UK.
- Discuss the declassification of homosexuality and transgender as mental illnesses by the World Health Organization.
- Explore the history and meaning of the rainbow flag.
- Study the LGBT+ Holocaust and Pink Triangle.
- Study the Matthew Shepard story in *The Laramie Project* (Kaufman et al., 2014).
- Study the 1999 nail bombings in Soho, Brick Lane and Brixton.
- Explore the legalisation of homosexuality and age of consent.
- Discuss the emergence of the Equality Act and LGBT+ human rights abroad.
- Study pioneering out Members of Parliament and peers, for example Chris Smith and Maureen Colquhoun, Lord Michael Cashman and Baroness Elizabeth Barker.
- Using the film *Hidden Voices* as inspiration, undertake a hidden LGBT+ project.
- Consider how LGBT+ identities can be used as a political lever to dehumanise political opponents.
- Study LGBT+ people in the military.
- Explore the erasure of LGBT+ identities and histories in relation to equivalent experiences of indigenous populations.

Humanities

- Study the diversity, spectrum and variation in human beings, how we are received in the world as a result and intersectional global examples of how this can result in stories of success over adversity.

- Ensure teaching and learning about LGBT+ identities.
- Seek opportunities to make intersections between the experiences of minority groups.
- Use stories of those who have experienced prejudice.
- Explore the link between austerity and the scapegoating of minority groups.
- Study LGBT+ Pride events around the world and why they exist.
- Study LGBT+ rights around the world.
- Develop in students a sound knowledge of how democracy works and how to participate fully.
- Look at the impact of culture, ethnicity and religious attitudes upon LGBT+ people and legislation.
- Study the impact of equal marriage legislation.
- Explore the impact of being forced to live in secret, such as flags, codes and language.
- Run a project on LGBT+ migration and treatment of refugees.
- Study the link between misogyny and the dislike of effeminacy.

Maths

- Use recorded bullying and hate crime data for statistics projects, for example comparing local and national data or predicting trends.
- Study pay inequalities.
- Include exercises using local and global LGBT+ statistics and demographics.
- Ensure you break down stereotypes.
- Discuss the difficulties that may arise when quantifying statistics around LGBT+ identities and why these arise, for example accurate employee or student demographics.
- Explore maths and science role models at www.500queerscientists.com.

Music

- Study LGBT+ musicians and pop stars, such as Years and Years, Elton John, Freddie Mercury, Wendy Carlos, Dusty Springfield and Anohni.
- Explore LGBT+ youth culture and the intersection between music and fashion.
- Understand how music is used in politics and activism, such as 'Glad to be Gay', by Tom Robinson.
- Explore LGBT+ stereotypes in music, such as Village People.
- Study the influence of LGBT+ identities and music on mainstream music, fashion and youth tribes, for example Mods (1960s) and New Romantics (1980s).
- Discuss LGBT+ allies in music, including Kylie Minogue, Lady Gaga and Madonna.

- Study the emergence of mainstream musical trends from LGBT+ club culture, including disco, house, high energy and the vogue dance movement.
- Explore homophobia and sexism in music.
- Consider the emergence of 'out' country singers, including k.d. lang and Drake Jensen, and 'out' rap and R&B artists, including Frank Ocean and Janelle Monáe.
- Run inclusive choirs.
- Discuss musical theatre as a stereotype and a career choice.
- Discuss the effect of transitioning on vocal range.
- Explore the potential for popular music to influence attitudes in mainstream society, for example the growth of synthesiser and gender non-conforming pop stars in the early 1980s, such as Annie Lennox and Boy George, and more recently Troye Sivan.

Religion and faith

- Establish the principle for respectful, non-judgemental dialogue.
- Explore current equalities legislation pertaining to faith and LGBT+ identities.
- Develop an awareness of the negative impact prejudicial views can have upon other human beings.
- Bring awareness to the intersection between faith and non-faith identities and the need to develop strong, respectful relationships in society.
- Make links to the persecution of people due to faith and LGBT+ identities.
- Debunk the notion of LGBT+ 'lifestyles' whilst exploring the notion of faith as a choice.
- Explore our ability to deploy ancient texts to conceal anxieties around difference.
- Signpost LGBT+ faith organisations, such as lgbtimission.org.uk, gaysikh.com, lgbthumanists.org.uk, jglg.org.uk and inclusivemosque.org.
- Reinforce the school as a safe space for all students.
- Download the Church of England anti-LGBT+ bullying resource 'Valuing all God's children' and the 'Made in God's image' resource produced by St Mary's University, Twickenham, which explores the Catholic context (see page 224).

Science

- Explore maths and science role models at www.500queerscientists.com, such as Polly Arnold, Alan Turing and Ben Barres.
- Look at biochemistry and an exploration of gender identity and LGBT+ identities.
- Examine shared human characteristics, genetic make-up and variance.
- Discuss links to the animal world.
- Study the medical response to the HIV/AIDS crisis (and Dr Mathilde Krim).

LGBT+ youth groups

LGBT+ youth groups or gay–straight alliances are student-led community groups that provide a safe space for LGBT+ youth in schools. Traditionally run in secondary schools, I am increasingly seeing a need for them in primary education as more LGBT+ pupils identify at a younger age. A study by the University of British Columbia (2019) found that in schools where gay–straight alliances existed, feelings of safety increased year on year. The researchers also reference previous research from 2014 that shows that when a gay-straight alliance has existed in a school for three years or more, there's a lower rate of suicidal thoughts in both LGBT+ and non-LGBT+ young people.

Setting up such a group involves talking to young people about their needs; will the group be exclusively LGB? Or T? Or LGBT+ or LGBT+ and allies? Their views must be heard. Carefully consider matters of confidentiality and the potential for students to be 'outed' simply by being seen at the club or being outed by teachers or other students. There are so many elements to these clubs to explore; here are some cues to get you started:

- The need to act with compassion but without shame.
- Regularity: for some the club may be their only authentic space for self-identification.
- Physical space: where will it be held and what message does this send?
- Timing: if the club is after school, some children may be forced to either lie or come out to parents before they are ready in order to attend.
- Training is essential for all the staff running the club.
- Terms of reference: involve the students in devising this to give the club structure, intention and direction.
- Establishing staff and student roles, giving young people ownership and responsibility.
- Leadership and ambassadors: could LGBT+ leaders and role models be nurtured as part of the group roles and activities? These can be deployed not only to provide leadership and peer support within the group, but also to take a lead in raising awareness and visibility across the school.
- Defining and sharing what 'ally' status actually means in and out of the group context.
- Linking to other network groups in school and having joint learning sessions.
- Linking to LGBT+ groups in other schools and in local businesses.
- Inviting in LGBT+ former pupils and business role models as speakers.
- Attending best practice conferences and events.
- Offering assemblies and visibility campaigns.
- Young people can work with curriculum leaders to help embed LGBT+ experiences, histories and lives through teaching and learning.

- Inviting in LGBT+ speakers from a variety of faith backgrounds.
- Positioning the group as part of a wider human or civil rights movement, making links to Amnesty and Unicef.
- Offering one-to-one and peer-to-peer support.
- Holding a fundraising and film night, with a film like *Love Simon*.
- Organising an LGBT+ icons competition, raising awareness across the school and taking a vote to establish the top five or ten LGBT+ icons from history and relating this to other minority groups and civil rights figures.
- Young people gain experience of working and socialising cross-phase.
- Opening the invitation to LGBT+ staff and allies.
- Resilience training and training to deal with online bullying.
- Links to local LGBT+ youth provision.
- Reporting hate crime.
- Ally badges and lanyard schemes.
- Producing a school newsletter or bulletin.
- Writing a gender neutral make-up policy that includes and represents the gender spectrum.
- Being inclusive, not exclusive.

The more you empower your LGBT+ group to become something that shines brightly in your school, the more rapidly it gains kudos amongst the whole school community.

Resources

Any work we do across the curriculum must be supported by a broad range of quality texts about diverse identities and family groups, which are not only accessible in school libraries but are also used to deliver text-based units and to go home in book bags. This will model school ethos and expectations to families and communities beyond the school gates.

I have collated an 'Inclusion For All' book pack about LGBT+ lives and families aimed at Key Stage 1 and 2 children with Lettterbox Library, a non-profit bookseller that specialises in books in which all children can see themselves and which reflect our world community in all of its diversity. Find it at: https://www.letterboxlibrary.com/acatalog/Inclusion-for-All-Pack.html.

You will find a list of recommended LGBT+ texts for secondary schools on the Stonewall website: www.stonewall.org.uk/sites/default/files/reading_list_secondary_ lo_res_final_v2.pdf.

I would also flag up Gay's The Word bookshop in London: www.gaystheword.co.uk.

I hope you find the ideas I have presented in this chapter useful in terms of stimulating thinking for lessons and themes. There is a wealth of opportunity for you to explore LGBT+ lives, histories and experiences in your own contexts. I am in a privileged position in that I am regularly invited to visit faith and non-faith schools and witness many inspiring initiatives. Perhaps one day I might visit your school to do the same. I would enjoy seeing your own wonderful practice!

Finally for this chapter, let's hear from a school who have worked to embed LGBT+ inclusion in their teaching and learning, and look at the results this has had in their setting.

Barnston Primary School, Wirral

We planned differentiated circle time teaching for the whole school and bought a selection of books to help with teaching and discussion too. Shaun's training and our subsequent teaching definitely opened children's minds more and gave them the tools to discuss the issues and appreciate the importance of inclusion at every level. The teaching gave the children more understanding and therefore more acceptance, which in turn led to better behaviour when dealing with such issues in the playground for example. Educating, educating, educating was the way forward. This has continued, year after year, and has been woven into our rich curriculum tapestry. It is now part and parcel of everyday life in our school.

Children have definitely become more open, understanding and accepting in their thinking. The children in school have always been protective of children they see as vulnerable, but now they can see how people could be the target of bullying by non-accepting children. They thoroughly appreciate that children who may be perceived as different are not different but that just because they can see this it doesn't mean everyone can see this. They appreciate signs to look out for and how to help support anyone who may need help in life. It has been amazing to see the transition from issues not being discussed with the children openly to mature discussion and support of each other. Staff feel comfortable to discuss issues openly. Year 6 children teach the younger children about issues through 'human rights club' at lunchtime. The achievements are extremely important in growing our young citizens for the future.

Young LGBT+ people definitely feel more confident and supported. We have always propelled a very supportive environment and ethos in our school, but being able to be open, with parents and staff on board, does bring another dimension to the wonderful ethos that has grown in our school. In terms of British values, we also changed the value of tolerance to the value of acceptance and we have adopted this value in our school. This work has been embedded with our LGBT+ work.

Time to reflect

Before turning the page, please take a moment to reflect.

Things to think about:

- How might you empower all members of your school community to serve as open role models to other community members? How much time do you really take to get to know students, staff and parents as individuals and what activities and approaches empower this?
- What barriers currently exist in your own school context that serve to prevent or restrict the freedom of LGBT+ individuals to be their authentic selves whilst at school? How might you begin to remove these barriers?
- The transition between primary and secondary schools can result in significant changes in children's experiences and attitudes as they explore their roles with peers and staff. Consider how you might plan for transition with your partner schools to ensure that the themes and positive attitudes towards LGBT+ inclusion are not lost once secondary provision begins? How might you support an LGBT+ student from one context into another?
- How can teachers work collaboratively with subject coordinators to develop lessons that celebrate LGBT+ identities?

Things to do:

- Explore the potential for an 'Our heritage' topic to start your next school term or year and to embed longer term.
- Plan a three-year programme of whole-school themes, assemblies and events that incorporate some of the diversity foci listed above.
- Identify internal and external speakers and begin a rolling programme of inspirational role models presenting in assemblies and in classrooms but also on posters and on the school website, including some openly LGBT+ role models. Encourage them to talk about their lives and journeys and whether they have overcome adversity.

Chapter 9
Teaching tolerance, nurturing acceptance

'When people use the word gay to cuss other people what they really mean is that gay is bad. I am gay; I am not bad.'

Frankie, aged 15, Liverpool

This chapter continues our Tier 4 journey of implementation, with a particular focus on tackling language and bullying related to LGBT+ identities, something that is not only very important but also potentially life-saving.

Dominic Crouch and Roger Crouch

This is not an easy story to write, nor is it easy to read. If reading it triggers you, please afterwards talk to a support service like the Samaritans or perhaps a trusted friend. However, it *is* important that this story continues to be told.

In 2011 whilst at a Stonewall conference I met a man called Roger Crouch. Roger was interested in my work and journey and expressed an interest in working together one day to share the message that homophobic bullying has no place in schools. During the conference Roger read out loud a suicide note from his 15-year-old son Dominic. It was a moment I will never forget, nor want to experience again.

Roger's son Dominic had been attending a secondary school in the English town of Cheltenham. Dominic, in the main, seemed to be enjoying school and was looking forward to life and new challenges. The school facilitated a residential trip that Dominic attended. During the trip a group of students gathered in a field to play a game of 'spin the bottle', which as you may or may not know involves dares and usually unpleasant 'forfeits'. As part of the game Dominic was dared to kiss another boy, which he did. It was a single momentary act that would have tragic consequences.

Students recorded images on their mobile phones and circulated them amongst other students back at school. Dominic (who was dyslexic) became the subject of homophobic jokes, teasing and 'banter' on returning to school. Things rapidly became very difficult for Dominic, as indeed they do for any child teased in this manner.

In May 2010 Dominic left his school without his teachers' knowledge; he committed suicide by jumping off the roof of a six-storey block of flats. A section of one of three suicide notes he left read: 'I'm so sorry for what I'm about to do. I have been bullied a lot recently.' With that, the potential and joy of a unique living being with his life stretching out before him was terminated – as a result of a 'game'.

In the months after Dominic's suicide, Roger Crouch bravely campaigned on his son's behalf, speaking to schools, lobbying politicians and speaking at conferences and, as you now know, that is how we met. In late 2011 Roger and I were booked to speak at a conference in Birmingham. But Roger never arrived; that morning Roger Crouch had hung himself in the garage at home.

Roger was 55.

What started as a childhood game destroyed not only a father and his son but stole away a brother, a father and a husband. A family was shattered, and lives were destroyed forever.

I often wonder how many of the perpetrators who mocked Dominic had kissed their parents at bedtime, their brothers and sisters on a birthday, or their mates after scoring a goal. In a world where people pay to see grown men punch one another, is a kiss between two people, even if for a dare, really worthy of such derision?

There is no evidence that Dominic was gay; Roger was married to a woman and had children, yet despite this, the disgust, shame and hate that some human beings harbour towards LGBT+ people was able to infiltrate the Crouch family and tear it apart. And what of the perpetrators? How must they have felt? What about the teachers who led the trip or didn't see it coming? There are no winners in this story, only a widow and a daughter who lost her father and brother.

Since Roger passed, whenever I train teachers and speak to young people in secondary schools, there is a tangible connection, because I met and spoke on the same bill as Roger, and I could so easily have been a Dominic myself. Dominic and Roger deserve to be able to make a positive difference, even in death.

This is a story that repeatedly moves me to tears as I speak it and indeed as I write it now. It is a story I will continue to tell. I hope you will now tell it too, for it can change hearts and minds.

And this in itself is important learning.

When I am training teaching colleagues, I work through the rationale for positive LGBT+ inclusion, presenting research, personal experience and statutory expectations. Despite all this, some educators will still sit with a disapproving face, challenge me repeatedly or simply disengage. However when I tell the story of Roger and Dominic, and I point out that to our best knowledge, Dominic wasn't actually gay and nor was Roger, suddenly they engage. My heart breaks a little every time, for whilst it is positive that finally they are engaged, in doing so they have revealed to me that they place a hierarchy on human identities, with 'hetero-sexuality' at the top of the pile.

It happens repeatedly, and it is the most difficult part of what I do, to see education professionals only engage when it is their own 'kind' who is being affected. What an awful shame.

I have recounted this heartbreaking story to staff and young people across the land, and in turn it has been explored by colleagues as a teaching resource, such as in Rosendale School:

'In Key Stage 2, I delivered an assembly that focused on the story of Dominic Crouch and his father Roger. I agreed with the head that I should tell this story. It had a significant effect. The incidents of homophobic language and bullying virtually stopped.'

Dominic and Roger may never know the huge difference they have made to the lives of so many young people, but I hope this book, in some small way, honours their memory. Rest in peace, Dominic and Roger, along with all those who have lost (and continue to lose) their lives to prejudice, hate and bullying.

Tackling the use of homophobic language

Since 2009, many schools have contacted me to help tackle the use of homophobic language and in particular the use of the word 'gay' as a pejorative term, a trend in the adolescent and subsequently adult lexicon that emerged in the UK from around 2003 onwards.

If we are not careful, we can merely instruct or direct young people to conform with our behavioural expectations (such as not using prejudicial language) *without* offering a rational or moral imperative. Thus we attain no real 'buy-in' from students who then adapt their behaviours to become more covert or find other strategies for being unpleasant!

The first time I heard the use of the word 'gay' used pejoratively was from a colleague in a staff room, who upon dropping her microwaved lunch on the floor exclaimed with disgust, 'That's so gay.' Even as a 40-something-year-old man, the use of this particular word to define a situation as something rubbish, not cool or crappy made me wince internally. My colleague actually knew I was gay and was seemingly fine about it, so I knew she wasn't taking an intentional pop at me. She wasn't for a moment intending to hurt me and yet, without even knowing it, she had equated being gay with being bad, triggering memories of events that almost led to my suicide. The second time was from a child talking with his mother on the bus; sat behind me they were discussing a school football match in which the child's team had apparently lost an all-important penalty due to some questionable footwork by a fellow team member. 'He was so gay to miss that goal,' said the child, and he and his mum laughed. I felt a familiar tightening in my stomach. In both cases,

I considered what message would be sent to a child overhearing these comments who was emergent LGBT+ or who had LGBT+ friends or family.

Having lived my life on the sharp end of LGBT+ prejudice, it does not take a degree in rocket science to work out how this particular word might find itself being widely used to describe something as 'less than', for this is what some people think and feel about LGBT+ people. The use of the word gay in this way is still very common. The Stonewall 'School report' (2017a) found that 86 per cent of LGBT pupils regularly hear phrases such as 'That's so gay' or 'You're so gay' in school.

A child who is gay or who is questioning their sexuality may already have low self-esteem, feel shameful and be fearful of rejection by their teachers, family, society, or cultural or faith group. The use of the word 'gay' as a replacement for rubbish, uncool or crap can add to a young person's sense of shame. A University of Michigan study (2012) found that the use of the word gay in this manner could have negative consequences for LGBT+ students. The study examined the impact of hearing 'That's so gay' amongst 114 LGBT students between the ages of 18 and 25, with the resulting data showing that LGBT students who heard the phrase frequently were more likely to feel isolated and experience headaches, poor appetite or eating problems than those who didn't. Michael Woodford, who co-authored the study, concluded that the use of the word gay as a pejorative term conveys that there is something wrong with being gay.

Take a pause

Think about the following questions and write some notes:

- Where and how do you hear the word gay being used in and around schools?
- When do you see and hear it being used openly and respectfully to talk about people who are gay?
- In what contexts and situations have you heard the word gay being used to *intentionally* hurt or cause disrespect to gay people?
- In what contexts and situations have you heard the word gay being used not with the intention to hurt or cause disrespect to gay people but in a manner that nonetheless might cause offence or hurt especially to gay people or those with gay family members?

Now place yourself for a moment in the mindset of the young LGBT+ person as they hear and read the word gay used in a pejorative way.

- How might hearing the word gay used in a pejorative way make you feel?
- What message is the person using the word gay as a negative 'cuss' sending about people with gay identities?
- Is the person being homophobic?

Now think about how you might respond if you were in a conversation with a colleague who used the word gay as a negative. What about in conversation with a parent? Or a student?

Reflecting on your current practice

The 2014 NatCen research (Mitchell et al.) found that recording and reporting of homophobic, biphobic and transphobic (HBT) bullying was seen to work better by school staff where there were clearly agreed definitions of these types of bullying in school, where action was taken in all cases and where responses to reports of HBT bullying were consistent, so that teaching aimed at preventing such bullying wasn't undermined. Consider your current practice in this area:

- Apart from the negative use of the word 'gay' what other prejudicial, mocking and negative language do you hear in school from parents, staff or students with regard to LGBT+ identities? (Some examples might be 'lezzer', 'dyke', 'tranny' and 'faggot'.)
- How does your school currently communicate to all stakeholders that this kind of language is unacceptable and *why* it is unacceptable?
- How does your school communicate the potential damage of using negative or mocking slurs in reference to LGBT+ identities?
- How confident are you in challenging homophobic, biphobic and transphobic language? Do you know what language to challenge and when?
- How confident are your staff in challenging homophobic, biphobic and transphobic language? Do staff know what language to challenge and when?
- How confident are your students in challenging homophobic, biphobic and transphobic language? Do they know what language to challenge and when?
- Do you or anyone else on your staff 'back off' from dealing with incidents of homophobic, biphobic and transphobic language or even bullying out of a lack of confidence (due to a lack of formal training) or the feeling that you might 'not say the right thing'?

Saying the 'right thing'

In the Stonewall 'School report' (2017a), seven in ten LGBT pupils reported that teachers or school staff only 'sometimes' or 'never' challenged homophobic, biphobic and transphobic language when they heard it. Seven in ten LGBT pupils said their schools told them homophobic and biphobic bullying is wrong, but just four in ten reported that their schools said transphobic bullying is wrong.

When I first started teaching practices as a student, I worked in several rural schools close to the outlying areas of the very diverse city of Leicester. As more BAME children attended our schools, incidents of racist language and bullying increased. In many of these situations I observed teaching and supervisory staff tactically ignoring incidents through fear of 'saying the wrong thing' and either causing greater offence or being 'labelled a racist'. The result was that some children got hurt, others went unpunished and new arrivals with BAME identities felt excluded from the outset.

Otherwise well-meaning staff also felt shameful, as whilst they knew they should *in theory* intervene, they did not feel empowered to do so. The same patterns of behaviour existed in the schools (including my own) that I initially worked with around the use of homophobic language; staff *knew* what they should be doing, but they needed help and permission in order to do it consistently and with confidence. Where staff do not feel confident to be proactive in tackling prejudicial language, it quickly escalates into more serious bullying.

Enter the Allport's Scale. Gordon Allport was a psychologist who created the 'Allport's Scale' in 1954. The scale provides a measure of the manifestation of prejudice in a society. It identifies five stages of prejudice, ranked by the increasing harm they produce.

Stage 1: Antilocution

This occurs when a 'socially acceptable' individual or 'in' group communicates negative messages and images of a less socially acceptable group or individual, for example those with LGBT+ identities or those who do not conform to societal 'norms' in terms of gender stereotypes. 'Banter' and hate speech are included in this stage and where banter and hate speech go unchallenged (for whatever reason) confidence grows within the perpetrators; this in turn sets the stage for more severe forms of prejudice. In a school this might manifest itself as stakeholders openly using prejudicial language or saying, 'That's so gay.'

Stage 2: Avoidance

Members of the 'in' group socially exclude or avoid those in the 'out' group. Isolation may result in feelings of shame and impaired mental wellbeing. In school this might involve children who are LGBT+ (or perceived to be) being excluded from popular peer groups or activities purely because of their LGBT+ identities.

Stage 3: Discrimination

The 'out' group or individual are discriminated against by the denial of opportunities or services, preventing them from education or employment. Section 28 was an example of this kind of prejudicial discrimination in education. The USA,

Russia and other countries are currently deploying legislation intended to discriminate against LGBT+ people, and future UK governments seeking a popularist vote may not be immune to the reintroduction of such legislation.

Stage 4: Physical attack

The 'in' group engages in violent attacks on individuals or groups, resulting in physical harm. A relatively recent example of this kind of attack in the UK is the case of 18-year-old Michael Causer from Liverpool, who was openly gay. In July 2008 as he lay in an upstairs bedroom at an after-pub party, sleeping off the effects of a night's drinking, he was physically assaulted, and his bleeding body dumped outside in the street. The perpetrator was alleged to have shouted, 'You little queer faggot' and 'He's a little queer. He deserves it.' Michael later died after undergoing extensive emergency surgery to his brain.

I too have been physically attacked for walking through the street with my partner, when we were not so much as holding hands. Furthermore, as someone who has lived in the apparently tolerant city of London since 2000, since the 'Brexit' vote on the EU Withdrawal Bill in 2016, a number of my LGBT+ friends have been targeted verbally and, in some cases, attacked physically whilst out in public or using the London Underground. Whilst so-called 'gay-bashing' is perhaps less prevalent than it was when I was growing up in the 1980s, attacks on LGBT+ people still occur in the UK. Transgender people are particularly at risk and hate crime in general has risen by 48 per cent over the last three years, with the number of recorded hate crimes and incidents based on sexual orientation rising by 70 per cent over the same period (Home Office, 2018).

Stage 5: Extermination

Members of the 'in' group seek to exterminate members of the 'out' group or remove them entirely. Examples include the Holocaust in Nazi Germany, in which the 'pink triangle' was placed on prisoners to mark that they were homosexuals. An estimated 55,000 were executed and many more experimented on and castrated. Even in recent history, attempts at mass extermination of LGBT+ people have been made. In Chechnya, from around early 2017, it was widely reported that more than 100 males were abducted, imprisoned and tortured by authorities based purely upon their perceived status as gay men. An unknown number reportedly died after being held in what some eyewitnesses identified as 'concentration camps'.

The Allport's Scale demonstrates the potential for unchallenged verbal abuse or language dismissed in school playgrounds as 'banter' to evolve into something far more pernicious and potentially deadly. Where schools fail to tackle low-level prejudice head on, they could be enabling the bashers or exterminators of the future. Stating, 'I don't mean to be homophobic when I say the word gay to describe something rubbish' is no defence at all. How might it be construed if instead of saying 'That's so gay' when I dropped my pencil case in class I said 'That's so black' or 'That's so Muslim' or 'That's so disabled'?

The UK Crown Prosecution Service (2017) defines hate crime as: 'Any incident/criminal offence which is perceived, by the victim or any other person, to be motivated by a hostility or prejudice based on a person's sexual orientation or perceived sexual orientation' and 'Any incident/criminal offence which is perceived, by the victim or any other person, to be motivated by a hostility or prejudice against a person who is transgender or perceived to be transgender'. In terms of UK hate crime legislation then the law is less concerned with the *intention* of the perpetrator and more with the *perception of and impact upon the victim*. As school leaders we are preparing young people for life in an adult world with sometimes serious repercussions for those instigating hate crimes. We must instil in them whilst still at school a sense of responsibility and ownership for their language choices and educate them as to the impact of their lexicon upon others.

Changing language

Language is ever changing; it changes across geography, across social groups and over time. Over successive generations, pronunciations evolve, new words are invented and old words are repurposed. Young people are especially adept at shaping language to their own needs and tribes. The introduction of personal and online texting and mobile communications has only served to accelerate the process of morphing language; the lexicon used to describe LGBT+ identities is not immune to this process, nor indeed is the language used to mock, cuss or denigrate LGBT+ identities.

This book is about making lasting organisational change, but for organisational change to remain robust and sustainable it needs to have within it the capacity to respond to emergent issues over time. In the case of language trends, such as the current use of 'That's so gay', I have no doubt that over time this will pass by and a new method of cussing LGBT+ identities 'without intending to' will emerge; it always does. I am also in no doubt (for I have seen it happen in my own and other schools) that the moment we undertake a school-wide initiative to outlaw the use of 'That's so gay', young people will adapt and find another way of cussing LGBT+ identities or they will simply continue to do it more covertly.

This tells us two important things: firstly that it is *attitudes* we need to change and secondly that we as school leaders must regularly survey our young people (in person and anonymously) in order to capture at least some of their current lexicon. This formed part of the initial audit you completed on page 121 but it must be ongoing. A school leader who fosters open, ongoing dialogue with staff and pupils around prejudicial language is more likely to be able to stay current and informed. A school leader who cannot define current trends in unacceptable or prejudicial language will not, as a result, be able to define these language choices with young people in order to stop and police them.

How do we tackle prejudicial language?

If pupils report the pejorative use of the word gay it is our statutory and moral duty to proactively tackle it. You should lead staff through training, asking them to consider their own use of the word gay and their own experiences of hearing derogatory language aimed at gay people in school and in society. Use the stories, strategies and research you have gained from this book to help illustrate the potentially damaging impact this can have.

Next explore with staff your pupil surveys and audits to help them understand what current unwelcome prejudicial language sounds like. Staff will find that whilst some language is clearly transphobic, biphobic or homophobic, on other occasions it can be difficult to identify what counts as prejudicial language. This is why conversations with LGBT+ students are so vital.

One issue that can arise is well-meaning lunchtime staff attempting to manage incidents of the pejorative use of the word gay but, due to a lack of training, actually adding to the culture of negativity around LGBT+ identities by saying to children, 'Don't say "gay"'. It is not a very nice thing to say.'

Take a pause

Imagine for a moment you are a child in your first year of secondary school who is already aware that he is gay. You have not yet told anyone. You are in the playground at lunchtime playing with two other friends, a boy and a girl. The boy without warning snatches the girl's hairclip out of her hair, pulling some hair out as he does so. Shocked and visibly upset, the girl tells the perpetrator, 'You are so gay for doing that.' Worried that the situation is going to escalate you do the right thing and call over the lunchtime supervisor, but on recounting the story of what has just happened she turns to the girl and says, 'Well, that wasn't a very nice thing to say.'

What might the impact upon you be of this statement and why? What is the implication of this statement? What was the supervisor's intention? What else could the supervisor have said in this situation?

Working with staff

Try a role play activity with staff in which they can explore their choices in terms of the scenario above. Ask them to attune to language that will help resolve the situation and language that will compound any sense of negative associations with LGBT+ identities. Feedback from this activity can help compile a whole-staff guidance document that can be used by all staff in order to develop a consistent approach to handling such incidents. Include questions and statements such as:

- 'What did you mean by saying that?'
- 'Do you understand what you were saying?'
- 'Why did you choose that word in particular?'
- 'Would it be a problem if someone in our school was gay?'
- 'What were you feeling and why?'
- 'What was it you really wanted to say?'

This process is hugely supportive in developing a consistent and confident approach amongst staff when dealing with incidents of LGBT+ bullying and incidents relating to other forms of prejudice. When I conducted it in my own school, incidents of all forms of prejudice-related bullying and language fell sharply. It is an investment of time, of course, but the training enables staff to develop greater self-awareness in terms of their own language choices and that pays huge dividends, impacting upon children's lives positively in the long term.

Working with children

Once you have undertaken surveys and audits to see what unwelcome language is being used, it is important that you make it very clear to young people what is not acceptable, why these words and expressions are not acceptable and the likely damage they can cause to other human beings. You should also offer alternatives. Then you can recruit young people to lead on educating the whole school community. It helps if we challenge the attitudes and language, rather than the individual.

If I take 'the gay cuss' as an example, the process is simply this:

- Surveys and audits identify 'the gay cuss' as a problem in the school.
- This language is identified as unacceptable with children in assemblies and classrooms and with staff and parents via newsletters, staff meetings and social media. It's important to establish that this is a shared responsibility.
- The impact of using 'the gay cuss' is made real using real-life stories of young people whom it has affected negatively. Listening to perpetrators and those who have experienced unwelcome behaviour is important.
- A gay role model speaks in a whole-school assembly and in classes about how hearing the gay cuss has affected them and how homophobic bullying has seriously impaired their life.

- An assembly is held to model to teachers a simple lesson on the history of the word 'gay' and how it originally meant 'happy' or 'carefree'. Images of poems using the word in this way are shown and children are asked to generate their own. The teacher then displays images of gay people and gives the children permission to tell others (including parents) respectfully that, for example, 'Mr Dellenty, our teacher, is gay.' Next the teacher clarifies with children that the more recent use of the word gay to mean crappy and unworthwhile is hurtful and damaging to people who are gay. The teacher then gives the whole class permission to use the word gay in the 'carefree' way and in the 'gay teacher' way but bans the 'cuss' completely and unequivocally. Finally, the teacher asks the children what action should be taken when children are heard to say, 'That's so gay.'
- The children themselves then lead on a whole-school visibility and education campaign around the prejudicial use of the word gay and any other language. Work could include poster campaigns, podcasts, slogans for the website, video reports, child-led assemblies, theatre in education projects, song competitions and much more. It never ceases to be inspiring.
- The school council seeks opinions on appropriate sanctions and restorative approaches with students and staff around LGBT+ prejudicial language and bullying. Once agreed, expectations and sanctions are clearly shared via newsletters and the school website. Policies can then be revised with a renewed sense of ownership.

In a short space of time, pupils will take charge and become confident in informing newly admitted pupils, 'We don't say the word gay in a negative way here, but you can use it to say "happy" and to say someone is gay who is gay.'

Around all the above the school must be engaging in specific LGBT+ awareness training and campaigns for staff, parents and governors, and realigning policies and procedures to ensure that a school-wide, robust and consistent message is sent. This process can be applied to any type of existing or emergent prejudicial language. There are many other words used to hurt and disrespect, so also challenge the use of unwelcome words such as 'faggot' or 'tranny', in addition to labels that place limitations and reference gender stereotypes, such as 'tomboy' and 'wuss'.

I am happy to say I have now worked with many children who have no issue with using the word gay to describe a carefree, happy, sunny day freely again in their writing, because I have taken the time to explore the ways in which the word can be used, positively and negatively, and to set clear expectations. I also meet many young people happy to tell their class about their own identities or LGBT+ people in their families, because the school now sends a clear message that the word gay brings no shame whatsoever; safer spaces open up around children and young people as a result. Let's look at how this has worked for one school.

Rosendale Primary School, Lambeth

The school, staff, children and parents have become much more open in the way they deal with difference. Rhetoric around gender stereotypes and expectations has been questioned and dialogue around male/female or girl/boy has reduced. For example, we have a football team comprising girls and boys.

The use of derogatory language associated with LGBT+ issues was reduced dramatically and immediately. Because we experienced a significant shift in attitudes towards difference we saw that the teasing and bullying of all pupils dropped.

We haven't had any pupils or parents tell us yet directly that they are LGBT+ but I think our culture makes it easy for them if they decided to. I don't think you can underestimate equality in marriage either. Whilst laws may not change attitudes straight away, they do lay the foundations for change. I think our pupils see themselves as unique people first, as smart or fast or kind or courageous.

Time to reflect

Before turning the page, please take a moment to reflect.

Things to think about:

● Reflect on the story of Dominic and Roger and how you might share it sensitively.

Things to do:

● Be seen to visibly tackle LGBT+ prejudicial language.
● Agree sanctions with students around LGBT+ language and bullying. (These should of course be equivalent to sanctions around racism or any other form of prejudice.)
● Ensure expectations around LGBT+ language and bullying are clearly communicated to all stakeholders along with sanctions.

Chapter 10
Speaking out

'To be effective, learning has to be emotional.'

Sir John Jones

In this chapter, I will explore how we can support ourselves, our staff and our pupils to speak out about LGBT+ identities in order to nurture a culture of openness in schools. This is a key part of our Tier 4 implementation process, which will underpin our work in celebrating diversity and tackling prejudice for the safety and wellbeing of all our young people. We will consider how we give ourselves, colleagues and pupils 'permission' to speak about LGBT+ lives, how to support a student who is coming out as LGBT+, and how we can speak out with compassion against unwelcome behaviours and any challenges that might arise.

Permission to speak

The all too common perception amongst those working with children and young people is that they don't have permission to speak about LGBT+ lives and stories and as a result they say nothing. Alternatively, they so fear saying the wrong thing that they say nothing as a result. This leaves young people vulnerable.

In the UK and overseas I aim to give educators permission to speak about LGBT+ identities, or more specifically I give colleagues permission to speak about all, not just some, of the wonderful young people for whom they are responsible, their parents and their colleagues. This involves me modelling language and conversations about LGBT+ identities and same-sex families as naturally as I talk about what I ate for dinner.

In 2018 I led an impromptu assembly to pupils in a Catholic primary school in the north of England where many staff were lacking confidence in even using the word gay or lesbian out loud, despite the fact that some children were already identifying as such. In the assembly, which was watched by all teachers, I read a short story on the theme of 'difference' and after exploring some of the themes with young people I casually told them I was looking forward to getting home to my husband and dog. Teachers around the room looked visibly worried as children's hands started going up to ask questions. They asked: 'What kind of dog do you have?', 'Is your dog a boy or a girl?', 'Can we see a picture of your dog?' and 'Where do you live in London?'

The simple fact that I am gay and married to another man was the *least* interesting thing about me to children, just as it should be! This is a common experience of working with young people in schools; they are either not particularly interested in the fact I am gay, or, if they are, they want to know how and when I met Mike and whether I am happy. Many young people (after listening to my story of surviving bullying) will shake my hand and say, 'I am so glad you are still here' or 'I am so glad you found someone who loves you for being you.' I may have just shed a tear as I wrote that, but it is joyful and true.

In the staff room after the assembly I was greeted by teachers, some also in tears, who expressed huge and tangible relief that it now felt easier to slip into conversation examples of LGBT+ and same-sex identities. They felt empowered by this simple act of permission. Please give your whole school community the permission today to talk openly, without shame and using respectful language about LGBT+ people. This simple act could change or save a life and will result in immediate and more open dialogue from those who either are LGBT+ or have LGBT+ people in their lives.

I don't believe in the main it is children and young people we have to worry about; rather it's parental prejudice and our own fears. If we present the injustices of human suffering in the right way, children simply 'get it' and are naturally compassionate. In schools of strong faith identities, once I have outlined my own suffering as an LGBT+ child, young people consistently show kindness and empathy. As educators we can worry too much about how young people might react – 'They will become confused about their own identities' is a common cry from those who secretly harbour prejudice but won't admit it. We can also allow fear of challenge by parents to shut down conversations before they have even started, which is dangerous.

Our focus should not be upon political, personal, theological or cultural sensitivities, but upon the safety and wellbeing of our diverse and brilliant young people. Educators must be told without any doubt that they have permission to speak about LGBT+ people, same-sex families and relationships, in exactly the same way as they do about other kinds of people and relationships. Never take it for granted that your staff feel that they have this permission or that they feel confident in opening conversations up; school leaders need to model this throughout every aspect of daily practice.

Inspirational speakers

An ongoing programme of diverse in-school inspirational speakers is an absolute must as part of your ongoing drive to allow the school community permission to speak out. In London schools we are blessed in terms of access to high-quality, high-profile speakers. If you live in a part of the world where it is a challenge to source speakers then the whole diverse world community is available online.

I would advocate at least a speaker a month, to speak to all children and young people where possible, although it may sometimes be necessary to differentiate according to age. When inviting speakers into school it is important that you consider not only the demographic of your school community, but also the need to expose young people to those whose lives might resonate with their own, as well as those whose lives might contrast with their own. In this way we aim to explore *similarities* and *diversity*.

In my own school we invited Claire Harvey, Olympic volleyball Paralympian, in to speak to young people. After recounting her personal journey (Claire had a serious accident in 2008 that left her partially paralysed), Claire casually revealed that she is a lesbian, by mentioning her female partner. During questions not one enquiry from the children was concerned with her lesbian identity. Children instead brought compassion to her suffering, asked gory questions about her accident and asked about her medals!

As an experienced school speaker myself, I find school talks most effective when all staff are present, when lead-in and follow-up of themes in lessons have been accounted for and when the speaker is also invited to pay a more in-depth follow-up visit to one or two classrooms after the assembly in order to work more fully with young people.

School speakers play a key role in developing listening and questioning skills. They can model strategies for overcoming adversity and act as role models for breaking down professional stereotypes. If invited to share just a little of themselves beyond their professional roles, speakers who are openly LGBT+ can expose young people to the simple fact of life that LGBT+ people exist and that they live, work and play alongside us; in fact, they *are* us, never 'them'.

There is also great power in a member of the student, staff or parent community sharing their own personal story in class or assembly. I have witnessed many young people being validated and empowered when a school leader 'came out' as dyslexic and when an inspirational young man explained to a whole school about a facial disfigurement and how he felt when he was mocked in the street. School is not just about learning for exams (although that is very important too); it is also about learning to live as a compassionate, empathetic human being.

Young people are fantastic, but if they do not see trusted adults who are fully empowered to openly celebrate their diverse identities, how on earth will they feel able to come out to you when and if they need to?

Coming out as LGBT+

In the 21st century we are familiar with celebrities or sports people 'coming out' as LGBT+. When reading coming out stories, I am saddened that our core identity is still so much of an issue that we even feel the need to undertake a public coming out process. Of course, I am proud of those who do publicly come out, and I wish them safe onward transit, but *why* should it be necessary to make such a public proclamation in the first place? When Princess Diana was introduced to the world in the 1980s she did not apparently feel the need to 'come out' as heterosexual. It is *very* common for me to be asked, 'Why do gay people feel the need to come out in the first place?', a question that is usually asked with a hint of judgement, as if LGBT+ people should keep ourselves to ourselves or maintain a low profile. The words 'forcing it down people's throats' are still often used. If we apply this logic to Princess Diana, by announcing her marriage to Prince Charles was she then forcing her sexuality down the public's throats, or was she just sharing a core part of who she was? People in public life may choose to come out for a number of reasons, but sometimes that choice is taken away. The press has a long and chequered history of 'outing' public figures and putting pressure on them to the point where they feel they have to out themselves first. Even after the partial decriminalisation of homosexuality in 1967, LGBT+ identities were used against people in order to gain control or blackmail.

Under UK human rights law LGBT+ people have the right not to be discriminated against; yet despite these apparent protections, many people still refrain from being open about their identities, especially in schools, due to a fear of bullying and prejudice. When some choose to come out – and it must *always* be their choice – they may do so after many years of reflection, contemplation and perhaps a considerable amount of suffering. Coming out means partly taking control and whilst it can leave a person feeling authentic and empowered (perhaps for the first time in their lives), it can immediately render them vulnerable to harassment, bullying and hate crime, and in some territories even death. Transgender people especially know this only too well. Teachers who come out in one school may find a supportive environment cannot always be guaranteed with subsequent employers; LGBT+ people often have to come out and go back into the 'closet', and some have to come out in new situations regularly.

Coming out is a considered decision for school staff, which in some cases is taken out of a professional's hands. I spoke in 2018 with a teacher who had come out in confidence to her manager, only to discover that same manager had outed her to the governors of her faith school, leading to serious issues with harassment and discrimination. If a colleague comes out to us, this information absolutely stays confidential if they wish it to, or we too could rightly face accusations of harassment.

Children and young people coming out

What of our young people? Coming out for young people can be a complex experience. Where it goes well it can empower young people in their authentic identity, enable them to meet other LGBT+ people and help them become a positive LGBT+ role model for others if they wish. Please be aware, however, that not everyone who is LGBT+ will want to be a role model the moment that they come out; this can bring additional pressure.

Coming out can also bring rejection from friends, who can equate LGBT+ identities with 'I just want to get in your pants', or from families, who might say, 'I so wanted a wedding and grandchildren', or from cultural or faith groups, who could say, 'A demon has entered you and we must drive it out.' In some contexts, coming out could mean a child is taken for 'corrective rape' or 'conversion therapies', which cause additional lifelong trauma. My own parents, you may recall, suggested taking me for electro-convulsion therapy in their desire to see me live 'a normal life', such is the fear in some people's minds, teachings and cultures about LGBT+ identities. As those entrusted with the safeguarding of children, we must be aware of these possibilities when working with children, parents, youth services and social workers.

Coming out whilst still at school can muddy the waters even more. At school in the 1980s we had nothing in the way of open discourse about LGBT+ people or role models. Now in our online world young people have access to a range of diverse identities, including pop and soap stars, from the outset and this is resulting in more young people self-identifying at an earlier age. We need to be there for them. When we create an open and accepting school culture into which young LGBT+ people can emerge naturally at their own pace, it is more likely that more young people will do so, something I have seen time and time again. Remember, this should *never* be confused with the misguided view that talking about LGBT+ identities in schools magically 'makes children turn'.

I can still recall the very first time a pupil in school came out to me. It was in the late 1990s and I was working in a middle school; I was not yet out myself to the students or parents. One day a young man asked if he could stay behind to see me after a discussion in a religious education lesson drifted towards acceptance and tolerance of difference. As part of the lesson a Year 7 child had announced, 'Jesus hates poofs', possibly because it was written on the local bus stop. The young man asked me if he could tell me something 'in private', as I seemed 'a good person to tell', and in that moment I can remember instinctively sensing where things were headed. He then told me he thought he was gay and that he knew his parents wouldn't like it.

Take a pause

Consider the following, writing notes to record your thoughts:

- What do you think the boy's needs were in this situation?
- How might you react in this scenario?
- What might your initial feelings be?
- What might your initial thoughts be?
- How might you respond?

Truth be told, I reacted badly and to this day (although I am able to bring compassion to my younger self) I feel that I let this young man down with a very bland and unhelpful response. A child coming out to a non-LGBT+ staff member can raise challenges for that person in knowing how to manage their own feelings in response to the situation and this is why awareness training for all staff is vital. For some members of staff who are LGBT+ such a disclosure has the additional potential to trigger some deeply personal thoughts, feelings, experiences and anxieties. In the scenario above, for example, my own thoughts and feelings were:

- Has he realised I am gay? Will he tell anyone?
- Will this conversation compromise me professionally?
- If I have this conversation will people think I am a paedophile?
- If I tell him it's okay to be gay and he tells anyone else will I get sacked?
- Could this be a set-up to try to get me to disclose my own identity?

I must stress this was the late 1990s, Section 28 was yet to be repealed and I was still over a decade away from entering long-term therapy to finally work through the suffering I had encountered growing up gay. The young man's disclosure landed in a raw place and this informed my unhelpful and rather awkward response. I cannot now recall the details, but I know that I went very red, became very flustered, avoided eye contact and directed the poor young man to another colleague.

Take a pause

How do you think my inadequate (but hopefully understandable) reaction might have affected this poor young man? What short- and longer-term implications could my response have had?

When we create a school culture in which LGBT+ staff can be fully authentic, there is a chance that young LGBT+ people may be drawn to come out to them as LGBT+ role models; as school leaders we must facilitate a culture in which all staff are empowered to deliver a consistent and compassionate response in these high-stakes situations. This is a matter for staff training and discussion in staff meetings. When it happens, leaders should also 'check in' with the staff and student involved to ensure things are proceeding positively.

Remember, if a young person makes a choice to come out to us it is a privilege and we must treat it as such. That young person stood in front of us may have spent a lifetime working things through in their heart and mind, to reach the time and space within which they feel they can trust us with information about a joyful core element of their identity. You may well be the very first person a child has had the confidence to tell, so if they are gifting you with this information, please honour and respect it; respond with dignity and compassion.

Visibly model compassionate listening, without making any assumptions. Instead explore their feelings and thoughts, with acceptance and respect for their identity and journey thus far. Praise them for reaching out and assure them that they are welcomed unconditionally within the school community. Ask open questions about how they feel, what kind of support or advice they would like and how they want to move forward. You may explore whether or not they have been subjected to any negative and unwanted behaviours in and around school as a result of perceptions about their identity. It is appropriate to signpost supportive resources and groups (these should be quality-vetted and agreed as a whole school) and reinforce how grateful you are that they have shared this part of themselves with you and that your support and that of the school is unconditional, both morally and (depending on your context) statutorily.

Avoid saying anything that diminishes or appears to question their identity. Even if you don't fully understand the terminology, they can explain it to you without being made to feel that you are suggesting 'that they might need time to work things out' or that they are 'going through a phase', which is downright insulting. Also avoid saying, 'Are you sure?' Would we really ever say to a child, 'Are you sure you are heterosexual?' Don't do anything without consulting them and ensure they are fully aware of the limitations around confidentiality. It's vital to ensure they know you won't do anything without consulting them. Tell the young person that you won't inform their parents, other students or even your colleagues (unless you detect a child protection issue). LGBT+ in itself is not a safeguarding issue, any more than heterosexual identity is.

Pointing out to the young person the structures and processes intended to keep all children safe in school as part of this conversation is important. Be wary of signposting counselling based purely upon LGBT+ identities, for this can imply to the young person that there is something wrong with their mental health; the focus must always be on how they are received within the school community as a result of their LGBT+ status and it is important that young people have confidence in all staff members to be LGBT+ inclusive – not just one who might happen to be gay themselves. Try to put yourself in the place of a young person who desperately needs love, validation, freedom and permission to be themselves without compromise and needs not to face rejection.

Every child and every coming out situation will be different; when I am working with schools I advocate role play within which young people come out as LGBT+ as part of staff training situations.

Coming out role play

Find a group of three and name yourself A, B or C:

- A is the child.
- B is the staff member.
- C is the observer.

A role plays coming out as LGBT+ to B. B engages as best they can with the situation, with a focus upon supporting as opposed to diminishing the child and their LGBT+ identity in any way. The role play lasts ten minutes, during which C silently observes.

A then feeds back to B and C as to how the exchange made them think and feel. B then feeds back to A and C as to how the exchange made them think and feel and what challenges arose when asking questions or listening. C feeds back to A and B as to what they have observed and what thoughts and feelings arose as they watched.

If time allows the scenario is repeated, with each person having a turn at each role. At the end of the activity conclusions can be drawn in terms of what strategies served to support the child in this scenario and what diminished them. If working as a whole school, these conclusions can be shared as a school in order to draw up some guidance for all staff in terms of managing these coming out scenarios with confidence and compassion, because they will happen and how we respond as professionals has the power to make or break another human being.

Children and young people identifying as LGBT+ may not always have a strong sense of secure attachment at home, due to parental attitudes and prejudices or perhaps cultural or faith attitudes and prejudices. I was appalled to hear the story of one particular student at a secondary school who came out as lesbian to her teacher. The teacher informed her parents (the teacher had received no relevant training) and as a result the child was rejected on faith grounds, taken out of school and sent to family in another country to be 'healed'. The child wasn't seen again.

The stakes really are that high.

Speaking out against unwelcome behaviours

We must support the development of resistance factors in young people who already might have spent a good deal of their lives feeling rejected by ensuring all our staff, and in some cases our students, feel confident in speaking out against unwelcome behaviours. For that, we need robust strategies that the entire school community understands, respects and knows will be implemented consistently. All the strategies that exist within schools to prevent and tackle unwelcome behaviours equally apply to LGBT+ identities, but a realignment is required to make your expectations around LGBT+ very visibly specific with all stakeholders on a school-wide basis. You are not starting from scratch here; you will, I am sure, have many existing structures and strategies in place that simply need reframing, some of which you will have considered when action planning in Chapter 7, page 137.

Consider how you might adapt and implement the following strategies in your journey towards LGBT+ inclusion:

- behaviour and bullying policies
- posters around school targeting specific unwelcome language or modelling expectations
- pupil voice
- anti-bullying week
- school council
- human rights club
- conflict resolution forums
- friendship stops
- safe spaces
- gay–straight alliances
- buddy systems
- speakers in assemblies
- use of online case studies
- use of student role models
- restorative justice to develop empathy and reach root causes of unwelcome behaviours
- rainbow lanyards for staff allies
- celebration of Spirit Day in October: www.glaad.org/spiritday.

Restorative justice

'I was worried that if I told my teachers I was being bullied they would punish those who were doing it and it would only get worse, meaning they would like people like me even less.'
Karmen, aged 14, South London

Staff training in restorative justice is important. Our aim is not to merely discipline young people into saying and doing the right things in order to avoid punishment; instead we are using incidents of unwelcome language and behaviours as opportunities for staff and students to talk openly, thus facilitating new learning, empathy and awareness of the experiences of LGBT+ people. Through mediation, the person experiencing unwelcome behaviours and the perpetrator can negotiate a positive resolution for participants.

A punitive approach to a young person who is being unpleasant or prejudicial about LGBT+ people can actually lead to a fortification of their feelings of fear or dislike. Therefore a more empathetic approach from both sides is required, allowing for shared experiences of suffering and intersections between identities to be explored. This of course can be time-consuming, but it is an investment of time, for you will not only be challenging unwelcome behaviours, you will also be changing thinking.

Dismantling barriers with compassion

'I once spent a whole afternoon counselling a transgender youth who was feeling suicidal. On leaving my office that evening I was met with an angry parent asking why we were "wasting time" observing IDAHOBIT on 17 May. On that occasion, I am not ashamed to say that I saw red.'

Janice, deputy headteacher, North London

What holds schools back from undertaking the joyful, life-changing journey I am advocating in this book is often *fear of challenge*. LGBT+ inclusion makes schools safer for young people, and this simple fact has guided my heart and mind through every challenge I have faced.

Take a pause

Consider the following questions, jotting down any thoughts:

- Who might provide challenge to your work? Why might challenges arise from them?
- What key personal skills do you currently have that enable you to meet challenge positively and robustly?
- What emotions and physical sensations do you experience when being challenged?
- What personal skills would you like to develop further in terms of meeting challenge?
- How can you apply all that you have learned in this book to meet these challenges positively and robustly?

As educators, we are challenged about too much homework, not enough homework, messy or lost uniforms, 'grossly unfair' punishments and much more. You know the score! There may occasionally be some situations (especially when we are stressed or have an awful lot on our plates) when we tactically remove ourselves from conflict in order to have a quieter life. However, if we are challenged by the press, education authorities, dioceses, colleagues, parents, pupils, politicians, school governors or even our own fears and prejudice, and we back away and do nothing to further positive LGBT+ inclusion in schools, where does that lead? It leads quite simply right back to everything you told me in the 'impact of LGBT+ bullying' activity on page 40.

And for me that is not okay.

We must speak out about challenge to our LGBT+ inclusion work, and encourage and support our staff to do the same. Try now to apply your learning from this book so far to a number of challenge scenarios drawn from my own experience. You are advised to deploy them in the form of a staff training role play exercise in order to facilitate a robust, consistent and confident school-wide approach to diffusing challenge positively. Take ownership in order to come to a consistent view that complies with moral and statutory expectations and is infused with the ethos of your own school culture and vision.

Keep your responses as simple and as child-centred as possible, placing the safety and wellbeing of young people foremost in your mind. Aim to defuse rather than inflame the challenger and aim to inspire rather than repel them. It might sound challenging, but it can be done if you are secure in your moral, statutory and human rights rationale and the potential positive impact of the work upon all school stakeholders. I'm not looking for 'right answers' but for deepening awareness and empathy.

Challenge scenarios

From students:

- 'Why should we learn about gay people at school? It's disgusting.'
- 'LGBT+ people are not natural; my faith teaches me this.'
- 'Our teacher said she is going to come back to school as a man. I don't want to be in *her* class anymore.'
- 'I admit I was saying, "That's so gay", but I wasn't being homophobic.'
- 'My teacher told us he is gay. I don't want to be in PE with him anymore in case he looks at me like he fancies me when I am changing.'
- 'This book has got a character in it with same-sex parents. It is illegal to have that kind of book in primary school. My dad told me.'

From the press:

- 'We heard you are teaching children to be gay. Why is this?'
- 'You let a teacher come out to the children. Do you think the teacher should be talking about their private life in this way in front of children?'
- 'I gather a teacher at your school is undergoing a sex change. What do the parents think about this?'
- 'You are celebrating LGBT History Month. Why would you celebrate one minority lifestyle in this manner?'
- 'Your focus on openly LGBT+ role models will surely result in more gay LGBT+ young people.'

From governors:

- 'Why are you singling out LGBT+ bullying as an issue? All bullying is important.'
- 'If that member of staff comes out as lesbian we can't support her.'
- 'You can't seriously be expecting to do a project on Alan Turing and mention his homosexuality. What will the parents say?'
- 'I notice you have posters up featuring same-sex parents. This is asking for trouble. Please take them down.'
- 'If you insist on having training for staff on gay issues (and I don't see why that is really necessary) then you must hold a meeting with parents upfront to warn them.'
- 'We don't have any LGBT+ young people in this school.'
- 'We don't have any homophobic, biphobic or transphobic bullying in our school.'

From staff:

- 'Staff member A is a lesbian, so I always send any incidents of homophobic bullying straight to her to deal with.'
- 'I am too busy to talk about gay stuff.'
- 'I don't agree with people who choose to be LGBT or whatever it is called, so I am certainly not talking about them in my classroom.'
- 'To be honest, if a boy chooses to join ballet class, he must expect to be bullied and called names. What do you want me to do about it?'
- 'A child reported to me that another child had said the word gay in assembly. I told him off and said it wasn't a nice thing to say.'
- 'I don't think children at primary school know who they are, so why even talk about these things?'
- 'I have a child who wants me to call her by a boy's name tomorrow and change the pronouns I use. I have too much to do already. I can't do that as well.'

From parents:

- 'Why are you talking about gay sex with children?'
- 'My personal beliefs tell me that LGBT+ people are wrong and unnatural. I don't want my child to learn anything about them.'
- 'I gather a teacher read a book in assembly about gay people. Why was this?'
- 'Why are you promoting LGBT+ "lifestyles" in your school? Don't children come to read and write?'
- 'I gather you let my son wear a dress in the school play. Are you trying to turn him gay?'

- 'I know for a fact that your assistant headteacher is in a relationship with another man – they live in my road – but he keeps it a secret at school, I gather. What has he got to hide?'
- 'Why are you promoting LGBT+ "lifestyles" by doing LGBT History Month? Other people get bullied too. Don't you care about them?'
- 'My parents taught me that gay men working in primary schools are paedophiles. Why do you have one working in your school?'
- 'I am going to my MP (or the press) because you told children it is okay to be gay.'
- 'I have a petition here from the majority of parents at the school who don't believe that LGBT+ lifestyles should be promoted in schools in order to sexualise children.'

Finished? Well done and thank you. Please do revisit these scenarios over time. Your reactions and responses to them will change as you become more confident and experienced in meeting challenge, just as they have done for the following case study school.

Ramsey Grammar School, Isle of Man

There has been a clear shift in the language used by some students. As a school we are trying to ensure that there are no negative attachments or associations with 'being gay' and staff and students are challenging any such behaviours with confidence. Suddenly it was like a weight had been lifted off some students' shoulders. For example, non-uniform days are now seen as an opportunity to celebrate difference. What exactly is conformity for? We have set up a highly visible LGBT+ group at the school.

In the next chapter we reach Tier 5, an opportunity for you to strategically reflect on and review your school's journey thus far.

Time to reflect

Before turning the page, please take a moment to reflect.

Things to think about:

- How can you as a leader best seek support when challenge becomes overwhelming? What local and national support exists?
- How can you strategically share new learning from this book to best up-skill all staff in terms of meeting challenges specifically around LGBT+ inclusion?

- Have you taken the time to speak to your governing body, dioceses, management board or local authority to agree the process and level of support you will get in the event a parent decides to complain about your LGBT+ work? Take into account (although relatively uncommon) the possibility they might make a complaint to the press, TV or Ofsted or threaten to take a child out of school.
- Do you and your staff feel confident in supporting young people when they come out? Be honest with yourselves. Have you had this open conversation with staff? If not, you may need to broker specialist support.

Things to do:

- Appoint a dedicated member of staff (or two) to act as researchers and points of contact for inspirational speakers. They could be a member of the steering group or other staff.
- Undertake a school-wide questionnaire in terms of what kinds of diverse role models and diverse business role models young people would be interested in meeting and listening to. These can be drawn up into a schedule of talks for the year. Ensure staff attend and teachers plan for lead-in and follow-up lessons whilst making broader links to skills and career paths.
- Consider inviting speakers to deliver an additional session for your parent community in order to facilitate aspiration and knowledge of diversity.

Tier 5
Evaluation and realignment

Chapter 11
Reflect, review and realign

'If your actions inspire others to dream more, learn more, do more and become more, you are a leader.'

John Quincy Adams

We have reached Tier 5, the penultimate stage in the process. In this chapter I will explore how schools can evaluate their practice, realign their intentions and implement action for maximum impact. In the first part of the chapter I will share some examples of reviewing impact at whole-school level. Later in the chapter we will hear from Dr Joseph Hall, who will share more detailed scrutiny of the impact of my own work at classroom level with the teachers and pupils in my school between 2011 and 2013. Where LGBT+ inclusion work has historically not happened, you have the potential to make rapid, positive change.

Leaders must maintain a key role in planning, implementation, evaluation and review. It is not enough for the action plan to be handed over to a steering group comprised solely of teachers; leadership and governance must play an active role throughout. Learning walks, lesson 'drop-ins' and observations offer a picture of visibility of LGBT+ identities and themes whilst providing invaluable opportunities to witness teachers leaving their own fears, misconceptions and prejudices behind. They also afford the joy of witnessing young people identifying and working through their own prejudices. After visiting lessons, offer praise, constructive feed-back and signposts to additional support; peer observation should be implemented and student feedback on lessons taken into account.

If you did not plan for review and evaluation opportunities as part of your ini-tial action plan in Chapter 7, page 137, you must revisit it and ring fence dedicated review time. Aim to strike a balance between informal evidence-gathering on a weekly basis and ensuring fortnightly opportunities for the steering group to meet, at least in the first year. If this is too much of an ask, consider allotting time in existing management or staff meeting time. The more precisely you link actions to outcomes at the initial action-planning stage, the smoother the evaluation and review process becomes.

Many staff feel passionate and motivated once they have permission to undertake LGBT+ inclusion work and progress at a robust pace. It is important we capitalise on this, whilst modelling our ongoing expectations and awareness that the journey forms part of strategic school improvement. With careful tracking and monitoring, schools can gain a picture of impact upon attendance, academic outcomes, lasting shifts in attitudes and mental health outcomes; these factors take longer to shift but be patient and resilient. These are complex matters with high stakes and as such are worthy of ongoing close scrutiny over time. From the moment you first lead an assembly or lesson on LGBT+ people, you will *already* be changing lives for the better.

Take a pause

Think about the following, writing any notes you would find helpful:

- What existing strategies for measuring impact will support you in gathering impact data around LGBT+ inclusion? Will they need to be adapted?
- What new strategies for measuring impact will you need to develop to support you in gathering impact data around LGBT+ inclusion?
- Who will be your key players in gathering data?
- What existing opportunities do you have in school to review, analyse and realign strategic action plans and school self-review? How will you adapt these to include your LGBT+ action plan?

It's vital to capture ongoing evidence of impact in a number of ways, partly to record our pathways for posterity; there will be lessons learned and strategies developed that will absolutely assist in disempowering future manifestations of prejudice and bullying, against which we must always be on our guard. Additionally, it is important that we are investing our already overstretched energies and resources into teaching and learning, as well as whole-school procedures and strategies that are precise, are robust and facilitate rapid results.

Self-review

We can apply existing in-school opportunities for self- and peer-assessment to review:

- the journey you have been on as an individual
- the journey you have taken staff on as individuals
- the journey you as a staff team have been on
- the journey your entire school community has been on
- the journey you are taking the community beyond the school gates on
- how your work is impacting nationally and globally.

To facilitate this, you should encourage self-awareness in yourself and others and strategically plan for moments of honest self-reflection throughout your journey. This will enable young people and staff to become more adept at noticing even the smallest changes in thinking, attitudes, reactions and responses. Learning logs or thinking logs for staff and students support this process of challenge and change. Mindfulness is also a powerful self-diagnostic tool that can be utilised in order to let the subconscious reveal itself; only then can we truly know whether our hearts and minds have really shifted, or whether we are simply playing the game to appear compliant.

Consider the following from the perspective of staff, students, parents and carers, using the initial audit materials you gathered in Chapter 6, page 115, as discussion prompts:

- How did your school look and feel at the outset?
- How does your school look and feel now?
- What has already changed and why?
- What is currently changing and why?
- What will you change next and why?
- What are the attitudes to this change?
- What is the impact of this change?
- What resistance has there been to this change?
- Has change brought about positive, negative or neutral outcomes?
- What rewards and benefits is your journey bringing?
- What has challenged you?
- What has inspired you?
- How have your actions to date made the school a safer place to be?

It is important to capture this data and strategically deploy the resulting feedback, just as you would for any other form of school improvement.

Whole-school review

Leaders are responsible for monitoring the action plan and reporting to the governing body on how the plan is being enabled and upheld. Governors are in turn responsible for monitoring the effectiveness of the plan via termly governor meetings and by in situ monitoring, such as learning walks, lesson observations and involvement in focus groups with pupils.

Hard and soft data must be regularly monitored and analysed by the designated staff responsible for mental health, anti-bullying, equalities and inclusion. Trends in homophobic, biphobic and transphobic bullying and language should be analysed, and your data and the analysis should be regularly reported along with resulting actions to the steering group, governors and your local authority.

You will have your own whole-school review process for school improvement. Regular review of your strategic LGBT+ action plan forms part of this cycle, but discrete opportunities must also be found to maintain and realign the action plan as a live document. Data is all well and good, but what is really important are the questions and dialogue that go on around it and the improvements that are made as a result. Here your steering group can play a key role in:

- measuring impact
- sustainability
- action planning for the future
- reflecting on, evaluating and further developing practice
- reporting back to leadership, governors, pupils and parents
- gathering evidence and reporting to outside bodies (such as Ofsted or the local authority).

Some of this is very tangible and easy to collect. The essential recording and reporting of progress measures, attendance, exclusions and incidents of homophobic, biphobic and transphobic bullying can easily be summarised and shared with staff, school governors, students and parents. Capturing shifting attitudes amongst a particular student or staff demographic may seem subtler, but by using anonymous questionnaires, circle time, focus groups, PSHE and philosophy for children it can be done.

It is important to review your initial action plan in terms of the kinds of data you wish to capture as an organisation. At the initial action planning stage this can feel rather abstract, so as your journey develops and you begin to see impact in a range of ways it is important that you also revisit your strategies for collection and analysis of this information. Remember to measure the diversity of your school community (the diversity of the demographic), in addition to inclusion (the strategic vision you deliberately deploy to make your organisation safe, inclusive, representative and celebratory of human diversity). Sometimes schools confuse or merge the two. Relate your impact measures to outcomes wherever possible as this will help to focus the subsequent analysis, review and realignment.

Ultimately, whoever is in charge of leading on the action plan needs to be robustly accountable; I am a strong advocate of the successfully implemented LGBT+ action plan forming part of the headteacher's appraisal targets.

Areas to review

The following are all areas in which you can gather data and information to evaluate and assess your whole-school progress in the short and medium term of your journey:

- attitudes and perceptions
- use of prejudicial language

- incidents of bullying
- confidence and understanding of what LGBT+ identities are
- number of LGBT+ stakeholders who are authentic at school
- visibility of LGBT+ lives and experiences
- school aims, ethos and vision: are they fully LGBT+ inclusive?
- policies, home–school agreements, behaviour contracts and the school website: are they realigned to be fully LGBT+ inclusive?
- staff action and awareness: are they implementing strategies from whole-school training and are they aware of statutory, human rights and inspection requirements?
- curriculum and whole-school foci: are they in place?
- focus groups: are these taking place with children?
- reports from steering group
- levels of self-awareness of individual bias and prejudice
- confidence in meeting challenges and incidents of unwelcome behaviours
- visibility of LGBT+ lives and experiences in teaching and learning and whole-school assemblies and foci
- visibility of a variety of family groups in lessons, texts, models and images
- PE departments: are LGBT+ sporting role models being deployed and are prejudicial language and stereotypes being challenged?
- awareness in the school community of what LGBT+ bullying looks and sounds like
- uniform and facilities: do they enable transgender and non-binary children to exist with dignity and safety (after relevant staff training)?

Keep a detailed running record of the actions the school is taking in all these areas and deploy this to guide the action plan review process. Leadership, governors and the steering group must then pose the question, 'So what?', in response to every action to find out what has changed as a result. How do you know? What evidence do you have? It's also important to note down the sources of the evidence for your answers and your next steps. For example:

Action: PSHE and literacy coordinators purchased books featuring same-sex characters for all classrooms and libraries.

'So what?': Children are becoming more familiar with LGBT+ identities from nursery onwards. Teachers report a 20 per cent increase in the number of children with LGBT+ identities and same-sex families coming out in school. We have also experienced a 76 per cent decrease in the number of children who are being bullied for having same-sex parents and a 58 per cent reduction in the use of the word 'gay' as a negative.

Evidence: Bullying records and anecdotal feedback from teachers.

Next steps: Invite the organisation FFLAG into school to speak about their work to support families with LGBT+ children to staff and parents. Continue to seek a wider range of texts that feature intersections between BAME, SEND and LGBT+ identities to be deployed in teaching and learning. Older children to make books about LGBT+ families and historical figures for younger students.

Evaluating objectives from the action plan

In terms of objectives, not only is it important to scrutinise their impact and relevance during formal review opportunities but schools must also track the development of objectives over a term, a school year or a series of years. If an objective remains static for a number of terms, something isn't working and additional analysis is required to ascertain why.

Here is an example objective from an actual strategic action plan: 'To reduce incidents of transphobic language by 75 per cent by the end of summer term 2015.' In reviewing this objective the school should seek to understand the following:

- The triggers for writing the objective and the causes behind them.
- The actions and strategies that have been taken to meet the objective, who was responsible for them and the relevance of their skillset.
- The timescale allocated: was the objective realistic in the time allotted?
- The resources that were deployed.
- Whether the objective was met:
  - If the objective was met, what went well and how was this achieved? What challenges were met, what new learning took place and what key strategies enabled success?
  - If the objective was not met, why was this? What challenges were met and who or what was responsible for the failure to meet the target on this occasion? Was it a case of lack of training, time, resources, confidence or skillset or was it due to other factors? How might these factors be overcome in order to ensure the objective is now met?
- What will happen as a result of the objective being met or not being met.
- How the negative impact of the objective not being met will be minimised.
- How the success of the objective being met might be celebrated.
- Whether the objective has been unmet on a previous action plan.
- How the objective might be realigned to ensure it is met within a revised time period; what additional resources or support are required?

Application of review

Each time formal review takes place, action plans must be annotated and realigned. It is helpful to break a copy of the plan up and transfer the objectives physically into separate sections in a folder (or folders) in order for evidence and best practice examples to be stored alongside them. In terms of process, once you have gathered evidence of impact, reflected carefully upon it and realigned the strategic plan, it is time to disseminate revised intentions, actions and roles to all staff and seek any additional resources and support that are needed to implement the revised plan.

Outside accreditation

External validation schemes and 'quality mark' schemes are increasingly available for schools wishing to validate their LGBT+ inclusion journeys. Whilst these schemes have many merits, especially the chance to form a supportive good practice network with other schools, please do be discerning; in my last school we were encouraged to pay an awful lot of money for a brand name on our website and an initial audit tool that was inferior to our own internal audit tools. Be wary too of organisations offering strategic LGBT+ inclusion development training for schools who have never actually been involved in teaching, let alone school leadership. You will, I am sure, be able to spot them when you meet them! Be careful and trust in your own expertise and, when you have it, set about celebrating and sharing it proudly.

Impact over time

As a result of this process of reflection, review and readjustment, your LGBT+ inclusion work can have a significant impact over time. As an example of this, Dr Joseph Hall now shares some findings from his scrutiny of the initial suites of LGBT+ inclusion work I instigated in my then own secular, state-run primary school. This contribution also provides an example of gathering and analysing data from interviews and focus groups, which I hope you find helpful as you review your own work. I wish to express sincere gratitude to Dr Hall and all the staff members and young people who contributed ideas and feedback for this scrutiny.

Impact upon teaching and children, by Dr Joseph Hall

I undertook doctoral research in Shaun's school between November 2011 and May 2013 to explore 'The formation, implementation and reception of gender and sexualities education in English primary schools' (see Hall, 2015). Here

---

I reflect on some of the interview and focus group data from teachers and children in Shaun's school to demonstrate the impact of gender and sexualities education on teaching and learning.

Shaun's initial training began to establish the strategic importance of situating homophobia, biphobia and transphobia in an anti-bullying context. Indeed, as the following quote from a teacher demonstrates, positioning gender and sexualities education in this way not only allows staff to get onboard with this work, but also encourages children to make connections between sexism, homophobia, biphobia and transphobia and other forms of bullying:

> 'They [the children] didn't see that calling someone names was necessarily homophobic bullying, so if he's not gay then how is it bullying, but after discussion they can now see that calling people names is a form of bullying. I think it has brought it out in the open more and children are more willing to talk about it, either to let you know it's happened to them or they will just come up and say, "You know what we did the other day? Can you explain to me this...?" They're much more open.'
>
> *(Year 6 teacher, 2011)*

Much like the teachers and governors, children had not previously considered the pejorative use of the word gay directed towards others as a form of bullying. However, when these links were made, children regarded sexist, homophobic, biphobic and transphobic bullying as no different to other forms of bullying, such as racist bullying, and would describe how they could potentially affect *anyone*. As the second part of the quote illustrates, discussion of these types of bullying broke a silence and brought gender and sexual prejudice out into the open, with children subsequently feeling more able to broach these issues. Indeed, as the next quote demonstrates, this gave teachers a good indication of children's moral compass and over time it reversed prevailing attitudes in and beyond the classroom:

> 'I really enjoy delivering it... it makes children think outside the box and it gives me a good assessment of children's options and ideals and experiences [and] you do see them change, whether it's even just the fact that they become used to hearing the words [gay, lesbian, bisexual, trans]. [W]e were hearing, three or four years ago here, "You're so gay" in a negative way in the playground and I think with some of those children that are still here, if we said that now they would react with, "Oh no, we don't use gay", so it has completely reversed and turned around their perceptions and options, I think.'
>
> *(Year 4 teacher, 2011)*

As this teacher notes, even just using the words gay, lesbian, bisexual and trans can be powerful and, as I explore below, in hearing appropriate use of these terms children became more familiar and comfortable with them. As a group of Year 4 children explain, reflecting on the book *The Sissy Duckling* (Fierstein, 2014):

Harry: I think they say it in American. They say a sissy and it is kind of like when you say, 'Oh, you're so gay.'

Merlin: If someone says, 'You're gay', maybe they are gay but it doesn't give you the right to take the mickey out of someone.

William: If someone is gay it don't matter, it is what they want... it is not what other people want them to do.

Merlin: Yeah, it doesn't mean they have to go out with a girl.

(Focus group with Year 4, 2011)

This profound exchange took place between a group of Year 4 boys and demonstrates how terms like gay can be reclaimed from pejorative use and imbued with positive meanings and associations. Hearing teachers confidently use terms like gay, lesbian, bisexual and trans is reassuring for children, but hearing peers articulate these sentiments *once they have been given permission to do so* is incomparable. Indeed, as Renold (2005) and others have shown, peer group culture in primary schools can be a hotbed for (hetero)sexist social relations. Yet, such open and frank exchanges, which occurred elsewhere, go some way to challenging heteronormativity. As a Year 5 girl reiterates:

'If you are like gay or lesbian or something like that you shouldn't really make fun of them 'cos maybe when you're older you might be the same and maybe you heard it off someone else and you shouldn't just say that if you have heard it.'

(Focus group with Year 5, 2012)

We perhaps underestimate the maturity of children in being able to have these kinds of discussions. Indeed, as focus groups, classroom observations and teacher testimonies confirmed, children of all ages empathically embraced a range of work, including trans awareness:

'[A Year 6 teacher] did a lesson on transgender people and whether they should be discriminated against [and they were] really grown up... you could almost see them sitting there... oh, I hadn't thought about that before.'

(Year 6 cover supervisor, 2011)

Such lessons gave children skills in critical thinking and the ability to recognise and challenge everyday, taken-for-granted norms and values. This enabled children to move beyond the wrongs of bullying to engage more deeply and meaningfully with gender and sexual stereotypes, assumptions and expectations. This is clear in the final exchanges between a group of Year 6 girls and a mixed group of Year 4 children who reflect on the book *The Sissy Duckling*:

Callum: *A sissy was basically when other people think you should behave different…*

Abigail: *To what you normally behave…*

Callum: *In a different way to how you are behaving.*

Abigail: *Like a sissy means when you want someone to do something differently to how they behave so you don't think it is correct.*

Elly: *Don't judge someone just because they're different because everyone's special and unique.*

(Focus group with Year 4, 2011)

Kate: *I remember the ballet one… we had to write a newspaper report.*

JH: *What did that involve?*

Kate: *I think it was about… like ballet is normally classed as a girl's thing.*

JH: *Do you all agree with that?*

All: *No!*

Ruth: *People label it as a girl's thing and sometimes it is what girls like to do but sometimes boys like to do it as well.*

JH: *So what was the point of that activity?*

Kate: *I think it was to realise that you shouldn't label things because it is for both genders.*

JH: *Does everyone agree with that?*

All: *Yeah.*

(Focus group with Year 6, 2012)

These exchanges stand as testament to a sustained, 'whole-school' approach and they illustrate how children can become active agents in societal change when afforded opportunities to engage meaningfully with gender and sexualities.

Dr Joseph Hall, May 2019

Thank you again to Dr Hall for this insight and to the students and staff who took part in his research.

The long-term impact of positive LGBT+ inclusion work is also evident in many of the schools with whom I have worked, including St Gabriel's Church of

England College. The following case study also highlights some methods they have used to assess the outcomes of their work.

St Gabriel's Church of England College, Lambeth

Negative behaviour reports regarding LGBT+ prejudice have almost been eradicated. The few that remain tend to be use of the phrase 'You're so gay' in a negative way by our younger students or students who are new to the school. We continue to work to ensure that this type of behaviour is eradicated, and we do this through our behaviour systems and through our curriculum.

Students are more confident in discussing LGBT+ issues, as are our staff members. It's difficult to assess attitudes but we are confident that our students' attitudes have improved. Our teachers now feel confident to tackle LGBT+ prejudice head-on without 'upsetting parents'. Every member of staff knows their responsibility in sustaining a truly inclusive school community and our known LGBT+ students are visibly more confident in being themselves. We continue to take immediate action against any prejudice that is reported or encountered. Teachers feel confident in highlighting the LGBT+ community in their schemes of work. For example, Alan Turing makes an appearance in computing and we discuss attitudes to LGBT+ more confidently in humanities. We continue to embed LGBT+ across our curriculum and we discuss LGBT+ issues as part of our PSHCE programme. The planning of LGBT History Month now appears on one of our middle leader's job descriptions to demonstrate how important this month is and we have also calendared an LGBT+ Inclusion Week; our successful LGBT+ Inclusion Week has been our biggest achievement since the training. Whilst we were planning this, some of our LGBT+ students volunteered to deliver assemblies alongside their peers. We are proud that our students felt confident and safe in the knowledge that our entire school community is supportive of them and that they can be free to be who they are without fear of prejudice or discrimination.

We feel that our LGBT+ students are more comfortable in being themselves. We are also more confident that our students can challenge each other in a calm, safe manner on LGBT+ views. We continue to place LGBT+ inclusive posters around our school and we continue to discuss LGBT+ issues across the curriculum to show all of our students that school is a safe space.

In this chapter I have shared some ideas for capturing impact and realigning your action plan accordingly. I do hope that you shine proudly and brightly to celebrate and disseminate how you have succeeded on your journey in order to inspire others, which brings us neatly to Tier 6 and Chapter 12, which is all about sharing best practice online and outside of your school gates.

Time to reflect

Before turning the page, please take a moment to reflect.

Things to think about:

- What termly opportunities can you find to reflect upon progress and impact?
- What termly opportunities can you find for key players to feed back to leadership, whole staff and governors in order to share what is working well and what might not be?
- How will you communicate ongoing barriers, challenges and success to all stakeholders?
- Is there a way in which you can share your journey from the start with colleagues from other schools in your network, sharing costs as well as expertise and experiences?

Things to do:

- Ensure review, evaluation and realignment of your action plan is robust and meaningful. Be sure all stakeholders know of any realigned intentions.
- Revisit aims and intentions of any steering groups and focus groups; are they still relevant and providing the evidence of impact you need?
- Identify opportunities to share emerging good practice beyond your own school and incorporate this into your action plan.

Tier 6
Celebration and dissemination

Chapter 12
Inclusion for all

'All young people, regardless of sexual orientation or identity, deserve a safe and supportive environment in which to achieve their full potential.'

Harvey Milk

We now reach Tier 6, a space for gathering, celebration and dissemination. In this final chapter, I consider how you can celebrate and disseminate your own best practice so you can inspire others and play a key part in the wider global educational journey towards positive LGBT+ inclusion. In other words, be proud!

Where are we now?

Before exploring how you can contribute to the journey the education community is on towards LGBT+ inclusion, it is first important to discuss where we are on that journey currently. Upon launching my professional LGBT+ journey back in 2009, I struggled to find any established organisation willing to undertake any significant work in the primary sector, resulting in me devising my 'Inclusion For All' strategy. Ten years on, professional, public and governmental feedback highlights that my work (in many respects) 'blew open' the field for larger LGBT groups to work in the primary and faith school sectors especially. If this is indeed the case then I am very happy and privileged to have undertaken this journey, with all of its challenges and successes. I was merely doing what I felt was right for our pupils at the time. I wonder what your own LGBT+ work in schools will look like ten years from now?

There are happily now increasing numbers of organisations (some funded by the UK government) undertaking positive LGBT+ inclusion work in schools. This is good progress, although recent experience has shown that *more* is not always better; do be discerning and ensure that those delivering training have at least worked within education! We have many years of inaction and a vast training deficit to catch up on, but quality is important too.

In the UK it can sometimes be easy to rest on our laurels in terms of advances in equal marriage and equality legislation, but legislation (in itself) does not always change attitudes. I once recorded a video message (available at https://itgetsbetter.

org/story/cvcxcqypzau, if you wish to watch it) for a very well-meaning project called It Gets Better, which sends hopeful messages to LGBT+ people struggling with rejection and bullying, their key message being that over time, if LGBT+ youth are resilient and access good support, life gets better. But is this intention *really* good enough for our young people? Don't they deserve life to be 'better' from the start of life and education?

Young people (who have *no choice* over their LGBT+ identities) are often told, 'Hang on in there. It will get better.' However for many, frankly, it doesn't; many self-harm and countless LGBT+ people around the world, even as I write, are being made homeless, and are being abused, rejected, raped and killed. Is this the world we *really* wish to facilitate through our teachings as a global education community?

To spare future generations from prejudice and suffering, governments must ensure without exception that colleagues entering the education profession (at whatever level) undertake high-quality training on how to facilitate positive LGBT+ inclusion at initial training stage, with refresher training and targeted strategic training for middle leaders, leadership, management and governors. Those entrusted with inspecting schools must too undertake dedicated and high-quality training. I work with universities and teacher training organisations, and I am often inspired by the open attitudes of many trainee teachers who express surprise and dismay that LGBT+ bullying in schools 'hasn't been sorted yet'. Nonetheless, I also meet trainee teachers who are unsure as to 'how they feel' about LGBT+ identities, in addition to vulnerable, covertly LGBT+ teachers who aren't yet confident in expressing their authentic identities in the workplace. These colleagues all deserve our support and guidance; a lack or knowledge, confidence or sense of permission will likely mean that they fail to tackle LGBT+ bullying.

Newly qualified teachers and staff new arrivals must be met with clear expectations in terms of conduct and induction; school leaders must be proactive in asking what experience and training they have received in terms of LGBT+ identities. Where they have had none, leaders must prioritise it as part of continuing professional development.

University of Derby

Our post-14 education and training initial teacher education programme is ambitious, forward thinking and committed to providing excellent learning and teaching for students, underpinned and informed by research and practice. Shaun's work provides a strong challenge to heteronormativity and engages individuals from all backgrounds in positive discussions about inclusion. His exceptional training continues to transform the lives of our trainees and prepares them well for promoting equality, diversity and inclusion within their placement and beyond.

Shaun's work is inspirational, thought-provoking and something that I will definitely take forward within my teaching philosophy – be kind, be mindful and celebrate difference to make the world of education a greater place for every child and young person to flourish. Shaun's powerful, respectful and engaging delivery takes the learners on an 'emotional rollercoaster' through his own life and those of others within the LGBT+ community, where feelings, barriers and attitudes are explored before personal, micro and macro strategies are shared to promote inclusion for all. This forward-thinking commitment to equality chimes with our programme ethos and this is why we invite him back every year.

Staff are more knowledgeable and comfortable engaging in discussions that promote equality. This ensures that trainees are equipped with knowledge to enable them to challenge inequality in their working lives.

Trainee teachers have a greater appreciation for the challenges that marginalised young people may face and how to support and promote equality and inclusion from a macro (organisational) to micro (classroom) level.

Liverpool John Moores University

Shaun's approach has had a great impact on our initial teacher training programmes. Initially he provided training for trainee teachers, lecturers and also the wider university staff. He was also kind enough to facilitate a placement in his school for some of our undergraduate students, who upon returning then disseminated what they had learned at the university teaching and learning conference to a much wider university audience. The training and information given to staff from working with Shaun still forms the basis of university training sessions five years on.

Our student teachers are now often at the forefront of delivering change out in schools. I know that many of them have developed the confidence to challenge and educate in the area of tackling homophobic bullying out in our partnership schools, impacting on the lives of many pupils.

In 2018 I was very grateful to be invited by Professor Jonathan Glazzard to become a member of the advisory committee of the newly formed Centre for LGBTQ+ Inclusion in Education based at Leeds Beckett University. This groundbreaking centre is committed to challenging all forms of prejudice, discrimination and marginalisation towards those who identify as lesbian, gay, bisexual, trans, queer or questioning and others who have gender identities or sexual orientations that differ from the heterosexual and cisgender majority. It generates research into the issues that relate to LGBTQ inclusion in schools. In July 2018 I asked Professor Glazzard to share his own view on the need for relevant, specific LGBT+ training at the initial training stage for teachers:

'Statistics from Stonewall in 2017 demonstrate that 45 per cent of LGBT pupils experience bullying for being LGBT at school and nearly one in ten transgender pupils receive death threats at school. Worryingly, 68 per cent of young people who identify as LGBT report that teachers or school staff only "sometimes" or "never" challenge homophobic, biphobic and transphobic language when they hear it.

The figures are worrying. Whilst there is a slight improvement to the 2012 data, clearly there is more work to do. Initial teacher training has a critical role to play in developing the capacities of the next generation of teachers to foster inclusive cultures for young people who identify as LGBT. Not all teachers recognise homophobic, biphobic or transphobic abuse and, if they do, they are not always confident in responding to it. However, responding to bullying is not sufficient. Schools need to promote respect for LGBT identities and encourage children and young people to view diversity as an energising force that enriches the world.

Initial teacher training programmes should enable the next generation of teachers to recognise homophobic, biphobic and transphobic abuse. In addition, it should foster inclusive values and support trainee teachers to reflect critically on their own values in relation to LGBT identities. Finally, it should provide trainees with the confidence to teach children and young people about these issues, both as a discrete unit of work and through integrating LGBT inclusion throughout the curriculum.'

Professor Jonathan Glazzard, 2018

Be the change you wish to see

Educators should strive never to wait for positive change to be directed from departmental or governmental level. We must embody and model the change we wish to see in our schools and education systems, where possible 'going public' and working in partnership, whilst keeping our children, families, staff and *ourselves* safe and well.

Some educators privately tell me they always knew that LGBT+ youth were struggling badly in their schools, but without governmental direction or permission they were forced into denial, inaction and avoidance. Colleagues have also shared feelings of shame that over years many vulnerable young people have been allowed to suffer, slip through the net or even die.

In many cases, my work has resulted in colleagues bringing their awareness to working with their prejudices for the first time; this sometimes results in feelings of shame when realisation hits that their own prejudice and bias have, throughout their careers, impacted negatively upon young people, parents and their colleagues; if these reflections resonate with you my advice is this: acknowledge these feelings and let them go.

Judging, shaming and blaming ourselves (or each other) will not help us move forward positively; neither will resting in a place of shame, regret or rumination about past injustices, such as Section 28. Don't strive to change the past but learn from it whilst investing energies towards shaping a more compassionate future, one that shows resilience against the swing of the political pendulum. Our unconditional belief in equality and human rights must be modelled in all aspects of school life, from first contact to the final moments in which young people, parents and staff move on to the next phase of their lives.

Take a pause

Ask yourself the following, noting down any thoughts and feelings:

- How will you make sure that transition between primary and secondary schools ensures that the compassionate and open attitudes nurtured in primary education do not become 'skewed' by the pressures and peer pressures of secondary school?
- To what extent does your current LGBT+ inclusion and awareness strategy:
  - Support young people as they transfer into further education and employment in a diverse world?
  - Support young people to know when hate crimes have taken place and how to report them?
  - Support young people to seek support from LGBT+ specific organisations?
  - Support young staff to seek support from LGBT+ specific organisations (on behalf of themselves or family members) and trade unions?
  - Support parents to seek support from LGBT+ specific organisations or report hate crime?
  - Enable a protective and inclusive space for parents, governors, staff and pupils who identify as LGBT+?
- How can you most strategically employ the intersections between your organisation's work on positive LGBT+ inclusion and other protected characteristics?
- How can you bolster existing and newly developed strategies for positive LGBT+ inclusion in order to ensure they are robust enough to survive when you move to another school?
- If you left your current school and went to work in another context, what existing strategies, skills and strengths would you be able to transfer with you? Which (if any) might you leave behind and why?
- What will your current LGBT+ inclusion and awareness strategy look and feel like in three, five and ten years' time?
- When all the current staff, pupils, governors, parents and carers have moved on from your school, what will their legacy be in terms of positive LGBT+ and more general inclusion?

It is important to keep the plates spinning in order to ensure sustainability, for despite our hard work and strategic drive, taking our foot off the pedal can rapidly result in a deteriorating school culture for LGBT+ youth.

A school I worked with undertook great work around positive LGBT+ inclusion, and as a result attitudes improved and students became more open to celebrating diversity. This was highlighted in a 2012 Ofsted report, with students commenting that the school was 'happy and harmonious'. However, leadership changed and halted the work for two years, leading to a decline in attitudes. Visiting again in March 2017, Ofsted found that whilst pupils understood that using homophobic language was wrong, leaders had only recently introduced a process to eliminate this in school. As a result, this system was yet to be embedded and some pupils regularly used inappropriate, homophobic language.

Hayle, who was previously a teacher at the school, observes:

'Whilst LGBT training for staff and lessons for students are done frequently this can create a lasting and positive change for everyone in the school. However, once this training stops and lessons are not completed, attitudes can return to being negative very quickly. This shows that for any LGBT work to have a lasting impact it needs to happen consistently and be a priority in the school. It can't just be one person's pet project to push this work through, but it must be everyone's if we want to ensure that all students are able to achieve their potential.'

It is vital schools don't adopt a 'flash in the pan' approach and that the foundations of our work are solid and sustainable, in the wake of staff and student mobility. Other case study schools have thoughts on strategies for sustainability:

'This work clearly aligns with our school vision and aims and augments them so that LGBT+ becomes part of what we do, much the same as we promote other areas of diversity such as race, gender and disability.'

Victoria Road Primary School, Isle of Man

'[We] run training every year and ensure PSHE sessions are completed by all tutors.'

Chiltern Edge School, Oxfordshire

'[We] ensure sustainability through whole-school planning. As the children move through the school, they revisit and take on new learning. This learning ties in with lots of work on self-esteem, stress, self-image, emotional wellbeing and talking.'

Barnston Primary School, Wirral

Becoming an advocate for positive change

How might you use the results of your hard work to facilitate change beyond your own organisation in order to inspire change in wider society? Despite an increase of training providers, many school leaders still find newly qualified teachers and other non-teaching members of staff (including all-important playground supervisors) arriving at school with no relevant training. This deficit can be addressed in part by disseminating your best practice in order to teach and inspire colleagues.

Sometimes those looking at my work confuse being a 'hero' with 'courageous leadership'. School leaders should not have to be labelled 'heroes' for celebrating and including all our young people; it is surely a basic tenant of the role and associated responsibilities we have been entrusted with. That said, when we witness or achieve progress, it is important to acknowledge and praise it where it makes a positive difference to young people. In this way those who trailblaze know that their work is valued and celebrated, and their confidence grows; as a result, outcomes improve.

I will now share four examples of how I personally was able to broaden the reach of my work, in order to make an impact beyond one organisation. These are strategies that have had large-scale impact. Please consider similar strategies for sharing your own work. Leaders can inspire a whole school community, but the leadership skills we deploy on a day-to-day basis can also empower us to become advocates for positive change on a significantly larger scale. All it takes is passion, positivity, a social media account and a bit of time.

Model 1: Upscaling

Nottingham is a city in the north of England with around 20 schools, many of them academies. The increased prevalence of academies led to a significant reduction of strategic input and training offered by local authorities. A number of Nottingham academies therefore formed the equivalent of a local authority training hub, which identified a city-wide issue with homophobic bullying and language.

A one-day conference was scheduled, to which all city academies were invited. I led colleagues through a day of presentations, reflective activities and role play. In addition to wanting to reduce incidents of homophobic bullying, city school leaders wished to minimise the impact of prejudice-related incidents upon student attendance and outcomes. Strategic work was supported by the provision of a bespoke whole-school audit tool to guide thinking.

The day provided an opportunity for colleagues to distil core messages into a city-wide charter aimed at preventing LGBT+ bullying. The subsequent charter was shared across the city.

Take a pause

Reflect on this first model using the following questions:

- How might you work with local partner and feeder schools to establish consistency of messages and expectations?
- How could you share best practice in teaching and learning across schools and use this to assess progression and continuity?
- How can you involve students in developing a whole-school charter around LGBT+ bullying and inclusion?

Model 2: Online resources

In 2015 I was invited to lecture at The Open University, where I agreed for the session to be filmed. As a result, the university created a free online resource called 'That's so gay! Homophobic language and schools' (you can find it at http://www.open.edu/openlearn/languages/linguistics/thats-so-gay-homophobic-language-and-school). In this manner the university was able to get my messages to a much wider audience than just the colleagues in one lecture hall on one day.

Take a pause

Reflect on this second model using the following questions:

- An increasing number of universities are taking great interest in the work schools are undertaking around LGBT+ inclusion. How might you connect with the local business community and local educational institutions to disseminate your own good practice more widely?
- What online video and podcast resources could your school community produce in order to facilitate new learning around LGBT+ bullying, identities and history? How could these be shared online?

Model 3: Partnership working

Descriptions of three of my experiences with partnership working follow. In each case I delivered an initial suite of training to each organisation.

The Church of England

Subsequent to my initial suite of training with the Church of England, a suite of free resources was produced for Christian schools in the UK entitled 'Valuing all God's children', which broke new ground for faith schools. I helped launch the resource on television alongside the Archbishop of Canterbury and secondary school students who had experienced LGBT+ bullying. The Catholic Church has also now produced a resource for schools called 'Made in God's image'. These resources can both be downloaded for free:

- 'Valuing all God's children': https://www.churchofengland.org/more/media-centre/news/homophobic-biphobic-and-transphobic-hbt-bullying-tackled-new-guidance-church
- 'Made in God's image': https://www.catholiceducation.org.uk/images/CES-Project_Homophobic-Bullying-Booklet_JUN18_PROOF-9.pdf

Amnesty UK

Amnesty UK facilitate annual teacher training to equip educators with the expertise to engage students with human rights. This strengthens skills in teaching and training colleagues, and involves sessions from experts in human rights education. It inspires teachers to engage young people in key ethical, social and political issues. These teachers then become 'Amnesty Teachers', who advocate human rights education in their school and beyond. For over six years, I have delivered the LGBT+ inclusion element of the programme. Amnesty Teachers act as human rights teachers and leaders, and within their own schools they lead training and deliver lessons on LGBT+ identities, history and global human rights. I supported Amnesty with their free, downloadable LGBT+ resource, containing lesson ideas for primary and secondary schools. Find it at: https://www.amnesty.org.uk/files/lgbti_rights_activity_pack_february_2015.pdf.

Theatre in education project: BOY

BOY is a partnership project with a UK theatre company called HyperFusion Theatre, based partly upon my own training and testimony, and informed by the voices gathered during school focus groups. *BOY* is a lively 45-minute play followed by an interactive workshop, during which young people actively explore issues of 'banter', bullying and prejudice. Using their voices in a safe space, young people explore solutions to issues of LGBT+ prejudice and identity-based bullying.

After well-received performances in my own school, *BOY* received grants to upscale and has now been performed in a range of primary, secondary and faith schools across the UK. *BOY* was also performed in UK Parliament during 2016 and was attended by the parliamentary LGBT group, politicians and Members of Parliament. To perform the play in the same space that had been responsible for Section 28 in the 1980s was incredibly moving and for me a hopeful sign that we have come a long way.

The play is available for schools. See more at: http://www.hyperfusion.co.uk/tic-box-productions/boy/.

Take a pause

Reflect on this third model using the following questions:

- How might you network to seek work in partnership and upscale your own work in order to achieve wider impact locally and nationally?
- Theatre and drama are powerful mediums with which to explore empathy and real and imagined stories of bullying and prejudice; how might your school use performance and dance to explore and highlight these issues with a wider audience?

Model 4: System-level change

The Isle of Man is a self-governing British Crown dependency in the Irish Sea whose legal system was not always supportive of LGBT+ inclusion. Private and consensual acts of male homosexuality were still illegal in 1992 and equal marriage was introduced in 2016. An equivalent of the UK Equality Act began phasing in during 2017. The island is increasingly liberal in terms of diversity, but some strong negative attitudes amongst some islanders still exist.

In January 2018 I commenced a long-term project supporting the island's 37 schools – 32 primaries and five secondaries – to become fully LGBT+ inclusive. Due to the historical challenges and barriers to LGBT+ rights on the island it was vital that I structure my approach in order to ensure 'buy-in' from the outset. My initial training model was this:

1. training for the education department in the Isle of Man government
2. training for all senior leaders
3. training for all middle leaders
4. training for all youth services
5. meetings with LGBT+ youth group
6. meetings with young people in schools
7. meetings with parents of LGBT+ youth
8. meetings with local politicians and press
9. training for all staff in schools (in clusters)
10. speaking with young people in school assemblies.

Apart from it being a privilege to be entrusted with this project, which had the potential to make lasting positive change to an entire education community and country, what struck me was the pace at which change started to happen. The stimulus for change once again was the giving of permission and providing a space within which to work through individuals' feelings about and responses to diverse identities, which completes the circle and takes us right back to Tier 1!

Sharing your good practice

Aside from my examples above, there are of course many ways in which you can disseminate the wonderful work you are doing in your own school so it can have a significant impact outside of your school gates. To provide you with some more ideas, please allow me to introduce my A–Z of how to share good practice.

A   **Assemblies** for other classes, colleagues, parents and governors to share your great work on anti-bullying, LGBT+ history, identities and awareness. You can also use school bulletins, newsletters, the school website, television screens in the main lobbies or corridors – you name it! Remember, your work is nothing to feel shameful of. Awards and achievements can be shared publicly to celebrate good work and positive inclusive attitudes. You may also seek to obtain awards and recognition from outside bodies and organisations.

B   **Be proud** of your hard work to facilitate an inclusive school, but also of your authentic self and of your authentically diverse colleagues and students. Class books with diverse families or work based upon LGBT+ history and role models can be produced and left in public spaces and libraries for other classes and parents to read.

C   **Call your local and national newspapers, television and radio stations.** Act without shame, knowing that you are already changing lives for the better!

D   **Deliver presentations** about your own work alongside students and colleagues at education conferences and events, locally, nationally and internationally. Share your vision and share its impact!

E   **Enthusiasm and energy.** The days of hanging our heads in shame and anxiety about Section 28 are long gone, so focus instead on the present and the future, and bring positive energy to every and any discussion about your ongoing work to facilitate LGBT+ inclusion.

F   **Friends with finances.** By sharing news of your great work in school you can find other schools and organisations who share a similar vision. Some of these will share best practice and resources with you, and in the case of businesses with a community remit you may even attract some funding. Check out any local businesses with LGBT+ networks.

G   **Gather evidence.** The more evidence of tangible impact and best practice you can gather the better. This will enable you to inspire, as well as meet any potential challenge robustly.

H   **History Month.** LGBT History Month is a fantastic, focused, annual opportunity to undertake and share work in classes, across phases, with the whole school and with the community beyond. You might also link up with a school in another country in order to share work undertaken in different educational and geographical contexts. Remember, the aims and vision of LGBT History Month should never be consigned to one week or month of the year. Inclusion and celebration of LGBT+ history and identities should be embedded throughout all aspects of school life, all of the time.

I **Induction** of pupils, staff, parents, carers and governors provides a fantastic opportunity to set out your stall in terms of your vision and ethos and the work it results in. On showing any new prospective member of a school community physically around the building, proudly make a point of showing them work around 'Our heritage' (see page 155), diverse families, LGBT+ and BAME identities, and some of the books you use about human diversity.

J **Joy!** Please remember the joyful feeling of validation a closeted young LGBT+ person will feel when an openly gay teacher whom they respect invites their partner to the school concert. Nothing to see here. Nothing to hide.

K **Keeping everyone in the loop.** If an equality steering group is set up, or the role of an inclusion and equalities coordinator established, a calendar of themed days and events can be circulated to everyone in the school community. You may wish to adopt a three-year rolling programme of diversity and inclusion events in order to foster good relations and develop balance and intersectionality to your offer.

L **Lessons.** Invite colleagues to watch you teach about, for example, transgender identities. Adopting an open-door policy helps to make everyone feel that the work is shame-free and transparent and that best practice can be shared. Celebrate what is going well and work in pairs or small teams to refine practice around subjects that might still be relatively new for some colleagues. Be sure to extend an open invitation to management and governors.

M **Modelling.** If you have written and delivered a fantastic lesson or theme on LGBT+ awareness, please don't keep it to yourself; model it in a staff meeting or staff training session and inspire others whilst celebrating your great work. Bring along examples of impact and student work, and consider how your work might have contributed to changing attitudes.

N **National and international education conferences.** Please think big in order to inspire other educators around the world. Simply as a result of sharing my own work on social media, I now have the privilege of speaking to international audiences from across the globe, many of whom are still very hesitant to even speak about LGBT+ identities in education contexts. Whilst you may not be able to change the political or geographic context in which they are working, you might be able to inspire some small change and offer something hopeful to which they can aspire.

O **Online forums and education journals.** In our plugged-in, online world, getting your voice, and therefore your own practice, out there has never been easier. Blogs written for education forums or publications can then be made available to an even wider audience via social media.

P   Pride! Increasingly at LGBT+ Pride events I see young people, teachers and same-sex parents walking proudly through the streets in order to celebrate authentic identity. Organisations such as Stonewall lead programmes for LGBT+ youth in order to build pride and resilience, taking young people along to events such as London Pride. A UK organisation called Just Like Us has recently established a Schools Diversity Week, but you may also wish to hold a whole-school 'Pride in our authentic diverse identities' carnival event at the end of your 'Our heritage' whole-school project (see page 155). In this way, all identities in school are publicly celebrated at the start of every school year. What a joyful start to term!

Q   Quizzes and competitions. It's been my absolute pleasure to see wonderful creative writing, poetry, song and rainbow cake competitions all themed around LGBT+ history, identities, diverse families or anti-bullying. Opportunities to share and celebrate these with the whole school community, but also with parents and the press, all contribute to disseminating the culture of your inclusive school. Human rights organisations, such as Amnesty, hold annual competitions for young writers and journalists to write about issues they hold dear. Quizzes can be held about LGBT+ identities, history, key dates, music or even the protected characteristics.

R   Research and working papers. LGBT+ inclusion in education is still an emergent field. Organisations such as the Centre for LGBTQ+ Inclusion in Education are being established in order to research and guide best practice, and as such are usually on the lookout for working papers and research about existing good practice. That topic or theme on non-binary identities you developed to use with your tutor group could potentially reach a much wider audience.

S   Social media can be a terrible thing, full of negativity and bullying, and yet without it you would not be reading this book, as I wouldn't have been able to share my work with a now global audience. Schools have websites, Twitter feeds and Facebook pages, all of which are the perfect place to share work undertaken by pupils, whether through photos, artwork, videos or podcasts. In a world where social media misuse is so widespread, modelling the celebration of best practice work around LGBT+ inclusion work in schools is another way to bring a little light into the world. Don't be surprised if you get negative comments, as some people's prejudices may be triggered. Remember they are harbouring anxiety so try to bring compassion. If, however, you experience hate or threats (unlikely but not entirely out of the question in some territories, sadly), then police support may be required; be sure to keep the evidence. I have actually shared (age-appropriately) some of the more unwelcome Tweets and messages I have been sent over the years as part of a classroom discussion. For those who have not experienced prejudice directly, this can be enlightening and very powerful indeed in terms of developing empathy.

T   **Training.** Once you feel secure in your own rationale and practice and have evidence of positive results and impact, which you will, you might like to consider running awareness training for other local schools or youth services, social services, care systems or early childcare providers. You don't have to be an expert or a hero to do this; just know what you are doing and why, and bring heart and passion to the work – it really is as simple as that.

U   **Universities.** There are very many young people studying in universities who have a vested interest in our work in education to facilitate LGBT+ inclusion. Why? Because they had a hard time at school themselves and they are hoping to see things change. Strong links with universities open up your school to some existing diverse role models who might come and speak to young people. Additionally, you will find that many young student teachers, in particular, have a real interest in equalities and inclusion and they will take great pleasure in finding out more about your own work in this field.

V   **Visibility.** Throughout our journey together, I hope I have stressed enough the importance of the specific visibility of LGBT+ identities. High-profile visibility of our LGBT+ inclusive ethos is vital in modelling expectations within our own organisations and to our wider communities. To all those who might harbour prejudice, the expectations must be clear and consistently shared and upheld.

W   **Work experience.** Celebrating LGBT+ identities requires us to listen compassionately and with an open heart to all young people about their intended career path and choices. I can recall telling an 'advisor' at my secondary school careers fair that I wanted to be an actor. In return I was told that was 'for poofs' and to get a proper job. LGBT+ young people may be creative or they may not be. It's important that we listen and keep our own assumptions, stereotypes, bias and prejudices out of the equation when giving career advice. As we increasingly facilitate LGBT+ inclusive spaces in our schools, I think we now have a prime opportunity to identify and nurture a range of diverse role models from within our own school contexts, who may one day come back to school to talk about their experiences at work and how this works alongside their LGBT+ identities. Similarly, as LGBT+ students increasingly find their authentic voice, there is scope for role modelling between schools and active involvement in youth parliaments and the democratic system.

X   eXperiment! Find what does and doesn't work in your own context and then set about celebrating your hard work in order to inspire others. Bringing curiosity and an open, non-judgemental heart will enable you to meet new developments around LGBT+ identities and the changing socio-political landscape, and will enable you to bring compassion to the journey of those whose lives may (or may not) be very different from your own. In schools we can remain fixed and constant, or we can bring our awareness to new learning about all manner of things, and experiment and adapt to meet the needs of all our stakeholders. It's not change but the attitudes we bring to change that count.

Y   'Your Disco Needs You'. Laugh with your students, cry with your students, bring compassion to your students and teach them well. Most of all have fun and celebrate your own success and theirs. Be proud of them and in return they will be proud of you.

Z   Zombies are surely not what we are hoping to nurture in our schools: dull, monochrome, cookie-cutter human beings who all love, think, look, learn and feel the same. Our privileged position as educators is that we can teach and inspire diverse, authentic, self-aware, unique human beings who go out into the world with compassion and make it a better place to be.

We have reached the end of the alphabet. It is now time to process all that you have read and apply it in order to empower all of our brilliant young people to shine brightly, whoever they are. For this is the privilege of being a leader in education.

What next for LGBT+ inclusion in education?

In late 2018 the Scottish government announced its intention to become the first country in the world to embed the teaching of lesbian, gay, bisexual, transgender and intersex rights in the school curriculum. State schools will be required to teach pupils about the history of LGBT equalities and movements, as well as tackling homophobia and transphobia and exploring LGBTI identity, with no exemptions or opt-outs. France too have recently introduced a statutory expectation for all schools to tackle LGBT+ bullying. This sets the bar for the rest of the world. Well done, Scotland and France, and those who worked so hard to achieve this.

Worryingly, there is increasingly a sense that the UK government may be weakening in its resolve for LGBT+ inclusive guidance for independent and private schools. Our journey is not over yet. I invited Dr Joseph Hall to share his own thoughts and hopes for where LGBT+ education might be headed. This is what he said:

While anti-bullying provides a strategic framework for justifying and implementing gender and sexualities education, my hope is that work in schools will merely use this as an entry point and not an end in itself. As Shaun has demonstrated throughout this book, anti-bullying is just one aspect of this work and I would hope that as you embark on your journey you follow Shaun's lead in going beyond anti-bullying to challenge heteronormativity and everyday, taken-for-granted norms, assumptions and expectations (see pages 53 and 79 and Hall, 2018). You may wish to engage with *Safe Is Not Enough: Better Schools for LGBTQ Students* (Sadowski, 2016) and publications exploring 'LGBTQ-affirming schools' (Hall and Hope, 2018; Hope and Hall, 2018a; 2018b), where safety is not seen as an end in itself. More than anything else, I encourage readers to continuously reflect on their practice and strive towards greater and deeper inclusions for LGBTQ+ students, educators and families. We should not become complacent, nor should we take anything for granted.

Dr Joseph Hall, 2019

Thank you, Dr Hall.

As for myself, I hope that a statutory national LGBT+ awareness element is introduced at initial teacher training in the very near future, enabling more young people to feel safe and celebrated. I wish to see greater discourse around the limitations and implications of applying 'labels' to ourselves and others. I hope more LGBT+ teachers and parents will feel they can be authentic within schools, serving as role models in order to inspire change in wider society. I hope for an increased teaching and learning focus upon getting involved with democracy and human rights, and working with the potential for prejudice in all of us. I hope schools work harder to support those who exist on the intersections of LGBT+, SEND and BAME. I hope we are able to bring mindful awareness to our suffering as human beings and a compassionate response for all members of our education communities, including more nuanced discourse around those of diverse gender identities and sexualities. I hope human beings learn to deploy their faith compassionately as opposed to judgementally. I hope we can all be kinder and bring our awareness (and the overriding social media and news narrative) fully back to the light on behalf of our young people.

Finally, I hope your own journey (and that of your learning community) towards celebrating difference is joyful, inspiring, life-changing and profound.

Time to reflect

Before turning the page, please take a moment to reflect.

Things to think about:

- What are you thinking and feeling after reading this book and how do you know?
- What key learning will you take from this book?
- What additional learning and training needs might you and your school now have in relation to LGBT+ inclusion and identities?

Things to do:

- Plan a celebration event for your school and invite parents and members of your community.
- Plan a session for local colleagues to share best practice.
- Picture what you want your established LGBT+ inclusive school to look like at its furthest point of success and begin taking steps to get there.
- Now remove any ceilings and go even further!
- Take a long moment to be proud, as an individual and as a school, knowing that I am proud of you too.
- Get involved in equality campaigning, locally, nationally and globally.

Conclusion

In the weeks between finishing this book and it being sent to print, I took to social media to promote the fact the book would be published and, in addition to interest, I was also met with comments such as 'You deserve to be stoned' and 'You are a paedophile.' Sadly these kinds of comments are all too familiar in my line of work. Therefore, I cannot thank you enough for reading and engaging with my book. It is a privilege and great honour to have been afforded this opportunity to speak to you via the written word. I hope I have inspired you to make at least some changes. Do take this book as a starting point, a guide, and then deploy your own unique skills and selves. Where you identify room for improvement please do make it happen, and where you facilitate best practice please feel free to share it widely.

In the introduction, I posed three questions and asked you to reflect upon your thinking:

1. Why should schools ensure that all stakeholders within learning communities feel safe, supported and included, including those who identify as LGBT+ or those who are perceived to be?
2. How can schools ensure that all stakeholders within learning communities feel safe, supported and included, including those who identify as LGBT+ or those who are perceived to be?
3. What might the impact of this work be upon children and young people, parents and staff?

Now reflect again upon these questions and your responses and reactions to them. Hopefully you kept your initial notes and can use them to reflect upon your thoughts and feelings when these questions were first posed, as opposed to now.

Once you have done so, reflect upon where you will take this journey next and how you will secure its reliance and sustainability whilst ensuring it can respond to shifting need and attitudes.

In creating secure foundations, we always run the risk of becoming set in stone ourselves, something that can hinder an open attitude to change; we must always be aware of this, keeping an open heart and mind, and being patient when supporting others on their journey. In terms of a journey, before I finish, you may like to know that I was invited back to the same secondary school that I once walked out of feeling suicidal, to speak to students about my life and work. You may also like to know that on the day of our wedding, all of my surviving parents were in attendance. Whatever it is I have achieved, I have done so without sponsorship or formal funding. I merely deployed my passion, my existing skills and experiences, social media and my heart. You too have access to all of these things. What can you change for the better?

In March 2019, the House of Commons approved new guidance on sex and relationships education, including explicit mention of LGBT people at primary and secondary level. This is a positive step forward but must be supported by funds and training. There are also questions over the delivery of this in faith contexts, where schools are allowed to express negative views of LGBT+ relationships and identities based on faith. This will damage young people. Within faith schools LGBT+ students *will* emerge. Schools should stand as an unequivocal protective factor. As I hope my book has shown, teaching and learning about LGBT+ identities, history and experiences is so much more than just relationships and sex education; it should infuse and inform all that we do and say, for this is equality, this is how we change lives for the better and this is how, ultimately, we can enable a more compassionate future.

In January 2018, whilst still writing this book, I spoke to secondary students at Ramsey Grammar School on the Isle of Man. After talking about diversity and human responses and reactions to difference (as I always do) I showed a photo of my husband and my dog as a way of modelling that my family might differ from their own. I confirmed that I am married to Mike and that LGBT+ people, just like us, exist in the world. At the end of the session, just as I finished speaking, a number of students spontaneously rose from their chairs in tears, shouting, 'You are talking about *us*. Thank you. No one has spoken about us before in school.' The students were in tears, staff were in tears and I was in tears. Although this has happened throughout my ten years of work, nothing prepared me for the number of amazing young LGBT+ people who bravely and publicly came out in front of their teachers and peers that day. We must never forget that when our children come out as LGBT+, they are still our children.

This book is for them, and for any human being, whether young or old, who has been made to compromise their true self or been on the receiving end of bullying or prejudice, simply for being who they were born to be.

It has to stop, so please do all you can to help. This is a shared journey and we are all on it together. I have no doubt that collectively you will be able to produce a far more exciting range of activities, work and whole-school events than I. It would be wonderful if in order to inspire others, you would care to share this work visually via my Facebook group (www.facebook.com/shaundellentycelebratingdifference/). On behalf of the brilliant, diverse rainbow of young people, I thank you for the work you are about to do.

Be kind, be safe, be proud, be you.

Love and light,

Shaun Dellenty, May 2019

Glossary

Ally A person who is (typically) heterosexual and/or cisgender who supports the LGBT+ community.

Asexual (ACE) A person who does not usually feel sexual attraction or urges towards other people. Asexuality exists as a spectrum with variation in levels of romantic and sexual attraction, including a lack of attraction.

Bi An umbrella term used to describe an emotional, romantic and/or sexual orientation towards more than one gender. Bi individuals might also describe themselves as **bisexual, pan, bi-curious** or **queer**.

Bi-erasure Belittling or attempting to negate the existence of people who identify as bisexual.

Bigender A person who identifies as two genders, such as male or female; identities may be experienced distinctly or at once.

Binary An identification system that involves only two things, for example the commonly deployed term 'gender binary', meaning man and woman. The human race is *not* confined to two genders.

Birth name The name assigned to you at birth, which may or may not assign to your gender identity and core sense of self.

Cisgender (CIS) A person whose gender identity is the same as the sex they were assigned at birth or a person whose assigned-at-birth gender identity aligns with their gender identity.

Coming out When a person first tells someone or others about their LGBT+ identity. Some people *never* feel safe or able to come out; some are **outed** by other people; some are only out in certain contexts. People who are not out are sometimes said to be **in the closet**.

Deadnaming Calling someone by their birth name after they have changed their name; usually with reference to transgender people who have changed their name in order to help with transition.

Demisexual A person who only feels sexual attraction when they form a strong emotional bond.

Dysphoria Unease or discomfort; often used in relation to 'gender dysphoria', the feeling that one's body doesn't match one's gender.

Female to male A person who has transitioned or is transitioning from the assigned sex of female to male.

Gay Homosexual; often used to describe a man who has an emotional, romantic and/or sexual orientation towards men. Also deployed as a term for lesbian sexuality; some women define themselves as 'gay' rather than 'lesbian'.

Gender expression How someone outwardly expresses their gender, within societal gender norms.

Genderfluid A person who has no set identity upon the gender spectrum.

Gender identity A person's innate sense of their gender, whether male, female or non-binary. Their gender might (or might not) correspond to the sex or gender assigned at birth.

Gender neutral A person who does not identify as one gender more than any other or something that is not intended for one gender or another (such as a toy or school uniform).

Gender non-conforming An umbrella term for individuals who do not fit in with societal gender 'norms'. Gender norms vary from culture to culture.

Heteronormativity The view that heterosexuality is the 'norm' or 'default' sexual orientation. Expressing this view belittles those who do not identify as heterosexual.

Heterosexual Romantic and/or sexual attraction or behaviour between people of the opposite sex or gender. Sometimes referred to as being **straight**, a term that can offend LGBT+ people as it reinforces heteronormativity.

Homophobia The fear and hatred of people who identify as lesbian, gay or bisexual. **Biphobia** and **transphobia** are the equivalent terms for fear and hatred of bisexual and trans people.

Homosexual A rather scientific word for gay, meaning a person who is sexually attracted to people of the same sex.

Hypermasculinity A term that denotes exaggerated forms of masculinity. Think Rambo!

Intersectionality The overlap of a number of social identities (gender, sexuality, race or class, for example) that contribute to the various forms and layers of discrimination that result from overlapping social identities.

Intersex People whose anatomy or physiology differs from the cultural stereotypes of what typically constitutes male and female, boy and girl. Find out more at http://www.ukia.co.uk/.

Lesbian A female who is romantically and sexually attracted to other females.

LGBT+ Abbreviation for lesbian, gay, bisexual, transgender and other non-heterosexual or cisgender identities (represented by the +).

Male to female A person who has transitioned or is transitioning from the assigned sex of male to female.

Non-binary A spectrum of identities for people whose gender identity doesn't sit comfortably with either 'male' or 'female'.

Norms Social or cultural expectations; often used to judge or police those who fail to conform. Norms vary from culture to culture.

Out An individual who has disclosed their LGBT+ identity to family, friends, in the workplace, to medical professionals, etc.

Outing When an individual's LGBT+ status is revealed without their consent by someone other than themselves; a form of harassment or bullying.

Pansexual A person who is sexually attracted to people of any gender.

Privilege A priority or advantage not enjoyed by everyone. A person may not be aware of their own privilege. People can have privileges whilst being disadvantaged by other factors.

Pronoun A word used to refer to people's gender conversationally, e.g. '**he**' or '**she**', '**him**' or '**her**'. Some people prefer gender-neutral language pronouns, for example '**they**' and '**their**' or '**ze**' and '**zir**'. An increasing number of people and organisations now signpost their preferred pronouns 'upfront' in order to create an inclusive space for transgender and non-binary people. For example, mine are 'he', 'him', 'his', 'they' or 'theirs'.

Queer A word that was too often said as I was being spat at as a younger man; therefore it still doesn't sit comfortably with me personally. Others within the LGBT+ spectrum have now reclaimed the word and it is commonly used as an umbrella term for non-heterosexual or cisgender identities. Take the time to explore the history of the word queer to avoid any misunderstandings or unintended (or intended) offence. You may also have heard of **queer study**, which explores the LGBT+ experience.

Questioning Someone who is unsure of their gender or sexual identity.

Sex Sex is usually assigned at birth based on primary sex characteristics such as genitalia and other reproductive functions. This often results in a baby being labelled as 'boy' or 'girl' based upon genitalia alone. This process does not take into account individual gender identity.

Spectrum A range of things.

Tranny A pejorative term to avoid. You will hear some transgender people or drag queens use the term, but we need to prevent its pejorative use.

Transgender An overarching term describing individuals whose gender is not the same as, or does not align with, the *sex* they were assigned at birth. Some transgender people prefer the following definition: an overarching term describing individuals whose gender is not the same as, or does not align with, the *gender* they were assigned at birth. Listen and take your cue from them.

Transition A process that an individual might undertake to affirm their true gender. This may involve surgery, cosmetics and name changes.

Transman Someone who was assigned female at birth but identifies as male.

Transsexual A more outdated term for transgender with roots in the field of medicine; can cause offence.

Transwoman Someone who was assigned male at birth but identifies at female.

Recommended reading and resources

Centre for LGBTQ+ Inclusion in Education, www.leedsbeckett.ac.uk/carnegie-school-of-education/research/centre-for-lgbtq-inclusion-in-education/

Dawson, J. (2018), *The Gender Games: The Problem With Men and Women, From Someone Who Has Been Both*. London: Two Roads.

DeJean, W. and Sapp, J. (2017), *Dear Gay, Lesbian, Bisexual, and Transgender Teacher: Letters Of Advice To Help You Find Your Way*. Charlotte, NC: Information Age Publishing.

De Witte, K., Holz, O. and Geunis, L. (eds.) (2018), *Somewhere Over the Rainbow: Discussions on Homosexuality in Education Across Europe*. Münster: Waxmann Verlag GmbH.

Diversity Role Models, www.diversityrolemodels.org (role model speakers for schools).

Dix, P. (2017), *When the Adults Change, Everything Changes: Seismic Shifts in School Behaviour*. Carmarthen: Crown House.

Families and Friends of Lesbians and Gays (FFLAG), www.fflag.org.uk (support for parents and their lesbian, gay, bisexual and trans daughters and sons).

Flynn, P. (2018), *Good As You: From Prejudice to Pride – 30 Years of Gay Britain*. London: Ebury Press.

Galop, www.galop.org.uk (LGBT+ anti-violence charity).

Hawkins, K. (2017), *Mindful Teacher, Mindful School*. London: Sage.

Jones, D. (2017), *50 Queers Who Changed the World: A Celebration of LGBTQ Icons*. London: Hardie Grant Books.

Kornfield, J. (2008), *Meditation for Beginners*. Boulder, CO: Sounds True.

LGBTed, www.lgbted.uk (network for LGBT teachers).

Price, D. (2015), *LGBT Diversity and Inclusion in Early Years Education*. Abingdon: Routledge.

Price, D. (2017), *A Practical Guide to Gender Diversity and Sexuality in Early Years*. London: Jessica Kingsley.

Stonewall, www.stonewall.org.uk (LGBT charity).

Van Dijk, L. and Van Driel, B. (eds.) (2007), *Challenging Homophobia: Teaching About Sexual Diversity*. Stoke on Trent: Trentham Books.

References

Allport, G. (1954), *The Nature of Prejudice*. Reading, MA: Addison-Wesley.

Ávila, R. (2018), 'LGBTQI inclusive education report'. Brussels: IGLYO.

Bedford, A. (2018), '"School can be the difference…"', 26 September, 6:37am, (Tweet), https://twitter.com/draprilwbedford/status/1044943999734358016

Burt, M. J. (2005), *Experience Is Impossible Without a Chance*. Baltimore, MA: PublishAmerica.

Catholic Education Service and St Mary's University Twickenham London, 'Made in God's image: challenging homophobic and biphobic bullying in Catholic schools', https://www.catholiceducation.org.uk/images/CES-Project_Homophobic-Bullying-Booklet_JUN18_PROOF-9.pdf

Church of England (2017), 'Valuing all God's children', https://www.churchofengland.org/more/media-centre/news/homophobic-biphobic-and-transphobic-hbt-bullying-tackled-new-guidance-church

Crown Prosecution Service (2017), 'Homophobic, biphobic and transphobic hate crime – prosecution guidance', https://www.cps.gov.uk/legal-guidance/homophobic-biphobic-and-transphobic-hate-crime-prosecution-guidance

de Haan, L. and Nijland, S. (2002), *King and King*. Berkeley, CA: Tricycle Press.

DePalma, R. and Atkinson, E. (eds.) (2008), *Invisible Boundaries: Addressing Sexualities Equality in Children's Worlds*. London: Trentham Books.

DePalma, R. and Atkinson, E. (eds.) (2009), *Interrogating Heteronormativity in Primary Schools: The No Outsiders Project*. Stoke on Trent: Trentham Books.

DePalma, R. and Atkinson, E. (eds.) (2010), *Undoing Homophobia in Primary Schools*. Stoke on Trent: Trentham Books.

Department for Education (2018), 'Keeping children safe in education', https://www.gov.uk/government/publications/keeping-children-safe-in-education--2

Department of Health and Department for Education (2017), 'Transforming children and young people's mental health provision: a green paper', https://assets.publishing.service.gov.uk/government/uploads/system/uploads/attachment_data/file/664855/Transforming_children_and_young_people_s_mental_health_provision.pdf

Ditch the Label (2018), 'The annual bullying survey 2018', https://www.ditchthelabel.org/wp-content/uploads/2018/06/The-Annual-Bullying-Survey-2018-2.pdf

Fierstein, H. (2014), *The Sissy Duckling*. New York, NY: Simon and Schuster.

Frankl, V. E. (1959), *Man's Search for Meaning*. Boston, MA: Beacon Press.

Gallup (2005), 'Gay and lesbian rights', https://news.gallup.com/poll/1651/gay-lesbian-rights.aspx

Gender Identity Development Service (2016), https://tavistockandportman.nhs.uk/care-and-treatment/our-clinical-services/gender-identity-development-service-gids/

George, M. (2018), 'Exclusive: 40% of LGBT teachers experience bullying', *TES*, 20 July, https://www.tes.com/news/exclusive-40-lgbt-teachers-experience-bullying

Government Equalities Office (2018), 'National LGBT survey: research report', https://www.gov.uk/government/publications/national-lgbt-survey-summary-report

Hall, J. J. (2015), 'The formation, implementation and reception of gender and sexualities education in English primary schools' (doctoral dissertation), https://hydra.hull.ac.uk/resources/hull:12624

Hall, J. J. (2018), '"The word gay has been banned but people use it in the boys' toilets whenever you go in": spatialising children's subjectivities in response to gender and sexualities education in English primary schools', *Social and Cultural Geography* (advance online publication).

Hall, J. J. and Hope, M. A. (2018), 'Lost in translation: naming practices and public feelings towards "gay schools"', in S. Talburt (ed.), *Youth Sexualities: Public Feelings and Contemporary Cultural Politics*. Santa Barbara, CA: Praeger, pp. 101–124.

Herek, G. (2005), 'Facts about homosexuality and child molestation', http://psychology.ucdavis.edu/rainbow/html/facts_molestation.html

Home Office (2018), 'Hate crime statistics', https://www.gov.uk/government/collections/hate-crime-statistics

Hope, M. A. and Hall, J. J. (2018a), '"This feels like a whole new thing": a case study of a new LGBTQ-affirming school and its role in developing "inclusions"', *International Journal of Inclusive Education* (advance online publication).

Hope, M. A. and Hall, J. J. (2018b), '"Other spaces" for lesbian, gay, bisexual, transgendered and questioning (LGBTQ) students: positioning LGBTQ-affirming schools as sites of resistance within inclusive education', *British Journal of Sociology of Education* (advance online publication).

Kaufman, M. and the Members of the Tectonic Theatre Project (2014), *The Laramie Project*. New York, NY: Vintage Books.

Kovacs, M. and Devlin, B. (1998), 'Internalizing disorders in childhood', *Journal of Child Psychology and Psychiatry*, 39, (1), 47–63.

Mitchell, M., Gray, M. and Beninger K. (2014), 'Tackling homophobic, biphobic and transphobic bullying among school-age children and young people', https://www.bl.uk/collection-items/tackling-homophobic-biphobic-and-transphobic-bullying-among-schoolage-children-and-young-people-findings-from-a-mixed-methods-study-of-teachers-other-providers-and-pupils

NASUWT (2015), 'Still far more to do to secure LGBTI equality in schools', https://www.nasuwt.org.uk/article-listing/still-more-to-secure-lgbti-equality-in-schools.html

Ofcom (2017), 'Children and parents: media use and attitudes report', https://www.ofcom.org.uk/research-and-data/media-literacy-research/childrens/children-parents-2017

Ofsted (2013), 'Exploring the school's actions to prevent homophobic bullying', Crown copyright, https://www.eani.org.uk/sites/default/files/2018-10/cpsss_exploring_schools_actions_to_prevent_homophobic_bullyng_0.pdf

Renold, E. (2005), *Girls, Boys and Junior Sexualities: Exploring Children's Gender and Sexual Relations in the Primary School*. Abingdon: Routledge.

Renold, E., Bragg, S., Jackson, C. and Ringrose, J. (2017), 'How gender matters to children and young people living in England', Cardiff University, University of Brighton, University of Lancaster and University College London, Institute of Education, https://orca.cf.ac.uk/107599/1/How%20Gender%20Matters.pdf

Rivers, I. (2011), *Homophobic Bullying: Research and Theoretical Perspectives*. Oxford: Oxford University Press.

Sadowski, M. (2016), *Safe Is Not Enough: Better Schools for LGBTQ Students*. Cambridge, MA: Harvard Education Press.

Sanders, R. (2018), *Pride: The Story of Harvey Milk and the Rainbow Flag*. New York, NY: Random House.

Stonewall (2017a), 'School report: the experiences of lesbian, gay, bi and trans young people in Britain's schools in 2017', https://www.stonewall.org.uk/sites/default/files/the_school_report_2017.pdf

Stonewall (2017b), 'LGBT in Britain: hate crime and discrimination', https://www.stonewall.org.uk/sites/default/files/lgbt_in_britain_hate_crime.pdf

Stonewall (2017c), 'Stonewall top 100 employers', https://www.stonewall.org.uk/sites/default/files/top_100_employers_2017-web.pdf

Tajfel, H. and Turner, J. C. (1979), 'An integrative theory of intergroup conflict', in W. G. Austin and S. Worchel (eds.), *The Social Psychology of Intergroup Relations*. Monterey, CA: Brooks/Cole, pp. 33–47.

Taren, A. A., Creswell, J. D. and Gianaros, P. J. (2013), 'Dispositional mindfulness co-varies with smaller amygdala and caudate volumes in community adults', *PLoS ONE*, 8, (5), e64574.

The Yogyakarta Principles (2016), 'Principle 16: The right to education', https://yogyakartaprinciples.org/principle-16/

UK Government (1988), 'Local Government Act 1988: Section 28' (as originally enacted), http://www.legislation.gov.uk/ukpga/1988/9/section/28/enacted

UK Government (2006), 'Education and Inspections Act 2006', https://www.legislation.gov.uk/ukpga/2006/40/contents

UK Government (2010), 'Equality Act 2010', https://www.legislation.gov.uk/ukpga/2010/15/contents

UK Government (2012), 'Bullying at school', https://www.gov.uk/bullying-at-school

United Nations (1990), 'Convention on the Rights of the Child', https://www.ohchr.org/EN/ProfessionalInterest/Pages/CRC.aspx

University of British Columbia (2019), 'Gay-straight alliances contribute to a safer school climate long-term', https://phys.org/news/2019-02-gay-straight-alliances-contribute-safer-school.html

University of Michigan (2012), 'Sticks and stones: "That's so gay" negatively affects gay students', https://news.umich.edu/sticks-and-stones-that-s-so-gay-negatively-affects-gay-students/

Weinberg, G. (1972), *Society and the Healthy Homosexual*. London: St Martin's Press.

Weinstein, N., Ryan, W. S., Dehaan, C. R., Przybylski, A. K., Legate, N. and Ryan, R. M. (2012), 'Parental autonomy support and discrepancies between implicit and explicit sexual identities: dynamics of self-acceptance and defense', *Journal of Personality and Social Psychology*, 102, (4), 815–832.

Zephaniah, B. (2002), *We Are Britain!* London: Frances Lincoln Children's Books.

Index